PERSONAL INCOME DISTRIBUTION

PERSONAL INCOME DISTRIBUTION:
A Multicapability Theory

Joop Hartog
Erasmus University Rotterdam

Martinus Nijhoff Publishing
Boston/The Hague/London

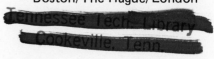

Distributors for North America:
Martinus Nijhoff Publishing
Kluwer Boston, Inc.
160 Old Derby Street
Hingham, Massachusetts 02043

Distributors outside North America:
Kluwer Academic Publishers Group
Distribution Centre
P.O. Box 322
3300 AH Dordrecht, The Netherlands

Library of Congress Cataloging in Publication Data

Hartog, Joop.
  Personal income distribution.

  Includes bibliographical references and indexes.
  1. Income distribution. I. Title.
HC79.I5H37   339.2'2   80-11851
ISBN 0-89838-047-2

Printed in the United States of America

To Marleen and to Johan Willem

CONTENTS

ACKNOWLEDGMENTS

The present monograph grew out of my involvement in a project on tax incidence that started in 1972 at Erasmus University Rotterdam and in which I encountered the need for a theory of personal income distribution. As it turned out, developing such as a theory was a major undertaking (which earned me a Ph.D. in early 1978), and although the theory was applied to questions of tax incidence, such questions could only be given modest attention. One should be very cautious in applying a theory that has barely been tested itself.

The project on tax incidence provided its participants with ample opportunity for on-the-job training, and I am grateful to the Department of Economics of Erasmus University for this addition to my human capital. The project created a fruitful research environment, and I gladly acknowledge those who helped create it. Throughout the project, the Fiscal Institute of Erasmus University was very hospitable.

Dr. Wouter J. Keller and Dr. Piet W. Moerland were colleagues with whom progress in research (and lack of it), successes and disappointments, as well as "human interest," could be shared without restrictions. They became close friends. Prof. W.H. Somermeijer, as chairman of the tax incidence project and later as a member of my thesis committee, with his usual effort, provided me with many detailed comments and criticisms. Although we did not always agree, many of his remarks led to improvements. I trust he welcomes the revision of the section on life-cycle labor supply. Finally, I am deeply indebted to my thesis supervisor, Prof. C.J. van Eijk, for the way he allowed me to carry out research without being distracted by other duties and for his supervision. His well-developed feeling for essentials and relevance and his incisive criticisms have guided me during the project.

Prof. J. Tinbergen deserves credit for the very stimulating discussions we had and for drawing my attention to the American data used here. Dr. J.B. Bracewell-Milnes, in an earlier stage, improved my English. Most of the typing was done by Ms. Schop-Hartmann, with superior skill; in the final stages, valuable help was provided by Ms. J.S. Krediet-Muilenburg and Ms. E.G. Bontenbal-Schuiten. The manuscript was carefully edited by Ms. Sarah Evans.

PERSONAL INCOME DISTRIBUTION

1 INTRODUCTION

Het is mogelijk dat het onmogelijk is om iets nieuwer en juister te zeggen, maar over al het geschrevene daalt het stof der tijden neer, en ik peins daarom dat het goed is als er om de 10 jaar een andere een kruis trekt over al die oude dingen, en de wereld-van-vandaag opnieuw uitspreekt met andere woorden.[1]

—Louis Paul Boon (1972)

1.1 THE PROBLEM

The distribution of labor incomes is a problem with two aspects, each of which has received ample attention in the literature. The first aspect relates to the shape of the frequency distribution of individuals according to their (labor) incomes. Analytical contributions include the so-called stochastic theories of income distribution, such as Gibrat's law of proportionate effect, Champernowne's and Rutherford's Markov-chain models, and Pigou's puzzle. The question is, If abilities are normally distributed, why should the distribution of incomes deviate from this shape? This deviation is the basic fact that these theories explain: income distributions, whatever the time and place of observation, are positively skewed.

1

The second aspect of the distribution of labor incomes is the problem of wage differentials: why do wages differ, why do all workers not earn the same wage? This question has been a standard problem ever since Adam Smith dealt with it. It is more in line with conventional economic analysis since it is simply the basic question of price theory. Any textbook on economic theory can be consulted for an exposition of scope and results. Most results stemming from this approach are old. As Dalton had already noted in 1920, "It is remarkable how early substantial truth was attained in this branch of economic theory and how little later writers have had to modify the conclusions of their predecessors" (1920, p. 252). Dalton himself then went on to give a good example of a straightforward supply and demand analysis in his chapter on "inequality of incomes from work."

Obviously, the two aspects of the distribution of labor incomes are related, but, unfortunately, economic theory has not bothered much to obtain a clear understanding of this link. And it would certainly be unwise to heed the words of Colin Clark, who simply stated, "What we wish to ascertain is solely what fixes the rate of wages, as such, and what fixes the rates of pure interest and of net profits, as such. When these rates are determined, a particular man's income depends on the amount and kind of work that he performs, the amount of capital that he furnishes, and the extent and kind of coordinating that he does" (quoted in Dalton, 1920). Clark's reasoning takes the entire set of latter variables for granted, assuming that they are static and price-independent. It also eliminates the analysis of the shape of the income frequency curve. In contrast to Clark's focus, the theory presented in this book will integrate the two aspects, thereby explaining both the shape of the frequency curve of incomes and the relative wage rates; the analysis will also incorporate the choices open to the agents in the labor market.

Other attempts have been made to link the two aspects. One such attempt is included in the theory of human capital, developed by Becker, Mincer, and others. This theory studies accumulation of human capital by workers and derives implications for the shape of the income density function from differences in annual earnings among individuals. The popularity of this theory warrants a further discussion in Section 1.5. Another attempt at linkage is that of Blinder (1974), who takes a model of economic behavior of the household over the life cycle as his starting point and then simulates the distribution of income from assumptions pertaining to the distribution of the characteristics of the households. Blinder is interested in a somewhat different problem from the one treated here, however, and he includes wage rates among the exogenous characteristics.

Last but not least, there is Tinbergen's (1956) analysis, which creates an income scale by postulating equality between the supply distribution and the demand distribution of worker characteristics. The theory to be presented here derives its main inspiration from that paper, as will become clear in the pages that follow.

1.2 SOME FACTS

Before theorizing any further about income distribution, it will be useful to survey briefly the variables whose effect on incomes has been established empirically and to indicate the nature of the relationships among those variables. Most of the evidence can be found in the standard publications of official statistical bureaus or in published wage scales.

1. *Job and Occupation.* Incomes differ significantly and persistently across jobs and occupations (job families). The variable is essentially qualitative, but a ranking by income level can be made. The general appearance of this ranking shows remarkable stability over both time and space.
2. *Industry.* Average wage levels vary by branch of industry. The cause of this variation is obvious inasmuch as industries employ the different labor categories in varying amounts. However, there also seem to be differences in the wages of similar occupations in different industries. To what extent these differences are temporary, rather than permanent, is not known empirically.
3. *Hierarchical Level.* Hierarchical levels are characterized by the direction of authority. Higher levels yield higher earnings, but the nature of the relationship is poorly known. There is some evidence that incomes increase progressively with increased authority levels.
4. *Sex.* Females earn consistently less than males, partly because they tend to occupy the lower-paying jobs and partly because they get paid less for performing the same job.
5. *Age.* As age increases, income increases, in a nonlinear relationship. Average income as a function of age has a negative second derivative, sometimes (in cross sections) even leading to decreasing income for the highest age groups.
6. *Education.* Individuals with more years of education generally earn a higher income and have a steeper age-income profile.
7. *Training.* Completion of training programs tends to increase wage levels.
8. *Experience.* Length of experience on a particular job or type of job tends to increase earning levels; the experience-income scale may or may not be linear. The impact of experience varies by occupation.
9. *Family Background.* Many studies have found that people raised in higher-status families earn higher incomes.
10. *Race.* Particularly in the United States, it is a well-established fact that some ethnic minorities, on average or in specific jobs, earn less than whites.
11. *IQ.* Individuals with higher IQ scores tend to earn more than those with lower scores.

12. *Regional Variables.* In most countries, different areas experience considerable variation in earnings. These differences are often quite persistent over time.
13. *Duration of Work.* The relationship between working hours and income is not completely unambiguous. If individuals are paid by the hour, more hours obviously imply more income. However, in some jobs (e.g., top management positions), hours do not bear a direct relationship to earnings.
14. *Output.* The volume of output may have an immediate impact on earnings (e.g., when wages are fixed in terms of piece rates or physically observable output).

"Sometimes economists content themselves with listing all of the factors which might influence the outcome of some phenomenon; but such 'theory' does not get us very far and is often discouraging in that it paints a picture of an impossibly complex world in which simple stable patterns of behaviour appear to be most unlikely" (Lipsey, 1962, p. 270). How, then, should the variables listed above be organized to bring out stable patterns of behavior? One possible classification is the following: Variables 1 to 3 indicate differences in the tasks that individuals perform, while variables 4 to 11 indicate differences among individuals. The first set of variables entails a distinction of labor demand, or tasks, while the latter set entails a distinction of labor supply, or people. Variables 13 and 14 relate to units of measurement, and variable 12 is somewhere between "task" and "people."

The classification of variables into those related to tasks and those related to people is important. It points in the direction of key questions in the problem of income distribution: If tasks differ and if people differ, how will people be allocated to tasks? What are the consequences of that allocation? What is the nature of the differences in tasks and in people? An analytical exploration of these problems will be given in the next section.

1.3 DIFFERENT JOBS, DIFFERENT PEOPLE

The empirical observations in the previous section were used to conclude that variables associated with income differences can be grouped into two categories: differences in tasks and differences in people. The consequences of those differences for income distribution can be highlighted in a simple model. Suppose, for example, that in a capitalist society, where free competition prevails, there are a great many different tasks to be done. Suppose also that the people in that society are all equally well equipped to perform any task—that is, they have the same skills. Furthermore, these people do not have a preference for one task over another; they are indifferent. In such a society, the wage rates for all tasks would be equal. Any deviation, no matter how small, from the standard wage rate would lead either to withdrawal of all labor supply or to overwhelming attraction of the labor supply. Hence, if people were identical, wage rates would be also, no matter how different the tasks that people performed, providing that they did not rank these tasks in terms of preferences.

Next, suppose that all tasks are identical, but that people's skills in performing this task differ. Skill differences among people will then lead to wage differences, provided the skill differences can be detected and are deemed relevant (as when skill differences lead to different output per time unit or to different product quality). The wage differences will be brought out by competitive bidding among the organizers of production. Suppose, however, that differences among people relate only to their tastes and not to skills; the utility or disutility attached to performing the task then varies among individuals. In this case, there is no reason for wage rates to differ among individuals. There will be just one wage rate, based on the marginal worker's disutility. The other workers have no interest in revealing their lower disutility and cannot be identified by employers as such. Hence, with identical tasks, differences in skill among individuals will produce wage differentials, but differences in tastes will not.

The analysis can be pushed a little further and related to some well-known concepts. Note that wages are understood as the amount of money per unit of time paid to individual i performing task j. Clearly, then, wage differentials can be associated with individual i or task j or both. Wage differentials can arise from two sources: *productivity differentials* and *compensating differentials*. Productivity differentials reflect differences in performance among individuals at a given task; some individuals are better than others in that they produce a better quality output or a larger quantity per unit of time. Compensating differentials are required to attract individuals to tasks that rank low in their preference orderings of tasks. In a perfect market, productivity differentials among individuals will be brought out by competitive bidding among employers, while compensating differentials will be forced out by individuals' potential moves toward alternative, more attractive jobs.

Table 1.1, which classifies the outcomes of varying assumptions regarding individuals i and tasks j, leads to the following conclusions:

1. Equality of all tasks does not imply equality of wages. Individual differences in productivity will be brought out by competitive bidding.
2. Different tasks do not necessarily imply different wage rates. If individual productivity at a given task does not differ and if individuals are indifferent in performing any of these tasks, wage rates will be equal. The

Table 1.1. Individuals, Tasks, and Wages

Tasks	Individuals Indifferent about Jobs		Individuals with Job Preferences			
			Job Preferences Identical		Job Preferences Different	
	Equal	Different	Equal	Different	Equal	Different
Identical	E	P	E	P	E	P
Different	E	P	C	C, P	C	C, P

Note: E = equal wages; P = productivity wage differentials; C = compensating wage differentials.

    equality will be established by individuals' moving toward jobs with the highest pay.

3. If individuals differ in productive abilities, there will always be wage differentials to reflect this difference (productivity wage differentials).

4. Whether individual preferences about tasks are identical or different is irrelevant with respect to the existence of wage differences. The only relevant distinction in the field of tastes is between the situation in which individuals are indifferent and the situation in which they have preferences about tasks. Compensatory earnings differentials can only exist if individuals have preferences requiring compensation and if alternative jobs exist. Note that compensatory wage differentials can only arise if individuals are utility maximizers, rather than income maximizers; income maximizers are indifferent about the characteristics of the task they have to perform.

1.4 RELATED APPROACHES

Table 1.1 shows the qualitative results of the conditions required for the existence of wage differentials, as well as the nature of those differentials. However, such an analysis lacks the detail necessary to produce hypotheses that can be tested and effects that can be measured. How can one specify a model that explains the allocation of differing individuals to differing tasks? How can the relevant variables be made operational?

    There is quite clearly a need for a model that can acknowledge the differences among individuals and among tasks and that can allow for analysis of wage rates and of the shape of the frequency function of earnings. The basic choice made in this book is to take differences in human abilities as the point of departure. Individuals have different levels of abilities, and their effectiveness in performing given tasks is determined by these levels. The latter condition can be turned around to state that, in some sense (see Chapter 3), different tasks demand different ability levels.

Much research on income distribution acknowledges the role of ability differences, but often in a rather marginal position—for example, as a variable that may bias estimates of the earnings effects of schooling (see, e.g., Griliches and Mason, 1972). Some theories, however, give prominence to abilities, and the most interesting of these will be mentioned to set the stage for the theory to be developed in this book. A full survey of the literature on income distribution will not be given since the interested reader can choose from a number of such surveys (Bjerke, 1961; Mincer, 1970; Sahota, 1978; Blinder, 1974; Lydall, 1968). There is also a choice of textbooks (e.g., Bronfenbrenner, 1971; Pen, 1971; Atkinson, 1975). The approaches discussed here are those of Roy (1951), Mandelbrot (1962), Sattinger (1975), Tinbergen (1956), and Lydall (1968).

Roy's analysis has some attractive features. In his model, individuals can choose between two occupations. In each occupation, output is physically measurable and earnings are the simple product of equilibrium unit price and quantity produced. Individuals choose the occupation that yields them the highest money income. The analysis leads to the conclusion that the distribution of income is shaped by the ranking of individuals by performance in each occupation, by the rank correlation among the individual rankings in the occupations, and by the dispersion of the individual output distributions relative to each other. In this model, the highest incomes will be realized by those who rank highest in the activity in which individual performance exhibits the greatest variance. Roy summarizes his results as follows:

> It will be shown here that whatever the rates of remuneration which either rational choice or irrational prejudice allocate to the units of output in different occupations, such scales of rewards exercise no more than a superficial distorting effect upon a basic pattern. . . . It depends . . . upon the varying relative effectiveness of human abilities when faced with different kinds of productive problems and can be altered only by changes in the technique of production in the various activities in which the human race engages. [1951, p. 136]

The analysis presented by Mandelbrot (1962) has some elements in common with Roy's model. Mandelbrot studies the relationship between the overall income distribution and the distribution in separate occupations. Incomes, or at least offers, are supposed to be linearly dependent on "factors," which are loosely associated with abilities. The rewards for these factors will generally differ among occupations. Individuals choose the occupation that gives them the highest income. If the overall income distribution is Paretian, with exponent α, then within each occupation n the income distribution will be Paretian, with exponent $w(n)\alpha$. For large values of $w(n)$, the distribution approaches the lognormal. The weight $w(n)$ relates to the number of factors that should simultaneously be large in order to observe an individual with a high income in occupation n. If a high income can only be obtained from simultaneously high levels for a number of factors, the weight $w(n)$ will be large, and this leads to a lognormal income distribution. Occupations that require a mixture of abilities will thus tend to a lognormal distribution, while "most of the highly paid people will be utterly specialized" (Mandelbrot, 1962, p. 69): Pareto tails emerge if high levels of only one factor are sufficient to generate high incomes.

Sattinger (1975) develops a model of labor allocation and earnings distribution based on the concept of comparative advantage. He defines ability as the number of units of a particular task that can be performed in a given time period. Labor is characterized by a grade that fully describes its abilities, and tasks are characterized by a degree of difficulty. Defining $t(g,h)$ as the time required to perform a unit task of difficulty h by labor of grade g, comparative advantage requires

$$\frac{t(g_1,h_1)}{g(g_1,h_2)} < \frac{t(g_2,h_1)}{t(g_2,h_2)}.$$

Thus, the ratio of the time required to perform two different tasks should deviate according to different grades of labor. As in Roy's model, individuals choose an occupation exclusively on the basis of maximum income, thus ignoring all the other characteristics of a job that may be important for the direction of individual efforts. The model predicts that individuals of higher grade will be allocated to more difficult jobs—that is, to jobs at which they have a comparative advantage. Sattinger's basic conclusion is that whenever comparative advantage exists, the distribution of earnings and the distribution of abilities will differ. In particular, the earnings distribution will be skewed to the right relative to the ability distribution.[2]

Tinbergen's (1956) contribution stresses that income differences essentially originate in differences in the distribution of demanded levels and supplied levels of a number of attributes. Allocation is brought in ingeniously by utility maximizing of occupational choice, with utility depending on the occupation's earnings and the squared difference between supplied and demanded levels of the attributes. The individuals prefer to take a job that exactly requires the attribute levels they possess, and they attach disutility to deviations, whether positive or negative. Earnings differentials can make up for this disutility; thus, these differentials are an allocational device to equate the distribution of supplied levels to the distribution of demanded levels. Since Tinbergen assumes both the supply and the demand distribution to be bivariate normal, he can work out a solution in terms of a few parameters (means, standard deviations, and correlations). His key result relates to the nature of the earnings equation. If the supply distribution and the demand distribution were identical, all incomes would be equal, since individuals would drift to their best jobs even without pecuniary stimulus and full equilibrium would be guaranteed. If only the means of the two distributions differ, the earnings equation will be log-linear in the required levels of the attributes, and if dispersions and correlations differ as well, the log-earnings equation will be quadratic in the required levels. The analysis also implies that a normal distribution of abilities (attributes) can easily lead to a lognormal distribution of earnings, as, for example, when only the means of the two distributions differ (the log of earnings is then a linear transformation of normally distributed attributes).

Lydall's (1968) view can be characterized as essentially a sorting model. He claims that individual ability or intelligence at very young ages has a rather small dispersion, but that later, as individuals are sorted and prepared for occupational roles through schooling and on-the-job training, dispersion and skewness increase dramatically. This development applies to "occupational abilities," not to "general ability." With respect to individuals at labor force age, reference to an overall distribution of ability is no longer warranted since there are now many different types of ability (by which Lydall, in fact, seems to mean occupational proficiency). Thus, Lydall states that "at the end of the phase of occupational specialization the original group of children will have been split up into hundreds of different occupational sub-groups, each of which is more or less non-competing with the others" (1968, p. 70). The individual's occupational specialization is strongly influenced by the social class of his parents, and, in Lydall's view, the effect of social background on later earnings is considerable.[3]

It is interesting to compare the models discussed above. Because it lacks a formal specification, which makes it difficult to apply rigorous empirical testing, Lydall's approach stands somewhat apart from the others. It should be noted, however, that Lydall's presentation contains what is by far the most empirical material. Nonetheless, the whole approach is somewhat tentative, indicating broad lines, rather than specifying a formal structure. A comparison of the other four contributions shows a distinction between Tinbergen's model, on the one hand, and the models of Mandelbrot, Roy, and Sattinger, on the other. The last three models are quite similar. They all postulate earnings maximization and stress the shape of the frequency distribution of income as their problems of interest; they do not give much explicit attention to occupational wage rates. However, their results differ somewhat. In Mandelbrot's world, high incomes follow from utter specialization, from occupations in which high levels of only one factor can yield the high income. In Roy's model, high incomes derive from occupations in which the dispersion in performance (ability) is largest; this is similar to Sattinger's conclusion that high incomes accrue to individuals who perform the difficult tasks, a difficult task being one in which the grade of labor is more critical (i.e., in which the dispersion of individual performance is greater). All three models interpret earnings differentials as productivity differentials, and this is their main point of departure from Tinbergen's model, which acknowledges only compensating differentials: individuals demand compensation for any tension between available and required levels of the attributes. An excess of available levels over required levels leads not only to a higher income, but also to a shortage of available, versus required, levels. This phenomenon violates what might be called the *principle of dominance*: an abler individual can perform at least as well as a less able individual, but a less able individual cannot reach the performance levels of an abler individual. This may be expected to lead to higher earnings for abler individuals unless, for one reason or another, these individuals decide not to utilize their ability to its fullest extent. That is exactly what happens in Tinbergen's model, but it seems quite implausible that a situation in which individuals of equal ability are paid more when their ability is underutilized than when it is fully utilized can persist.

Like Tinbergen's theory, the theory that will be presented in this book attempts to deal simultaneously with occupational wage rates and the shape of the income distribution. It acknowledges the principle of dominance and explains wage differentials basically in terms of differences in required attribute levels, in a simple linear specification. This seems a logical first step, which was, however, omitted in the theoretical contributions just discussed. Although Mandelbrot, Roy, and Sattinger implicitly acknowledge dominance, they do not give it its simplest, linear specification because their primary aim is to explain the shape of the income frequency curve and to reconcile a positively skewed earnings distribution with a symmetric ability distribution. The present theory attributes the difference between the distribution of earnings and the distribution of abilities to the fact that abilities are not necessarily fully utilized, a point that this theory shares with Tinbergen's formulation.

1.5 HUMAN CAPITAL THEORY

In human capital theory, all the differences among tasks and individuals are reduced to a unidimensional variable, the amount of human capital. This theory's basic postulate, which is quite simple, was clearly stated by Adam Smith:

> The wages of labour vary with the easiness and cheapness, or the difficulty and expense of learning the business. When any expensive machine is erected, the extraordinary work to be performed by it before it is worn out, it must

be expected, will replace the capital laid out upon it, with at least the ordinary profits. A man educated at the expense of much labour and time to any of those employments which require extraordinary dexterity and skill, may be compared to one of those expensive machines. The work which he learns to perform, it must be expected, over and above the usual wages of common labour, will replace to him the whole expense of his education, with at least the ordinary profits of an equally valuable capital. It must do this, too, in a reasonable time, regard being had to the very uncertain duration of human life, in the same manner as to the more certain duration of the machine. The difference between the wages of skilled labour and those of common labour is founded upon this principle. [1776, pp. 203–04]

Although the basic notions about human capital and its relevance to occupational training have thus been around for quite a while, their full development, stimulated and led by Becker (1964) and Mincer (1958), is recent; an overview is given by Mincer (1976). The approach has rapidly conquered a great part of the profession, particularly in the United States. It provides a fairly simple analytical tool by which a large number of the variables mentioned in Section 1.2 can be brought together in a united framework. It is embedded in conventional economic theory (by contrast to, e.g., stochastic theories) and has demonstrated its usefulness on many occasions in empirical work, where it has been used extensively.

Yet, human capital theory has its shortcomings as well (see Blaug, 1976, for a critical evaluation). So far, the formal analyses have usually been based on the income maximization of individual behavior rather than on utility maximization, acknowledging at best the utility value of leisure time. This type of analysis ignores individuals' preferences for different jobs relative to one another and, similarly, their preferences for different types of education. However, the framework admits easy adaptation to account for nonpecuniary effects. More fundamentally, testing the theory is hampered by the fact that its key concept, human capital, cannot be observed. It is unclear even a priori what constitutes an individual's human capital. To find out why employers are willing to pay a return to human capital and if and how human capital increases productivity, one cannot relate the individual's performance to his observed human capital. This can only be accomplished by going back to the variables of which human capital is composed (cf. Blinder, 1974, p. 15).

Human capital is essentially a value concept, but since it is not traded, one cannot use the market valuation. There are two ways to construct the value, which (under certain conditions) generate the same answer. One way is to calculate the present value of all future returns from future earnings differentials. However, this is not a useful approach here. Explaining earnings differentials from human capital boils down to explanation from earnings differentials. The other way is to calculate the cost incurred in creating the human capital. In many cases, the larger part of this cost consists of earnings foregone: the individual's time is needed as input in the production of his human capital. As long as the individual attends school, this time can be measured with reasonable accuracy. But the time devoted to on-the-job training, which is held responsible for the positive slope of age-earnings profiles, is usually not measured and, in many cases, involves situations of joint production of commodity output and increased worker proficiency. In this case, predictions about the shape of the age-earnings profile can be made, but earnings differentials cannot be related to observations concerning the amount of on-the-job training, the essential intervening variable. This precludes a direct test of the human capital explanation of age-earnings profiles. There is another serious shortcoming: human capital theory does not explain why some individuals invest more in human capital than others. Even though the theory formally predicts optimal investment behavior, these optimal patterns are not associated with observable individual characteristics, which would allow a direct test of the theory. In Sattinger's view (1978a), this aspect eliminates human capital theory even as a theory of earnings distribution. The assumption of lifetime earnings equalization implies a perfectly elastic supply curve of individuals with any particular schooling level. Thus, the numbers of individuals with given schooling levels cannot be determined from the supply side; they derive entirely from the location of the demand curves. But the demand curves are not analyzed. In fact, the assumption is usually made that individuals with different schooling levels are perfect substitutes (the efficiency units assumption), which implies perfectly elastic demand curves. Clearly, the two assumptions cannot be made simultaneously: "Horizontal demand curves and horizontal supply curves do not in general meet. The human capital school of thought must choose between explaining the earnings function (and assuming present values of lifetime earnings are equalized) and explaining the distribution of earnings (and adopting the efficiency units assumption)" (Sattinger, 1978a, p. 5; see also Sattinger, 1980, Chap. 2).

Human capital theory deserves credit for stressing the importance of the cost of learning a trade and for drawing attention to age-income profiles. But it does not dig deeply into the actual content of learning processes and does not give intrinsic content to the concept of human capital. This omission has led to the challenge that schooling is valued, not for its productivity augmenting function, but for the information it conveys about individual characteristics and expected performance (see Spence, 1974; for references and discussion of this screening and signalling argument, see the survey by Cain, 1976). It seems clear that to unravel human capital's constituent parts, it is important to discover the traits that make up an individual's human capital. In that sense, the theory developed here tries to fill the gap that human capital theory creates as it prices human attributes without knowing them.

1.6 CAPABILITIES

The research reported in this book is an attempt to provide a unified framework with which the two faces of income distribution (wage differentials and the shape of the income frequency curve) can be explained and to do so in a way that allows testing and measurement. The basic notion of the theory is that of a "capability." Capabilities are those characteristics of an individual that determine his productive potential. Both tasks and workers will be analyzed through capabilities as demand and supply categories, thus providing one set of variables with which both sides of the labor market can be treated. Tasks require capabilities; individuals supply capabilities.

The model draws its main inspiration from Tinbergen (1956), whose contribution is attractive for stressing the allocational aspect of the problem and for putting demand for labor on a par with supply. The inspiration applies to the view that the labor market is a market for individual characteristics. Tinbergen used a broad concept of individual characteristics, including personal relationships. In this book, a narrower view is taken: characteristics are limited to directly productive capabilities. Empirical implementations of the capability concept are given in Chapters 7 and 8. Examples are general intellectual ability, spatial orientation, motor coordination, dexterity, independence, and sociability. Measurement can be through such methods as testing of individuals and job evaluation.

Stressing the role of capabilities opens the way to a very important field of problems. The belief that capabilities are important in shaping an individual's position in society is widespread. The higher positions are supposedly occupied by those blessed with great talents, the lower positions by those with poorer endowments. This view is based mainly on casual observation and is clearly in need of solid scientific research. The problem touches on the important question of justice and efficiency. A society that allocates individuals according to their capabilities is clearly an efficient one. Moreover, many favor rewarding individuals according to their capabilities on the grounds of this efficiency: through optimal allocation of talent, output will be maximized. It may be added immediately that this view is not generally accepted and that according to others, justice should prevail by rewarding efforts rather than innate talents. Nonetheless, this view illustrates the important questions that relate to the problem of capabilities.

The main conceptual contributions of this book (some of which are novel) derive from the prominent position awarded to capability as a multidimensional variable. Such a multicapability framework has scope both for cognitive variables and for noncognitive variables. The latter are the subject of a growing body of empirical work, as illustrated by Edwards (1976). By treating capabilities in this way, one can devise a theory of income distribution that uses the conventional tools of microeconomic theory and that incorporates important choices open to economic agents in the labor market (such as job design and job choice). An important feature of the theory is the distinction between the individual's capabilities and his use of them in the labor market. This point will be clarified in Chapter 2, but it may be stated here that this distinction leads to an attractive specification of individual efforts: efforts relate to the extent to which an individual uses his capability endowments. This is a meaningful and intuitively appealing specification. Effective supply of individual capabilities is defined as the product of effort and endowment, and this also seems a very relevant approach.

The theory developed here assumes capabilities to be measurable on a ratio scale. This assumption implies a fixed origin and allows only positive, proportional transformations—that is, given a scale F, a scale $F' = aF$, $a > 0$, is also permitted. Admittedly, this is a strong assumption, but it is not adopted without reason. Note first of all that a "stronger" scale has advantages over a "weaker" scale (i.e., a ratio scale is better than an ordinal scale) since it adds a number of permissible operations (e.g., multiplication or addition). With respect to capabilities, it appears that with some imagination, it is possible to give an operational specification that allows measurement on a ratio scale. One way to accomplish this is to add a time dimension. For example, intellectual capabilities might be measured as the time required to perform a particular task or as the number of tasks accomplished per unit of time (cf. Sattinger's approach). But even without the time dimension, it is possible to use ratio scales. For example, responsibility may be measured as the number of subordinates or as the money value of the operations under the individual's control; the talent to convince people (a possible aspect of "commercial" talent) may be measured as the number of people converted to an alternative opinion in some experimental setup; and sociability may be measured as the proportion of the members of a given group that rates an individual as sociable. Of course, one may argue over the relevance of the operational specification with respect to the concept one seeks to measure, but the point is that it appears possible to devise some specification on a ratio scale.

A more important argument in favor of cardinal measurement is related to the concept of effort as that concept is employed in this book. Effort is defined as the proportion of a capability endowment that is put to work. This definition is based on the postulate that people are able to state to what extent they use a particular capability—whether they use half of it or 60 percent or 90 percent. It seems possible that people can make such evaluations, which, in fact, they are often asked to do in questionnaires.[4] However, the assumption implies that capabilities can be measured on a ratio scale. Otherwise, the whole operation of taking a proportion is meaningless: it does not make sense to apply proportions of use and nonuse to ordinal variables. Since the postulate mentioned above seems reasonable, the implication that capability measurement on a ratio scale is possible will also be accepted. Rejection of the postulate will not invalidate the basic notions of the theory, but it will be much harder to construct a formal model and to derive testable implications.

1.7 OUTLINE OF THE BOOK

The next chapter provides a model of the individual supplier of labor. This model makes an important distinction between the capability stock of the individual and his capability supply: the individual chooses in what proportions he will supply his capabilities. In Chapter 3, demand for labor is analyzed as capability demand. Chapter 4 is concerned with the determination of equilibrium, while Chapters 5 and 6 investigate consequences of the model with respect to the shape of the personal income distribution. Chapter 7 presents some first steps toward full testing of the model, reinterpreting some evidence found in the literature. Chapter 8 reports on testing and measurement performed on newly collected material. Finally, Chapter 9 evaluates the main assumptions that had to be made and indicates how they can be made less restrictive.

Throughout the book, there is a continuing interest in the role of income tax. Changes in the parameters of the income tax rate can provide an illustration of the applicability of a theory. However, there is another reason for interest in the income tax: the present theory grew out of the need for a tool with which to assess the effects of income tax changes. If the theory passes empirical testing, then measurement of the relevant variables allows prediction of such effects. In the meantime, although detailed predictions should await the empirical work, some general conclusions on tax effects can be stated, assuming, of course, that the theory is valid.

The theory developed in this book tries to establish a framework through which the facts enumerated in Section 1.2 can be understood. Not all the variables mentioned in that section will be explicitly treated. This is a matter of research strategy. Once a theory dealing with fundamental variables has been established, the next step is the use of that theory to analyze the effect of compound or derived variables (such as family background or region).

2 INDIVIDUAL LABOR SUPPLY

It is necessary to have both intelligence and energy to excel in any profession. A man of great intelligence, but at the same time extremely lazy is unlikely to accomplish anything worthwhile, and the same is true of the man of great energy but of low intelligence.

—C.H. Boissevain, quoted in H. Lydall (1968)

Individual behavior in the labor market is quite complex. The complexity derives from the wide range of choices open to individuals, caused by the division of labor that has been accomplished in our economic organization. Were labor a perfectly homogeneous good, the range would be narrowed to choosing the amount of work per unit of time, which could be analyzed simply as choosing the hours of work. Intertemporal allocation of work might be the only complexity added to this simple framework.

But labor is not homogeneous. Jobs differ greatly in the actual content of the activities that have to be performed, presumably matching at least to some extent the differences in individuals' aptitudes for performing these activities. In such a world of heterogeneous labor, the choice of hours of work is only a minor one. Far more important are the choice of a job and the choice about the way in which the individual will produce the desired output of the job.

The heterogeneity of labor has an important dynamic aspect. The very fact that an individual has filled a job for some time has changed his productive potential: he has learned something and he has gained experience. This augmentation has improved his performance in his present job and, in many cases, has prepared him for other jobs.

This chapter attempts to develop a framework of formal analysis that encompasses these views and allows measurement and testing of the assumed relationship. In this framework, the individual is supposed to be endowed with stocks of capabilities. These capabilities are the inputs in the individual's performance of a given job. Different jobs require different inputs, and the choice of a job can therefore be analyzed as the choice of capability supply. Individuals choose the proportion of each of their capability stocks that they want to offer in the labor market. This proportion is what really counts for the individual; it is a measure of his effort. Supply of these efforts is analyzed as the utility-maximizing combination of efforts by capability and by the consumption level that is made possible by the returns to capability supply, subject, of course, to a budget constraint. This means that the individual's job choice is determined by the reward of the job and by his preference for performing the actual job content, in terms of capabilities. Outspoken preference for particular jobs is included as strong preference for supplying particular capabilities; outspoken income maximization (i.e., consumption-level maximization) is included as indifference among the various capabilities and a high preference for consumption.

The analysis includes the dynamic aspects by postulating age dependence of capability stocks. With increasing age (or experience), capability stocks develop. They develop in different ways, and the individual's labor market positions therefore change with age. As the individual adjusts to his changed capability stocks, he traces out a career and an age-earnings profile. The model can generate the typically observed shapes. Differences in profiles are attributed to differences in capability development and in the capability mix supplied by individuals.

2.1 THE BASIC MODEL

2.1.1 General Formulation

It will be assumed that there exist a number of capabilities. Capabilities are defined as those characteristics of an individual that determine his productive potential. An individual is supposed to be endowed with stocks of capabilities, and the stock of capability m is represented as x_m ($m = 1,2,\ldots,M$). A capability stock is measured as the maximum flow of services per unit of time that the individual can supply.

The individual's labor market choices consist of the extent to which the individual will offer each of his capabilities for paid labor market activity. He will offer a proportion $(1 - f_m)$ of each of his capabilities, and he will retain a proportion f_m. The proportion $(1 - f_m)$ will be called his *effort* with respect to capability m, and the proportion f_m will be called his *leisure* with respect to capability m. Note that this definition of leisure has nothing to do with the number of hours in the day or the year that the individual does not work; in fact, it will be assumed that the number of hours per period that the worker should work is fixed for each job and is beyond the control of the worker. Leisure as defined here should be viewed as leisure on the job: supplying less of a given capability stock makes life easier for the individual. This would seem a very relevant way of defining an individual's efforts. It is also a good representation of the ordinary meaning of the concept of leisure in that it does justice to the connotation of doing something "at leisure" or "leisurely." The choice of capability supply expresses the choice of a position in the labor market—not only an occupation, but also a particular job position. It will be assumed that the individual can always find the job position that requires exactly the capability bundle that he desires to offer.

The individual will determine his efforts through the maximization of his utility function, subject to a budget constraint. The arguments of the utility function are: leisure by capability and consumption. The budget constraint expresses the necessary equality between expenditures and income. It will be assumed that the labor market provides the individual with given prices per unit of capability m, w_m. This implies that conventionally observed wage rates are not the basic prices that are determined, but the market operates as if prices per unit of capability were the basic units. These latter prices cannot be observed directly (i.e., they are not "quoted"); they can only be determined implicitly. The individual only observes job wage rates (the reward per unit of time for performing a given job) and capability requirements. It is assumed that these requirements are known exactly to the worker. Job wage rates are assumed to depend on capability requirements in a linear relationship. The conditions under which such linearity holds are discussed in detail in Chapter 4.

It will furthermore be assumed that the individual is subject to an income tax, with parameter vector Θ. It will be assumed that the individual's behavior responds to rewards after income taxes. In other words, it will be assumed that there is no "*tax illusion*"; if individuals were subject to tax illusion, their response to a given net wage rate would be different according to whether this net rate was equal to the gross wage rate or was the amount left after deduction of taxes from a higher gross wage rate (compare Keller, 1980, p. 15).

Defining C as the amount of the individual's consumption in a given period and p as the unit price of consumption, the individual's choices follow from

$$\text{max! } U(C; f_m, m = 1,2, \ldots, M)$$

subject to

$$pC = \gamma \{f_m, x_m, w_m, m = 1,2, \ldots, M; \Theta\}$$

where γ indicates the income-generating function. Within this general formulation, some conclusions on individual behavior might be deduced (marginality conditions for the optimum). However, more specific conclusions from an explicitly formulated model would be preferable, and such a model is presented in the next section.

2.1.2 Specific Formulation

The utility function will be made explicit by applying Keller's elegant formulation of the nested CES utility function (Keller, 1976). This function allows treatment of a wide variety of individuals according to ability and tastes, produces explicit demand functions, and permits immediate interpretation of the solutions.

$$U = \{\alpha_L^{1-\rho_0} L^{\rho_0} + \alpha_c^{1-\rho_0} C^{\rho_0}\}^{1/\rho_0} \tag{2.1}$$

where

$$s_0 = (1 - \rho_0)^{-1}.$$

s_0 is the elasticity of substitution. The following restrictions are imposed:

$$\alpha_L, \alpha_c \geqslant 0; 0 \leqslant s_0 < \infty; \alpha_L + \alpha_c = 1.$$

Leisure utility L derives in a similar manner from the leisure with respect to each capability, f_m:

$$L = \left\{ \sum_{m=1}^{M} \alpha_{Lm}^{1-\rho_1} f_m^{\rho_1} \right\}^{1/\rho_1} \tag{2.2}$$

where

$$s_1 = (1 - \rho_1)^{-1}.$$

s_1 is the elasticity of substitution. Again, the following restrictions are imposed:

$$\alpha_{Lm} \geqslant 0, \text{ all } m; 0 \leqslant \rho_1 < \infty; \sum_m \alpha_{Lm} = 1.$$

The utility function is thus of the nested CES type and shares its attractive properties. By varying the parameters, well-known functions emerge as limiting cases. For s_0 approaching unity, Equation (2.1) approaches the Cobb-Douglas with exponents α_L and α_c; for s_0 approaching infinity, it passes into a linear additive function with weights equal to one; for s_0 approaching zero, the function takes the Leontief form, with "input-output" coefficients equal to α_L and α_c.[1] In the present specification, the elasticity of substitution is equal for all pairs of leisure components f_i and f_j, but if desired, this can easily be changed by adding more levels in the utility function.

To represent income taxes, a linear tax function is chosen:

$$\text{tax} = \Theta_1 y + \Theta_0, 0 \leqslant \Theta_1 \leqslant 1 \tag{2.3}$$

where y equals gross income ($y = \Sigma_m (1 - f_m) w_m x_m$), Θ_1 equals the marginal tax rate, and Θ_0 is the intercept. By choosing appropriate values of Θ_0, the average income tax rate can be made to rise with income ($\Theta_0 < 0$), remain constant ($\Theta_0 = 0$), or decrease ($\Theta_0 > 0$), thus leading to what will be termed a *progressive, proportional,* or *degressive* income tax. If this tax function applies only to incomes beyond $-\Theta_0/\Theta_1$, and if the amount of income tax at lower incomes is zero, $-\Theta_0/\Theta_1$ would be equal to the *tax exemption level*. If the tax function applies over the entire range, with $\Theta_0 < 0$, then a negative income tax plan is fully integrated with the positive income tax at the same marginal tax rate. Incomes below $-\Theta_0/\Theta_1$ would receive a subsidy, and $-\Theta_0$ would be the guaranteed income—that is, the subsidy obtained if $y = 0$. Although government programs include some of these elements (such as income-related subsidies on housing in the Netherlands), there is no claim that this linear function represents the entire exchange of taxes and subsidies between government and individuals. It is only a simple specification used to obtain some analytical results on effects of tax rate parameter changes (see, however, Chapter 5, note 2).

The budget constraint can now be formulated as equality between income and the sum of consumption expenditures and taxes:

$$\sum_m (1 - f_m) w_m x_m = pC + \Theta_1 \sum_m (1 - f_m) w_m x_m + \Theta_0. \tag{2.4}$$

Income results from effective capability supply (i.e., the product of effort and capability stock) multiplied by the unit capability price and added over all capabilities. The income tax is taken from Equation (2.3), with the sum of capability rewards replacing y. Rearranging (2.4) yields

$$R = \sum_m f_m P_{Lm} + pC \tag{2.5}$$

where

$$R = \sum_m (1 - \Theta_1) w_m x_m - \Theta_0 \qquad (2.6)$$

$$P_{Lm} = (1 - \Theta_1) w_m x_m = \tilde{w}_m x_m. \qquad (2.7)$$

According to the formulation used in Equation (2.5), resources R should equal the money value of leisure and consumption. Resources R indicate the maximum after-tax income that can be obtained by offering all capabilities to their fullest extent ($f_m = 0$, all m). $\Sigma_m f_m P_{Lm}$ represents the opportunity cost to the individual of not choosing the job position in which he uses all his capabilities at their maximum levels (i.e., it indicates the income differential between income maximization and utility maximization). $\tilde{w}_m$ is the marginal after-tax wage rate for capability m.

The solution to the maximization problem is now a straightforward application of Keller (1976). The derivation will not be given here. Instead, the basic assumptions will be presented, together with the result.

The Basic Labor Supply Model. Maximization of the utility function

$$U = \{\alpha_L^{1-\rho_0} L^{\rho_0} + \alpha_c^{1-\rho_0} C^{\rho_0}\}^{1/\rho_0}$$

where

$$L = \left\{ \sum_m \alpha_{Lm}^{1-\rho_1} f_m^{\rho_1} \right\}^{1/\rho_1}, 0 \leqslant f_m \leqslant 1, \text{ all } m.$$

$$s_i = (1 - \rho_i)^{-1}, i = 0, 1$$

with the following constraints on the parameters:

$$\alpha_L, \alpha_c \geqslant 0; \alpha_L + \alpha_c = 1; 0 \leqslant s_0 < \infty$$

$$\alpha_{Lm} \geqslant 0, \text{ all } m; \sum_m \alpha_{Lm} = 1; 0 \leqslant s_1 < \infty$$

subject to the constraint

$$R = \sum_m f_m P_{Lm} + pC$$

where

$$R = \sum_{m} P_{Lm} - \Theta_0,$$

$$P_{Lm} = (1 - \Theta_1) w_m x_m$$

is obtained by

$$f_m = \alpha_L \, \alpha_{Lm} \, \frac{R}{P_U} \left(\frac{P_U}{P_L}\right)^{s_0} \left(\frac{P_L}{P_{Lm}}\right)^{s_1} \tag{2.8}$$

$$C = \alpha_c \, \frac{R}{P_U} \left(\frac{P_U}{p}\right)^{s_0} \tag{2.9}$$

where

$$P_U = \{\alpha_L \, P_L^{\rho_0'} + \alpha_c \, p^{\rho_0'}\}^{1/\rho_0'}$$

$$P_L = \left\{ \sum_m \alpha_{Lm} \, P_{Lm}^{\rho_1'} \right\}^{1/\rho_1'}$$

$$\rho_i' = 1 - s_i, \, i = 0, 1.$$

2.1.3 Some Implications of the Basic Model

The solution obtained above has a very elegant structure and lends itself to easy interpretation. Consider first some properties in terms of shares. Introducing the optimal values of f_m and C into the utility function yields, after some rearranging,

$$\frac{f_m P_{Lm}}{L \, P_L} = \alpha_{Lm} \left(\frac{P_{Lm}}{P_L}\right)^{1-s_1} \tag{2.10}$$

$$\sum_m \frac{f_m P_{Lm}}{L \, P_L} = 1 \tag{2.11}$$

$$\frac{L \, P_L}{R} = \alpha_L \left(\frac{P_L}{P_U}\right)^{1-s_0} \tag{2.12}$$

$$\frac{Cp}{R} = \alpha_c \left(\frac{p}{P_U}\right)^{1-s_0} \tag{2.13}$$

$$\frac{L P_L}{R} + \frac{Cp}{R} = 1. \tag{2.14}$$

Optimal "expenditure" shares are governed by preference weights and relative prices. These expenditures can be arranged along the lines of the utility function: nested utilities lead to nested expenditures. If the elasticity of substitution s_i ($i = 0,1$) equals unity, value shares are constant and equal to the relevant preference weight (the Cobb-Douglas case). If the elasticity equals zero, the volume share is equal to the preference weight (the Leontief case).

Note the implications with respect to the price indexes P_U and P_L. These indexes give the individual's weighting of prices corresponding to his optimum. Again, their nature depends on the elasticity of substitution. Consider the index P_U:

$$\lim_{s_0 \to 0} P_U = \alpha_L P_L + \alpha_c p \tag{2.15}$$

$$\lim_{s_0 \to 1} P_U = P_L^{\alpha_L} p^{\alpha_c} \tag{2.16}$$

$$\lim_{s_0 \to \infty} P_U = \min (P_L, p) \tag{2.17}$$

Hence, a Leontief utility function implies a linear price index, a Cobb-Douglas utility function implies a Cobb-Douglas price index, and a linear utility function implies a Leontief price index. This relation between price index and utility function can be expressed in condensed form by the inverse relation between their elasticities of substitution $s_i' = 1/s_i, i = 0,1$.

Consider next the meaning of the results with respect to labor market behavior. Equation (2.8) determines the individual's leisure by capability. His labor supply by capability (his effort) is given as its complement, and therefore his job choice is given by

$$\{(1 - f_m)x_m, m = 1,2,\ldots,M\}. \tag{2.18}$$

The individual will now select the job that perfectly matches this supply. By assumption, he is able to find this job without cost. Note that job choice is thus governed by endowments (x_m, $m = 1,2,\ldots,M$) and by preferences (through f_m, $m = 1,2,\ldots,M$, in particular through the preference weights α_L, α_{Lm}). He can never choose a job that requires more of any capability than he possesses.[2] In choosing a job, he may follow his capability endowments (if, e.g., $f_m = f$, all m, his labor supply will be composed in exact proportion to his endowments); however, his preferences may lead him to different arrangements. His relative leisure choice follows:

$$\frac{f_m}{f_n} = \frac{\alpha_{Lm}}{\alpha_{Ln}}\left(\frac{P_{Ln}}{P_{Lm}}\right)^{s_1} = \frac{\alpha_{Lm}}{\alpha_{Ln}}\left(\frac{w_n}{w_m}\right)^{s_1}\left(\frac{x_n}{x_m}\right)^{s_1}. \qquad (2.19)$$

Relative leisure demand follows from the preference weights and from (relative) capability prices, where these prices are determined by market prices (w_m, w_n) and by individual capability endowments. Note also that income-maximizing behavior is included as a special case. It occurs if $\alpha_c = 1$ and hence $\alpha_L = 0$; by consequence, $f_m = 0$, all m, and the individual will fully supply all his capabilities without buying any leisure.

If any price changes, the individual may be induced to a different labor supply. Consider some elasticities:

$$\frac{\partial f_m}{\partial P_{Lm}}\frac{P_{Lm}}{f_m} = (1 - f_m)\frac{P_{Lm}}{R} - s_0\frac{f_m P_{Lm}}{L P_L}\left(1 - \frac{L P_L}{R}\right) - s_1\left(1 - \frac{f_m P_{Lm}}{L P_L}\right). \qquad (2.20)$$

The elasticity of leisure with respect to its own price consists of three parts:[3]

1. An income effect, which is always nonnegative
2. An effect of substitution between overall leisure and consumption (through s_0), which is always nonpositive
3. An effect of substitution between leisure by capability (through s_1), which is always nonpositive

If the cross elasticity is considered, (2.20) reduces to

$$\frac{\partial f_m}{\partial P_{Ln}}\frac{P_{Ln}}{f_m} = (1 - f_n)\frac{P_{Ln}}{R} - s_0\frac{f_n P_{Ln}}{L P_L}\left(1 - \frac{L P_L}{R}\right) + s_1\frac{f_n P_{Ln}}{L P_L}. \qquad (2.21)$$

The substitution effect through capability substitution now turns out nonnegative, rather than nonpositive.

The elasticities of substitution s_0 and s_1, together with the expenditure shares, determine the sign of the elasticities. Consider some special cases:

1. $s_0 = s_1 = 0$; there is only an income effect, and both the direct and the cross price elasticity of leisure are positive.
2. $s_0 = 0$; the cross elasticity (2.21) is positive.
3. $s_0 = s_1 = s$; the cross elasticity (2.21) is positive.
4. $s_0 = 1, s_1 > 1$; the cross elasticity (2.21) is positive.

Simultaneous changes in a number of prices are also of interest. Note first of all that the solution is homogeneous of degree zero in all prices and the transfer level Θ_0. This implies that lack of adjustment of Θ_0 to inflation has real allocation effects. Next, consider the effect of an equiproportionate change in all capability prices w_m, $m = 1,2, \ldots, M$, in effect changing job wage rates by this proportion:

$$df_m = \sum_n \frac{\partial f_m}{\partial w_n} dw_n.$$
(2.22)

Writing

$$dw_n = \lambda w_n$$
(2.23)

and substitution of (2.20) and (2.21) yields

$$\frac{df_m}{f_m} \frac{1}{\lambda} = (1 - s_0)\frac{pC}{R} + \frac{\Theta_0}{R}.$$
(2.24)

As to the sign of the change in leisure component f_m, the sign and magnitude of s_0 and Θ_0 are critical:

$$\frac{df_m}{f_m} \frac{1}{\lambda} \begin{array}{c} > \\ = \\ < \end{array} 0 \text{ according to } s_0 \begin{array}{c} < \\ = \\ > \end{array} s_0^* = 1 + \frac{\Theta_0}{pC}.$$
(2.25)

s_0^* depends on the transfer level Θ_0:

Proportional income tax: $\Theta_0 = 0, s_0^* = 1.$
Progressive income tax: $\Theta_0 < 0, s_0^* < 1.$
Degressive income tax: $\Theta_0 > 0, s_0^* > 1.$

Finally, effects of tax rate changes can be analyzed. A change in the marginal income tax rate Θ_1 implies an equiproportionate change in all capability prices w_m, and this yields conclusions similar to (2.24). For convenience, the effect of a change in $(1 - \Theta_1)$ is calculated:

$$\frac{\partial f_m}{\partial (1 - \Theta_1)} \frac{1 - \Theta_1}{f_m} = (1 - s_0)\frac{pC}{R} + \frac{\Theta_0}{R}.$$
(2.26)

The effect of changes in $(1 - \Theta_0)$ on f_m thus depends in the same crucial way as above on s_0 and Θ_0.

The effect of a change in Θ_0 is straightforward:

$$\frac{\partial f_m}{\partial \Theta_0} = -\frac{f_m}{R} \leqslant 0.$$
(2.27)

An increase in Θ_0, being a reduction in real resources R, always reduces leisure f_m; this is, in fact, the income effect, which is always nonnegative. Note that an increase in Θ_0 implies a decrease in the exemption level. Thus, tax increases through a decrease in the exemption level increase efforts.

Tax rate changes may be so composed as to bring out the effects of an income-compensated price change.[4] Suppose $(1 - \Theta_1)$ is changed and Θ_0 is adjusted to keep resources R unchanged. This requires

$$dR = \sum_m w_m x_m \, d(1 - \Theta_1) - d\Theta_0 = 0, \qquad (2.28)$$

and hence

$$d\Theta_0 = (R + \Theta_0) \frac{d(1 - \Theta_1)}{1 - \Theta_1}. \qquad (2.29)$$

The simultaneous effect of the change in $(1 - \Theta_1)$ and Θ_0 may now be deduced to be

$$\frac{df_m}{d(1 - \Theta_1)} \frac{1 - \Theta_1}{f_m} = -\frac{1}{R}(R - \tilde{y} + s_0 \, \tilde{y}) \leqslant 0 \qquad (2.30)$$

where $\tilde{y}$ denotes after-tax income;

$$\tilde{y} = (1 - \Theta_1) \sum_m (1 - f_m) w_m x_m - \Theta_0 = \sum_m (1 - f_m) P_{Lm} - \Theta_0. \qquad (2.31)$$

As usual, a compensated price change has a negative effect on leisure demand.

2.2 OCCUPATIONAL CAREERS

In Section 2.1, labor market behavior was analyzed with individual capability stocks fixed. However, actual labor market behavior of individuals has some significant dynamic features, which express themselves as "occupational careers." Individuals do not normally spend their entire working life in one particular position; rather, they change jobs with age. In the simplest form, such an occupational career consists of an apprenticeship followed by promotion to skilled worker. In more elaborate form, a career may extend over a great many jobs, ending in some top executive position.

A great many job shifts during a lifetime may result from changes in preference parameters or in relative prices, or they may be related to search activities (since, contrary to the assumption made here, information in the labor market is not immediately available to all participants). But there is also a systematic career pattern in which certain jobs are held consecutively and in which most members of an occupation follow a similar development. This systematic pattern can be analyzed by making individual capability stocks age dependent. In this section, the immediate consequences of this assumption will be studied, while in the next section, some other assumptions will be added to arrive at a closed theory of occupational choice and age-income profiles.

If capability stocks are age dependent, capability prices $P_{Lm} = (1 - \Theta_1)$ $w_m \, x_{mt}$ change over age, and the individual will adjust according to his preferences.

First, recall Equation (2.19), add subscript t for time, and differentiate:

$$\frac{\partial \, (f_{mt}/f_{nt})}{\partial \, (x_{mt}/x_{nt})} \cdot \frac{x_{mt}/x_{nt}}{f_{mt}/f_{nt}} = -s_1. \tag{2.32}$$

Hence, an increase in a relative capability stock will lead to an adjustment of relative leisure away from that capability.[5] Actually, it is the product of effort and capability stock that is relevant for supply. Consider the following (which is the counterpart of effective supply, namely nonused capability):

$$\frac{\partial \, (f_{mt}x_{mt}/f_{nt}x_{nt})}{\partial \, (x_{mt}/x_{nt})} \cdot \frac{x_{mt}/x_{nt}}{f_{mt}x_{mt}/f_{nt}x_{nt}} = 1 - s_1. \tag{2.33}$$

Since the changes in the x_{it} also have an income effect, the changes in ratios of nonused capability are directed by $1 - s_1$ rather than $-s_1$. Relative nonused capability will change in the same direction as relative capability stocks if $s_1 < 1$, the opposite direction if $s_1 > 1$, and they will not change at all if $s_1 = 1$.

Finally, consider effective capability supply at age t as defined by

$$S_{mt} = (1 - f_{mt}) \, x_{mt}. \tag{2.34}$$

Then, S_{mt} changes over age according to

$$\frac{dS_{mt}}{dt} = (1 - f_{mt}) \frac{dx_{mt}}{dt} - x_{mt} \frac{df_{mt}}{dt}. \tag{2.35}$$

Realizing that (using 2.8)

$$\frac{df_{mt}}{dt} = \sum_n \frac{\partial f_{mt}}{\partial P_{Ln}} \frac{\partial P_{Ln}}{\partial x_{nt}} \frac{dx_{nt}}{dt}, \tag{2.36}$$

Equation (2.35) may be written out as

$$\frac{dS_{mt}}{dt} = (1 - f_{mt})\frac{dx_{mt}}{dt} - f_{mt}x_{mt}$$

$$\sum_{n} \left\{ (1 - f_{nt})\frac{P_{Ln}}{R} - s_0\frac{f_{nt}P_{Ln}}{L P_L}\left(1 - \frac{L P_L}{R}\right) + \right.$$

$$\left. - s_1\left(\delta_{mn} - \frac{f_{nt}P_{Ln}}{L P_L}\right)\left(\frac{dx_{nt}}{dt}\frac{1}{x_{nt}}\right)\right\} \tag{2.37}$$

where $\delta_{mn} = 1$ if $m = n$, and $\delta_{mn} = 0$ if $m \neq n$.

The effect of capability stock growth on effective capability supply is therefore made up of some potentially counteracting components, and its direction cannot be predicted unambiguously without further restrictions. However, the age-income profile resulting from adjustment to all these price changes can be predicted. First note that after-tax income equals consumption expenditures (take the budget constraint [2.5] and substitute Equations [2.6] and [2.7]):

$$\tilde{y} = pC \tag{2.38}$$

and, thus, from (2.9)

$$\tilde{y} = \alpha_c\left(\frac{p}{P_U}\right)^{1-s_0} R. \tag{2.39}$$

The change in $\tilde{y}$ over time then follows as

$$\frac{d\tilde{y}}{dt} = \alpha_c\left(\frac{P_U}{p}\right)^{s_0-1}\left\{(s_0 - 1) R \frac{dP_U}{dt}\frac{1}{P_U} + \frac{dR}{dt}\right\}. \tag{2.40}$$

Assuming only the P_{Lm} change over time (because of changes in x_m), with all other parameters constant, and noting that

$$\frac{dR}{dt} = \sum_{m}\frac{dP_{Lm}}{dt} \tag{2.41}$$

$$\frac{dP_U}{dt} = \alpha_L\left(\frac{P_U}{P_L}\right)^{s_0} P_L{}^{s_1}\sum_{m}\alpha_{Lm} P_{Lm}{}^{-s_1}\frac{dP_{Lm}}{dt}, \tag{2.42}$$

Equation (2.40) can be rewritten by substituting (2.41), (2.42), and (2.8) to yield

$$\frac{d\tilde{y}}{dt} = \alpha_c \left(\frac{P_U}{p}\right)^{s_0-1} \sum_m (1 - f_m + s_0 f_m) \frac{dP_{Lm}}{dt}.$$ (2.43)

Clearly, with an increase in (at least some) prices P_{Lm} due to increased capability stocks x_m, after-tax income will not decrease, since $0 < f_m < 1$ and $s_0 > 0$. Increased capability stocks may lead to substitutions among various efforts and hence to a different job, but such substitutions will never lead to a decrease in the individual's after-tax income. The same conclusion applies to before-tax income y, since $0 \leqslant \Theta_1 \leqslant 1$. Note that the converse also applies: if (at least some) capability prices fall, due to depreciation of capability stocks, effort substitution will not prevent a fall in income.

Further analysis of the age-income profile now requires some specification of the change in capability stocks x_m over time. Such changes will be investigated in the next section. A deliberate attempt has been made to find an independent empirical basis for these profiles, but the available evidence is rather limited. Only the literature on learning curves yields some useful documentation on the processes of individual development, learning behavior, and career lines.

2.3 CAPABILITY DEVELOPMENT

Empirically, many growth processes related to the individual's abilities exhibit an asymptotic pattern, with fast growth initially and small increases later until some upper limit is reached. Such development is reflected in the so-called learning curve, which measures worker progress in performing certain tasks. There is now a large body of literature documenting this curve and presenting estimates of its parameters (see Boehmer, 1970; Corlett and Morcombe, 1970; Crossman, 1959; Salvendy and Seymour, 1973).

Applications deal with worker performance in repetitive routine tasks in which certain simple operations are repeated to form a series of "cycles." Examples usually deal with the operation of machines: typewriters, cigar-making machines, capstan lathes, textile industry machinery, and so on. In its original format, the learning curve may be stated as follows:

$$h_n = h_1 n^{-\nu}$$ (2.44)

where

n = number of operations performed.
h_n = time required to perform the n-th operation.
h_1 = time required to perform the first operation.

Thus, the time required to perform an operation starts at h_1 and then reduces continually in log-linear dependence on the cumulative number of operations. The curve is often stated in terms of the reduction fraction: the reduction in operation time that occurs when the number of operations performed is doubled.

This fraction, r, is a constant:

$$r = h_{2n}/h_n = 2^{-\nu}. \tag{2.45}$$

Corlett and Morcombe (1970) indicate that estimates thus far have produced values of r ranging from .70 to .95.

The original format implies that operation time in the limit approaches zero. This implausible effect was remedied by De Jong (see Boehmer, 1970), who provides for asymptotic approaching toward an incompressible minimum operation time. His specification shows good empirical fit in a number of cases (Crossman, 1959). The curve may be reversed to throw light on the typical shape of capability over time. If the time required for some performance typically starts at some initial level and then asymptotically approaches some minimum level, then its inverse — performance per unit of time — will start at some minimum level and asymptotically approach some maximum level.

The nature of this particular capability development, relating to manual speed skills, is now assumed to be typical for capability development in general. It is thus hypothesized that individual capabilities start at some initial level and then develop over working life by asymptotically approaching toward some maximum level. The following explicit specification will be used:

$$x_{mt} = x_{om} + x_{dm} (1 - e^{-t\gamma m}). \tag{2.46}$$

The stock of capability m that the individual commands at age t, x_{mt}, develops from a minimum level of x_{om} to a maximum of $x_{om} + x_{dm}$, with a rate of convergence toward this maximum of γ_m. Typically, the parameters will be different for different capabilities. For example, manual capabilities may have a relatively limited scope for development, while intellectual capabilities may grow over a much larger range.

The capability profile (2.46) is related to age. Although it is conceivable that biological age is relevant for some capabilities, it seems that labor-force age or experience is usually the key variable. Since parallel development of age and experience in the labor force is the common situation (except for married women who return to work later in life), there is usually no problem in referring to age.

2.4   A LIFE-CYCLE LABOR SUPPLY MODEL

Having made some assumptions on the nature of capability development in Section 2.3, labor supply behavior in response to these developments can now be studied. The starting point is the earnings equation presented as (2.39), with time subscripts added for those variables that change with the individual's age:

$$\tilde{y}_t = \Pi_t R_t \tag{2.47}$$

where

$$\Pi_t = \alpha_c \left(\frac{p}{P_{ut}} \right)^{1-s_0}. \tag{2.48}$$

Equation (2.43) was already used to conclude that

$$\frac{d\tilde{y}_t}{dt} \geq 0. \tag{2.49}$$

To find the second derivative of the age-income profile, the components of (2.47) should be studied. R_t exhibits asymptotic development similar to the capability profiles:

$$R_t = \sum_m \tilde{w}_m \, x_{mt} - \Theta_0; \tag{2.50}$$

$$\frac{dR_t}{dt} = \sum_m \tilde{w}_m \, \frac{dx_{mt}}{dt} > 0; \tag{2.51}$$

$$\frac{d^2 R_t}{dt^2} = \sum_m \tilde{w}_m \, \frac{d^2 x_{mt}}{dt^2} < 0. \tag{2.52}$$

R_t moves asymptotically from $\sum_m \tilde{w}_m \, x_{om} - \Theta_0$ to $\sum_m \tilde{w}_m \, (x_{om} + x_{dm}) - \Theta_0$. The development of Π_t, the proportion of resources turned into income, is analyzed in Appendix 1, with the following conclusions:

$$\text{If} \quad 0 \leq s_0 < 1, \quad \frac{d\Pi_t}{dt} < 0 \text{ and } \frac{d^2\Pi_t}{dt^2} > 0.$$

$$\text{If} \quad s_0 = 1, \quad \frac{d\Pi_t}{dt} = 0 \text{ and } \frac{d^2\Pi_t}{dt^2} = 0.$$

$$\text{If} \quad 1 < s_0, \quad \frac{d\Pi_t}{dt} > 0.$$

$$\text{If} \quad 1 < s_0 \leq 2, \quad \frac{d^2\Pi_t}{dt^2} < 0.$$

Thus, net income as described by (2.47) is the product of two variables Π_t and R_t. R_t exhibits a positive asymptotic behavior, and Π_t is determined by s_0; it may be constant, it may asymptotically increase, or it may asymptotically decrease.

As to the resulting behavior of the age-income profile, the conclusion was already obtained that the slope is never negative. If $s_0 = 1$, the profile has the same, asymptotic profile as R_t. If $s_0 \neq 1$, $\tilde{y}_t$ is determined as the product of two variables that each exhibit asymptotic development. The second derivative of the age-income profile will then depend on the development of these profiles relative to each other, and the profile may include a point of inflection.

Combining these outcomes with the results obtained in Section 2.2, predictions on individual career lines can be made. Capability development with age allows the individual to adjust his labor market position, to take new jobs as he grows older. Depending on capability development and preferences, he will set new capability supply levels. However, he will never move to a job with lower earnings; his age-income profile always has a nonnegative slope. As the individual's maximum attainable level of income grows, he may decide to turn a larger or a smaller proportion of it into actual income, depending on the elasticity of substitution between leisure and consumption. As a result, the ensuing age-income profile may increase asymptotically, but it may also exhibit a point of inflection, depending on parameter values.

2.5 EVALUATING COMMENTS

This chapter on the behavior of individual labor supply may be concluded by summing up the main findings and by pointing to some shortcomings that had to be accepted. In the basic model, labor supply is determined for an individual with given capability stocks and with prices given. His labor market behavior consists of choosing a utility-maximizing position in the labor market. He chooses his optimum by offering optimal proportions of each of his capability stocks. This optimum is determined by his preference weights, elasticities of substitution, capability prices, and capability endowments. In this model, rewards for effort are individually determined variables; the market price of a capability is weighted by individual capability stocks.

The first result is a restriction on individual behavior: job choice is limited by capability endowments. A job that requires more of any capability than the individual can supply is beyond his reach. Other results deal with the impact of price changes on individual behavior. The elasticity of substitution s_0 turns out to be an important parameter for the signs of derivatives.

Once the assumption of static capability stocks has been relinquished in favor of age-dependent capability, the basic outlook changes. Labor market mobility becomes a natural thing; individuals move from one position to another to match their changing capability levels. This means that even with given market wage rates, the labor market is no longer a collection of fixed positions. At given market prices, individual rewards for effort will change. An equilibrium position of the labor market also involves a certain pattern of career development. Capabilities may develop differently, and the individual will adjust the capability mix of his labor supply. However, he will never move to a situation with lower income. Thus, his age-income profile is upward sloping.[6] Depending on parameter values, it may contain a point of inflection.

In evaluating the present model, one may stress its elegant treatment of the entire labor market system with a few variables and its integration of the optimizing behavior of individuals. The choice of occupation can now be treated by marginal analysis instead of, as is more common, by the analytically limited linear programming techniques (compare, e.g., Freeman, 1971). Other valuable accomplishments are the specification of effort as the extent to which a capability is employed, the distinction between capability supply and capability stocks, and the notion of effective capability supply as the product of effort and endowment.

Of course, the analysis had to incorporate a number of restrictions. One of these deals with job choice. Treating job choice as the choice of capability utilization has two important consequences. In the specifications developed here, it implies that labor allocation operates entirely through capability utilization. All other aspects of a job are ignored. This is a deliberate choice, which is aimed at stressing the role of productivity-related individual capabilities. The other aspects that may be relevant for job choice (such as degree of risk, working conditions, etc.) can be brought in later. On the supply side, this might be done by employing the present framework, but the demand side would require different treatment. With respect to demand, the symmetry between supply and demand would be disturbed because some aspects would be relevant only for suppliers, not for demanders (they do not affect productivity). It is not easy to draw the line between capabilities and preferences in these applications. For example, if an individual does not mind dirty jobs, one might also state that he has the capability to do it. Analytically, there would not be much difference.

Taking capability utilization as the effort variable in the utility function also implies that the notion of the individual's distaste for underutilization of his capabilities is rejected. Some authors argue in favor of this distaste (e.g., Tinbergen, 1956), but it would seem that much expressed preference for a good match between available and required capabilities is, in fact, a description of the optimum, not of the utility function. Hence, the stated preferences include the fact that higher utilization implies a higher income. One may therefore wonder if such preferences would hold if higher utilization would not lead to a higher income.

Another limitation is the assumption of exogenous capability development. The assumption was made as a necessary first step, which seems sufficient for the purpose of analyzing the personal income distribution (see Chapter 5). But a better explanation of labor market phenomena can probably be obtained by incorporating endogenous capability development, in which learning is an integrated and unavoidable element in job performance. A limitation of similar weight is the assumption of full and free information on prices and capabilities. Surely, many aspects of labor market behavior find their origin in the search for this information (screening and testing of job applicants, shopping around by laborers, accepting a job "to find out what it is like," etc.), and this search is certainly not costless. In fact, it is another aspect of "learning," learning about the world of work and about one's own capabilities. Future theoretical developments would therefore have to stress these learning processes.

With regard to learning, an important omission from the present model also comes to mind: the role of formal education has not even been mentioned. However, it is beyond any doubt that formal education has an overwhelming structural impact on the labor market. Formal education has not yet been included in this model because it is believed that the model suffices for the purposes for which it was erected: to analyze personal income distribution and to do so in a way that integrates it with a treatment of labor market phenomena and individual optimizing behavior. Moreover, it is felt that theory should not be pushed too far without first testing some of its basic elements. Once the conviction is obtained empirically that the model is worth pursuing in further detail, there should be no problem in incorporating the role of formal education. There are at least two ways in which this might be accomplished. First, analyses might begin after individuals have completed their formal education. Whatever the impact may be of education on capability stocks, this has been effected before labor market entrance and remains completely exogenous. Another approach, employing the lifetime labor supply model, would use the assumption that education and occupational choice are intimately related. Individuals may then be assumed to make their choices at some early age (e.g., upon leaving elementary school) and to choose an educational-occupational career plan as a capability supply plan. In this plan, the educational stage serves to build up the capability stocks that are minimally required to enter certain occupations. The lifetime reward to such a career plan would consist of the ordinary rewards during the working life and the zero or negative rewards during the schooling stage. In fact, then, the human capital model as developed by Becker, Mincer, and others can be integrated with the present multicapability theory.

The framework developed here should also be useful in analyzing a recent controversy about the income-augmenting role of schooling. Is income augmentation due to changes in the individual's productivity created in the process of schooling or just to screening—that is, to selection of individuals according to (given) marginal productivity? The alternative hypotheses might be framed in terms of capability augmentation versus capability screening and then be put to empirical tests. But such applications will be postponed until after the testing of the main hypotheses of the model in its present state.

3 LABOR DEMAND

It seems part of the natural order of the societies we know that occupations requiring greater skill, experience, and effort should be paid more highly.

—H. Phelps Brown (1977)

A theory of income distribution cannot neglect labor demand. A little reflection reveals that the great changes that have taken place in the last century both in the structure of the labor market and in the distribution of income cannot be explained by mere analysis of the labor supply. Rather, many such changes have been induced by demand. The changes in technology and in the organization of the production and development of new products have been responsible for the emergence of entirely new occupations and for the restructuring of old ones. These changes also require a theoretical analysis.

The analysis of labor demand, like that of labor supply, will be founded on the notion of capabilities. It will be argued that different jobs demand capabilities in different combinations and that a job is specified by the required levels of capabilities. Such a view is often implicit in economic approaches to the labor market, but it is made explicit in occupational psychology, occupational counseling, and the job evaluation system. The link with this empirical work will be made in Chapter 7.

The prime accomplishment of this section consists of making job content an endogenous variable. Rather than assuming that there exist a given number of jobs with fixed content, it considers the factor of job design. Those who organize the production can also choose how they organize labor. They can decide on the degree of division of labor and can specify which activities will be collected into one job and which will be separated. They cannot do so at will, of course, since they are subject to rules and restrictions set by technology and market conditions.

The view developed above is incorporated in a formal theory primarily through the specification of a production function. According to this specification, certain types of labor are "produced" by combining capabilities. Different combinations of capabilities yield different types of labor. Labor, capital, and intermediate goods may then be combined to yield commodity output. The production function is of the CES type; the nested CES specification is again chosen for its flexibility in covering different situations, its attractive structure, and its easy interpretation.

In this chapter, a "firm" is assumed to be an organization that produces one single commodity. The output level is fixed exogenously, and the firm tries to produce this at minimum cost. This formulation includes firms that try to maximize profits, as well as nonprofit organizations. This may seem a minor modification relative to profit maximization, but it is worth pointing out that an increasing proportion of the labor force works in such nonprofit organizations.

Labor demand and, in particular, capability demand can now be derived quite easily as the cost-minimizing input required to produce the given output level, and effects of price changes can be derived. These latter effects are presented in Section 3.4. First, the production function is explained, and the optimum solution is derived.

3.1 THE PRODUCTION FUNCTION

The production structure in which labor demand is embedded will be described by a multilevel production function. It is similar to the utility function applied in Chapter 2 (i.e., a nested CES structure). At the lowest level, capabilities are combined into particular *labor types*. To each labor type, capital goods and intermediate goods are added, yielding *production units*. And, finally, these production units produce the output.

To develop the production structure, it is easiest to start at the job level, where capabilities are combined into particular labor types. One unit of labor type j (where the unit is one man per standard working period—e.g., forty hours a week) can be obtained by alternative combinations of capabilities. The amount of capability m supplied by this man in job j during the standard working period will be denoted by v_{mj}. Let the isoquant be given by

$$1 = \left\{ \sum_{m=1}^{M} \beta_{jm}^{1-\rho_{aj}} v_{mj}^{\rho_{aj}} \right\}^{1/\rho_{aj}}. \tag{3.1}$$

This is the isoquant associated with the CES specification in which $s_{aj} = 1/(1-\rho_{aj})$ is the elasticity of substitution. The function is homogeneous of the first degree, and all isoquants are multiples of (3.1). The marginal rate of capability substitution is not affected by the number of laborers of type j, only by the input ratios. Therefore, the specification of the isoquant can be expressed in total output of labor type j and total inputs $\ell_{jm} = A_j v_{mj}$, where A_j is the number of units of labor type j:

$$A_j = \left\{ \sum_{m=1}^{M} \beta_{jm}^{1-\rho_{aj}} \ell_{jm}^{\rho_{aj}} \right\}^{1/\rho_{aj}}. \tag{3.2}$$

The following restrictions are imposed:

$$\left\{ \beta_{jm} \geq 0, \text{ all } m; \sum_m \beta_{jm} = 1; 0 \leq s_{aj} < \infty; \text{ all } j \right\}.$$

Hence, different types of labor are characterized by differences in the distribution parameters β_{jm} and in the elasticity of substitution s_{aj}. Equation (3.2) specifies the number of laborers of type j as a function of total capability inputs in job j. Capability input per worker (i.e., the capability composition of a type j worker) is found by dividing ℓ_{jm} by A_j. This method is permitted because the production function is linearly homogeneous.

The elasticity of substitution is an important structural parameter:

$$\lim_{s_{aj} \to 0} A_j = \{ \min_m \beta_{jm}^{-1} \ell_{jm} \}. \tag{3.3}$$

$$\lim_{s_{aj} \to 1} A_j = a \prod_m \ell_{jm}^{\beta_{jm}}, a = \prod_m \beta_{jm}^{-\beta_{jm}}. \tag{3.4}$$

$$\lim_{s_{aj} \to \infty} A_j = \sum_m \ell_{jm}.$$

(3.5)

Each labor type j is supplemented by capital goods and intermediate goods, combining into production units, indicated by the symbol E_j:

$$E_j = \{\beta_{aj}^{1-\rho_{ej}} A_j^{\rho_{ej}} + \beta_{kj}^{1-\rho_{ej}} K_j^{\rho_{ej}} + \beta_{nj}^{1-\rho_{ej}} N_j^{\rho_{ej}}\}^{1/\rho_{ej}}.$$

(3.6)

K_j indicates the amount of capital goods, N_j the amount of intermediate goods. Both are subscripted by the index j to indicate that they are specific to the production unit j.[1] A production unit j therefore combines labor type j, capital type j, and intermediate goods of type j. It is a very particular unit within the productive process, with its own labor, capital, and material requirements. For example, j may indicate a printing unit in which a printer, a printing machine, and paper are combined in a process whereby the printing unit, together with other production units, produces a newspaper.

As before, the elasticity of substitution s_{ej} is given by

$$s_{ej} = (1-\rho_{ej})^{-1}.$$

(3.7)

The restrictions are

$$\{\beta_{aj}, \beta_{kj}, \beta_{nj} \geqslant 0; \beta_{aj} + \beta_{kj} + \beta_{nj} = 1; 0 \leqslant s_{ej} < \infty; \text{all } j\}.$$

Finally, the production units are combined to yield output Q:

$$Q = \left\{ \sum_j \beta_j^{1-\rho_q} E_j^{\rho_q} \right\}^{1/\rho_q},$$

(3.8)

with

$$s_q = (1-\rho_q)^{-1}.$$

(3.9)

$$\beta_j \geqslant 0, \text{all } j; \sum_j \beta_j = 1; 0 \leqslant s_q < \infty.$$

3.2 EQUILIBRIUM OF THE FIRM

In the present section, labor demand in terms of capabilities will be derived for an individual firm that operates to minimize costs. A firm is understood as a particular organization: it produces only one commodity, and its level of output is fixed by considerations that are kept exogenous to the present model. By implication, then, the firm may be an industrial plant operating under profit maximization in a perfectly competitive market, but it may also be a nonprofit organization whose output level is determined by a government decision. The firm is assumed to operate under constant returns to scale at all levels of the production function. Input prices are beyond its control. The equilibrium position of the firm is then easily derived. (See Appendix 2).

The Labor Demand Model. Let technology be given by

$$Q = \left\{ \sum_j \beta_j^{1-\rho_q} E_j^{\rho_q} \right\}^{1/\rho_q},$$

$$E_j = \{\beta_{aj}^{1-\rho_{ej}} A_j^{\rho_{ej}} + \beta_{kj}^{1-\rho_{ej}} K_j^{\rho_{ej}} + \beta_{nj}^{1-\rho_{ej}} N_j^{\rho_{ej}}\}^{1/\rho_{ej}},$$

$$A_j = \left\{ \sum_m \beta_{jm}^{1-\rho_{aj}} \varrho_{jm}^{\rho_{aj}} \right\}^{1/\rho_{aj}},$$

where

$$s_i = (1 - \rho_i)^{-1}, 0 \leqslant s_i \infty,$$

$$i = \{q, (ej, j = 1,2,\ldots,J), (jm, j = 1,2,\ldots,J, m = 1,2,\ldots,M)\},$$

$$0 \leqslant \beta_i, i = \{j, aj, kj, nj, (jm, m = 1,2,\ldots,M), j = 1,2,\ldots,J\},$$

$$\sum_j \beta_j = 1; \beta_{aj} + \beta_{kj} + \beta_{nj} = 1, \text{all } j; \sum_m \beta_{jm} = 1, \text{all } j.$$

Let the price of a unit of capability m be given by w_m, per unit of capital j by r_j, and per unit of intermediate good j by p_j. Then, the level of output Q is produced at minimum cost O if

$$\varrho_{jm} = \beta_{jm} \beta_{aj} \beta_j \left(\frac{P_Q}{P_{ej}}\right)^{s_q} \left(\frac{P_{ej}}{P_{aj}}\right)^{s_{ej}} \left(\frac{P_{aj}}{w_m}\right)^{s_{aj}} \frac{O}{P_Q}, \tag{3.10}$$

$$A_j = \beta_{aj} \beta_j \left(\frac{P_Q}{P_{ej}}\right)^{s_q} \left(\frac{P_{ej}}{P_{aj}}\right)^{s_{ej}} \frac{O}{P_Q}, \tag{3.11}$$

$$K_j = \beta_{kj} \beta_j \left(\frac{P_Q}{P_{ej}}\right)^{s_q} \left(\frac{P_{ej}}{r_j}\right)^{s_{ej}} \frac{O}{P_Q}, \tag{3.12}$$

$$N_j = \beta_{nj} \beta_j \left(\frac{P_Q}{P_{ej}}\right)^{s_q} \left(\frac{P_{ej}}{p_j}\right)^{s_{ej}} \frac{O}{P_Q}, \tag{3.13}$$

$$E_j = \beta_j \left(\frac{P_Q}{P_{ej}}\right)^{s_q} \frac{O}{P_Q}, \tag{3.14}$$

where

$$P_{aj} = \left\{ \sum_m \beta_{jm}\, w_m^{\rho'_{aj}} \right\}^{1/\rho'_{aj}}, \tag{3.15}$$

$$P_{ej} = \{ \beta_{aj}\, P_{aj}^{\rho'_{ej}} + \beta_{kj}\, r_j^{\rho'_{ej}} + \beta_{nj}\, p_j^{\rho'_{ej}} \}^{1/\rho'_{ej}}, \tag{3.16}$$

$$P_Q = \left\{ \sum_j \beta_j\, P_{ej}^{\rho'_q} \right\}^{1/\rho'_q}, \tag{3.17}$$

$$O = \sum_j \left\{ \sum_m \ell_{jm}\, w_m + r_j\, K_j + p_j N_j \right\},$$

$$\rho'_i = 1 - s_i,\, i = \{q,\, (e_j,\, \text{all } j),\, (a_j,\, \text{all } j)\}. \tag{3.18}$$

3.3 SOME COMMENTS

The equations given in Section 3.2 present the optimal solution. Because of the nature of the production function, this solution has a very regular structure. Note that it consists of a chain of price ratios that may be rewritten to bring out the stepwise optimization. For example, starting from capability demand, the structure is

$$\ell_{jm} = \beta_{jm} \left(\frac{P_{aj}}{w_m} \right)^{s_{aj}} A_j; \tag{3.19}$$

$$A_j = \beta_{aj} \left(\frac{P_{ej}}{P_{aj}} \right)^{s_{ej}} E_j; \tag{3.20}$$

$$E_j = \beta_j \left(\frac{P_Q}{P_{ej}} \right)^{s_q} \frac{O}{P_Q}. \tag{3.21}$$

Alternatively, the solution may be given in terms of optimal cost shares:

$$\frac{\ell_{jm}\, w_m}{A_j\, P_{aj}} = \beta_{jm} \left(\frac{w_m}{P_{aj}} \right)^{1-s_{aj}}; \tag{3.22}$$

$$\frac{A_j\, P_{aj}}{E_j\, P_{ej}} = \beta_{aj} \left(\frac{P_{aj}}{P_{ej}} \right)^{1-s_{ej}}; \tag{3.23}$$

$$\frac{E_j\, P_{ej}}{O} = \beta_j \left(\frac{P_{ej}}{P_Q} \right)^{1-s_q}. \tag{3.24}$$

Finally, to complete this picture, it may be pointed out that at each level, shares add up to unity:

$$\frac{\sum\limits_{m} \ell_{jm}\, w_m}{A_j P_{aj}} = \frac{A_j P_{aj} + K_j r_j + N_j p_j}{E_j P_{ej}} = \frac{\sum\limits_{j} E_j P_{ej}}{O} = 1. \tag{3.25}$$

At each level, then, optimum quantities are determined in proportion to the quantity of the higher level of variable; the proportion is determined by the distribution parameter β and by relative prices. Varying the elasticity of substitution brings out some well-known results: if it equals unity, *value shares* are constant and independent of relative prices (the Cobb-Douglas case); if it is zero, *quantity shares* are constant and independent of relative prices.

At each level, input factors are combined in optimum proportions that are independent of variables at other levels. Consider the relative capability mix of labor type j:

$$\frac{\ell_{jm}/A_j}{\ell_{jn}/A_j} = \frac{\beta_{jm}}{\beta_{jn}} \left(\frac{w_n}{w_m}\right)^{S_{aj}}. \tag{3.26}$$

The quantity of capability m relative to capability n, both employed in labor type j, is determined only by the distribution parameters of the "labor-type level" of the production prices and the relative capability prices.

The present formulation makes job requirements endogenous. For given jobs j, the solution specifies what is required of a worker—in other words, what quality of worker will be hired for that job. The desired quality of the worker is composed according to two basic rules:

1. Capability use should be efficient across labor types; the marginal rate of substitution should be equal in all labor types, since cost minimization requires equality with the common wage ratio:

$$\frac{\partial Q/\partial \ell_{jm}}{\partial Q/\partial \ell_{jn}} = \frac{\partial A_j/\partial \ell_{jm}}{\partial A_j/\partial \ell_{jn}} = \frac{w_m}{w_n} = \frac{\partial A_i/\partial \ell_{im}}{\partial A_i/\partial \ell_{in}} = \frac{\partial Q/\partial \ell_{im}}{\partial Q/\partial \ell_{in}}. \tag{3.27}$$

The marginal rate of capability substitution in each labor type is independent of the number of laborers and is only determined by the input ratio and the technology parameters. (This is immediately clear from calculating $\partial A_j/\partial \ell_{jm}$ and $\partial A_j/\partial \ell_{jn}$ as used in [3.27].) Such a rule implies, for example, that if the marginal rate of substitution between intellectual and manual capability, at given input ratios, is always greater in management positions than in machine-operating positions, management positions will be characterized by higher (relative) intellectual requirements than will operator positions. This is an important result with respect to allocation.

2. The use of capability m in labor type j should follow Equation (3.19), which states that the amount of capability m in labor j is determined by the distribution parameter β_{jm} and the relative wage rate w_m/P_{aj}. Secular changes in technology might be reflected in changes in the distribution parameters β_{jm} and also in the elasticity of substitution. For example, clerical occupations may witness developments that lead to higher requirements of intellectual capabilities at given prices and elasticity of substitution.

As mentioned earlier, the type of worker demanded for a given job has become endogenous, responsive both to technological developments and changes in relative prices. Note, however, that the model deals with a given set of jobs j. For these jobs, secular changes are allowed for, as are price-related changes. With prices given, the capability composition of the job is also given.[2]

Like the labor supply model, the labor demand model yields price indices whose main characteristics are governed by the elasticity of substitution. The price index P_{aj} may be given some particular attention. A_j was defined as the number of workers of type j per standard unit of time. Now recall Equation (3.25)—that is,

$$\sum_m \ell_{jm}\, w_m = A_j P_{aj}.$$

The total wage bill paid to all capabilities employed in labor type j appears equal to the product of number of workers of type j and the price index P_{aj}. In the optimum solution, therefore, P_{aj} is equal to the average wage rate per worker of type j. The firm appears to demand so much labor of type j that its own wage index P_{aj} equals the market wage rate of labor type j.

Finally, it is worth stating that the structure of the solution is untouched if firm behavior is not restricted to cost minimization. Profit maximization, nonconstant returns to scale, and imperfect competition in the product market can be dealt with in the same elegant manner.

3.4 PRICE CHANGES

This section will deal with the effect of price changes. Emphasis will be on induced changes in labor demand, but because of the symmetrical structure of the solution, most effects apply quite similarly to other variables.

Note that the solution is homogeneous of degree zero in all prices; changing all prices by the same rate does not change any optimum quantity. If all capability prices w_m change in the same proportion, P_{aj} will change in this proportion. Equation (3.19) demonstrates that in this case the share of ℓ_{jm} in A_j is unaffected. However, the change in P_{aj} does affect the share of A_j in E_j. Define v_{aj} by

$$v_{aj} = \frac{A_j}{E_j}.$$

Then, Equation (3.20) shows

$$v_{aj} = \beta_{aj} \left(\frac{P_{ej}}{P_{aj}} \right)^{s_{ej}},$$

and the impact of a change in P_{aj} is

$$\frac{\partial v_{aj}}{\partial P_{aj}} \frac{P_{aj}}{v_{aj}} = -s_{ej} \left\{ 1 - \frac{A_j P_{aj}}{E_j P_{ej}} \right\} \leqslant 0. \tag{3.28}$$

An increase in all capability prices w_m by the same proportion reduces the volume share of labor type j in production unit j. The same applies to other variables. For example, let

$$v_{kj} = \frac{K_j}{E_j}.$$

Then,

$$\frac{\partial v_{kj}}{\partial r_j} \frac{r_j}{v_{kj}} = -s_{ej} \left\{ 1 - \frac{K_j r_j}{E_j P_{ej}} \right\} \leqslant 0. \tag{3.29}$$

Consider next the effect of a change in just one capability price, w_m. Recall

$$v_{mj} = \frac{\ell_{jm}}{A_j}.$$

Then,

$$\frac{\partial v_{mj}}{\partial w_m} \frac{w_m}{v_{mj}} = -s_{aj} \left\{ 1 - \frac{\ell_{jm} w_m}{A_j P_{aj}} \right\} \leqslant 0; \tag{3.30}$$

$$\frac{\partial v_{nj}}{\partial w_m} \frac{w_m}{v_{nj}} = s_{aj} \frac{\ell_{jm} w_m}{A_j P_{aj}} \geqslant 0, m \neq n. \tag{3.31}$$

An increase in capability price w_m reduces the share of ℓ_{jm} in A_j and increases the share of ℓ_{jn} in A_j. Finally, consider the effect on demand for capability m in labor type j:

$$\frac{\partial \ell_{jm}}{\partial w_m} \frac{w_m}{\ell_{jm}} = -s_{aj} \left\{ 1 - \frac{\ell_{jm} w_m}{A_j P_{aj}} \right\} - \frac{\ell_{jm} w_m}{O} +$$

$$-s_{ej} \frac{\ell_{jm} w_m}{A_j P_{aj}} \left\{ 1 - \frac{A_j P_{aj}}{E_j P_{ej}} \right\} +$$

$$-s_q \frac{\ell_{jm} w_m}{E_j P_{ej}} \left\{ 1 - \frac{E_j P_{ej}}{O} \right\} \leqslant 0; \qquad (3.32)$$

$$\frac{\partial \ell_{jn}}{\partial w_m} \frac{w_m}{\ell_{jn}} = s_{aj} \frac{\ell_{jm} w_m}{A_j P_{aj}} - \frac{\ell_{jm} w_m}{O} +$$

$$-s_{ej} \frac{\ell_{jm} w_m}{A_j P_{aj}} \left\{ 1 - \frac{A_j P_{aj}}{E_j P_{ej}} \right\} +$$

$$-s_q \frac{\ell_{jm} w_m}{E_j P_{ej}} \left\{ 1 - \frac{E_j P_{ej}}{O} \right\}, m \neq n. \qquad (3.33)$$

An increase in w_m leads to redesign of jobs so that the amount of capability m per unit of labor j is reduced, while total demand for capability m in job j, ℓ_{jm}, is also reduced, due to all the negative substitution effects. (Notice that the substitution effect at each level of the production function is separately identified in Equation [3.32].) The effect of an increase in w_m on the demand for capability n per unit of labor j is positive. However, the impact on total capability demand ℓ_{jn} is less clear-cut, since all the negative substitution effects at the higher levels of the production function in response to cost increases have to be compared with the positive substitution effect at the level of capability mix in A_j.

3.5 EVALUATING COMMENTS

This chapter has presented a model to deal with labor demand in a way that makes it suitable for use in a theory of income distribution. As in the model dealing with labor supply, this was accomplished by analyzing labor demand as demand for capabilities. In this way, job content has become endogenous. As stated in the introduction to this chapter, this is quite important in the light of the great changes that have taken place in the structure of labor demand over the last decades.

With given technology and given prices, cost minimization is a sufficient assumption from which to derive some clear results. Optimum capability demand is specified as demand for each labor type separately, and technological and price variables combine to a well-structured solution. Technology determines the impact of price changes. If the elasticity of substitution between capabilities at a given type of labor is zero, changes in capability prices have no effect on the capability mix of that labor type; if it equals unity, cost shares of each capability in labor cost of the particular type are unaffected by price changes.

Own-price effects at all levels are always nonpositive; an increase in the price of a factor reduces its (relative) demand. Cross-price effects are less unambiguous, since contrary effects occur. At its own level, a price increase stimulates the employment of the other factors; at the higher level, the cost increase tends to reduce demand.

The present theory, like any other theory, combines generality with limitations. It is general in its recognition of endogenous job design, in the scope for various values of the elasticity of substitution at the different levels of the production function. It is limited in the particular specification of the production function, in the way the production structure is assumed to be decomposable in the production units.

In the perspective of the theory presented throughout this book, this last specification is not essential. It could easily be expanded by allowing different elasticities of substitution at many additional levels. It could perhaps be reduced as well. For present purposes, it seems an attractive and adequate representation. But what is essential in the context of this book is the specification of labor demand on the assumption of decomposability into capability demand. This specification, which will be used in later chapters, justifies the claim that the theory of income distribution developed here does not neglect the demand side of the labor market.

In this chapter, job design was limited to determining the optimal capability mix within a particular labor type. This takes the job position as a given entity. However, the theory might be fruitfully expanded to cover the choices that are relevant in the field of the division of labor. This possibility is particularly relevant in the light of long-run changes in income distribution. Division of labor regards the composition of jobs in terms of the basic activities that have to be performed, the activities that will be combined into a single labor type, and the activities that will be separated. Such an expansion should specify the relationship between these basic activities and the required capabilities. It should also spell out the rules governing the combination or separation of activities. Undoubtedly, such a rule should acknowledge Adam Smith's observation on the fruits of division of labor—"the increase of dexterity" that comes with specialization (Smith, 1776, p. 112). In other words, the slope of the learning curve of a particular activity is essential: only if the curve is sufficiently steep will there be separation of an activity. Such expansions, however, will have to wait until the present simpler specification of the theory has been fully developed and empirical testing has warranted further theoretical work.

4 MARKET EQUILIBRIUM

Any parrot can become an economist, it has been said, if one simply teaches him to say the words "supply and demand."

— N. Arnold Tolles (1964)

Thus far, the analyses of individual supply and individual demand have assumed equilibrium capability prices to exist. In the context of those isolated analyses, the assumption was a perfectly acceptable one, but a complete theory of income distribution cannot ignore the problems associated with the determination of equilibrium prices.

The present chapter investigates the conditions of market equilibrium. Equilibrium in the labor market has some special properties in at least two respects. First, the assumption that equilibrium will be established may itself be inadequate. The nature of these markets may be such that equilibrium will never materialize, owing to institutional barriers, existence of noncompeting groups, and so on. The assumption of smoothly operating markets has come under increased scrutiny and criticism recently, both in general economic theory and in labor economics, where, for example, the dual labor market hypothesis has become popular (see the survey by Cain, 1976). Taken together, do these criticisms imply that the equilibrium approach should be abandoned altogether? Not necessarily. The assumption can still be instrumental in obtaining valuable insights that can serve as a basis for comparison with the outcome when equilibrium cannot be established. If equilibrium is impeded by some particular obstacle, such a comparison demonstrates the effect of the obstacle. Moreover, any theory requires assumptions to describe effects of changes in conditions—a guiding principle, so to speak. In comparative statics, this is the postulate of equilibrium restoration. In the present state of the alternative theories, such a guiding principle is not yet available; hence, these theories cannot yet fruitfully be made operational. Also, although persistent disequilibrium may be relevant in some situations, this does not imply that the assumption of equilibrium is irrelevant altogether. In fact, the equilibrium postulate is considered quite adequate for analyzing the main characteristics of income distribution problems. For example, the existence of persistent unemployment is not acknowledged in the present theory, but this is not considered a shortcoming since the theory does not aim at explaining that problem. Part of unemployment can immediately be explained by removing some of the other assumptions, such as those on costless information and mobility; part of it can be explained by considerations that are deliberately omitted, such as cyclical fluctuations. For these reasons, the assumption of equilibrium will be maintained.

The second special property of labor market equilibrium is the fact that labor services require the presence of the laborer and cannot be separated from their supplier in the way that ordinary commodities can. This may lead to a quite complicated price system, as is demonstrated in Section 4.1. In such a model, it would not be easy to analyze effects of parameter changes. Linearity of the earnings equation and the existence of a unit price for each capability that is identical throughout the entire labor market have great analytical advantages. Therefore, assumptions will be made to generate these results. Essentially, job divisibility appears to be required. Implications and assumptions are worked out in detail in the ensuing sections.

Once the assumptions have been accepted, the analysis through the method of comparative statics can be pursued, first in a single capability model, next in a multicapability environment. Predictions on the wage effects of changes in exogenous variables are derived; some of these results will be used in the next chapter on the frequency function of incomes.

4.1 DIVISIBILITY

Equilibrium is a situation that is unchanged as long as exogenous variables do not change. Assuming market prices to change as long as there is an agent who cannot satisfy his plans at the given parameter values, equilibrium requires that each agent can actually attain his optimum. In the present problem, this means that each individual can supply the capability combination he wants and that each firm can find the workers it wants—a perfect match between jobs and workers. However, labor services require the presence of the individual, and the individual cannot split himself to supply each of the different capabilities simultaneously in different jobs. Thus, to establish equilibrium in the entire labor market seems to require that supply and demand exactly match for each and every capability bundle. For each job (a demanded capability bundle), there should be a worker, and for each worker (a supplied capability bundle), there should be a job. More generally, then, for each capability bundle, the frequency of supply should equal the frequency of demand. There are no standard solutions for this situation. Only a few particular cases could be solved (see Tinbergen, 1956; Rosen, 1974), both depending heavily on the specifications chosen for the frequency functions. An illustration of such approaches will be given to point to some basic features. This will be done for a one-capability world.

Suppose there exists a density function of demand for labor varying by capability level, specifying the frequency density of demand for each level of the capability. Suppose also that there exists a given density function of available capability levels ("stocks")—that is, given densities for individuals with specified levels of their capability stock. Indicating by d the level of the demanded capability and by x the level of the capability stock with which an individual is endowed, suppose that the density functions of demand and available stocks are identical if available stocks are transformed as follows:

$$\frac{d - \mu_d}{\sigma_d} = \left(\frac{x - \mu_x}{\sigma_x}\right)^{\delta} \qquad (4.1)$$

or

$$d = \sigma_d \left(\frac{x - \mu_x}{\sigma_x}\right)^{\delta} + \mu_d. \qquad (4.2)$$

Thus, the gap between the demand distribution and the available stock distribution entails differences in means μ, standard deviations σ, and an exponent δ that can be used to express a twisting of one distribution relative to the other. The hypothesis implies that after proper adjustments for differences in mean and variance, the distribution of capability stocks can be transformed into the demand distribution through the application of just one exponent δ. This is sufficiently general to bring out the essence of the present problem.

Equation (4.2) indicates the transformation of available stocks x into effective supply as required for equilibrium. Next, assume that individuals have some preferences on efforts and consumption (income) and that they will seek a labor market position to match their preferences at given prices. This means that individuals are willing to transform their capability stocks x into effective supply of capability level s. Assume that this transformation depends on their capability stock x and on the marginal income $w_s = \partial y/\partial s$ that they obtain from supplying capability of level s:

$$s = x\, e(w_s). \tag{4.3}$$

One recognizes the analysis of labor supply in this specification; s/x conforms to $(1 - f)$, the proportion of the capability stock supplied. This effort is supposed to respond to the capability price w_s.

Equilibrium materializes if the density function of demanded capability levels and supplied capability levels coincide; hence, for each capability level, supply equals demand. Clearly, this occurs if the transformation required according to (4.2) is just produced by individual behavior according to (4.3):

$$x\, e(w_s) = \sigma_d \left(\frac{x - \mu_x}{\sigma_x}\right)^{\delta} + \mu_d. \tag{4.4}$$

Taking the total differential on both sides yields

$$e(w_s)dx + x\,\frac{\partial e}{\partial w_s}\,dw_s = \delta\,\frac{\sigma_d}{\sigma_x}\left(\frac{x - \mu_x}{\sigma_x}\right)^{\delta-1} dx. \tag{4.5}$$

Rearranging (4.5) leads to

$$\frac{dw_s}{dx} = \left\{\frac{\delta}{\sigma}\left(\frac{x - \mu_x}{\sigma_x}\right)^{\delta-1} - e(w_s)\right\} \Big/ x\,\frac{\partial e(w)}{\partial w_s} \tag{4.6}$$

where

$$\sigma = \sigma_x/\sigma_d. \tag{4.7}$$

Equation (4.6) gives the sensitivity of the equilibrium price function to the capability stock level. It indicates how the parameters of the model determine the changes in the marginal capability price w_s if different capability stock levels are considered. The first part of the numerator is, in fact, the derivative of d with respect to x, the change in d accompanying a change in x as required for equilibrium. The second term in the numerator is the change in supply s accompanying a change in x as determined by the individual's behavior. If these two derivatives are equal, individual behavior produces the transformation of capability stocks into supply as required for equilibrium spontaneously, independent of price incentives. Not surprisingly, in this case $dw_s/dx = 0$, and there exists an equilibrium unit price that is identical for all stock levels.

Clearly, this spontaneous equilibrium transformation is coincidental, and, in general, the unit capability price w_s will be different at different capability levels to induce individuals to the proper capability supply. Note that a deviation between stock level μ_x and mean demand level μ_d does not require a variable capability unit price, as might be expected. But note also that similarity of stock distribution and demand distribution ($\delta = \sigma = 1$) is neither sufficient nor necessary for constant capability unit price. This is so because the stock distribution is not of prime relevance, but the supply distribution (i.e., the stock distribution) is transformed through individuals' supply behavior ($\partial s/\partial x$). The unit capability price w_s may increase, as well as decrease, for increased capability levels. For example, if $\delta = 1$,

$$\frac{dw_s}{dx} > 0 \text{ if } \frac{\sigma_x}{\sigma_d} < \frac{\partial s}{\partial x} = e(w_s);$$

$$\frac{dw_s}{dx} = 0 \text{ if } \frac{\sigma_x}{\sigma_d} = \frac{\partial s}{\partial x};$$

$$\frac{dw_s}{dx} < 0 \text{ if } \frac{\sigma_x}{\sigma_d} > \frac{\partial s}{\partial x}.$$

This means that individuals with higher capability levels may receive a lower capability unit price, and, in fact, there is no guarantee that with equal efforts, individuals of higher capability end up with higher earnings. This violates the principle of dominance mentioned in Chapter 1, which states that if an individual of higher capability is at least as good as an individual of lower capability in the latter's job, the higher-capability individual may be expected to earn at least as much as the lower-capability individual.

The approach described above is built on the notion that each supplied capability bundle is a unique entity and that each demanded capability bundle is also a unique entity. The relationship between one supplied capability bundle and another supplied bundle is not investigated, the possibilities for substitution of different bundles in production are ignored, and the principle of dominance may be violated. Moreover, the unit capability price may vary with the capability level. This is a considerable complication for the analysis of supply and of demand, for the analysis of the shape of the income frequency curve (see Chapter 5), and for comparative static analysis of parameter changes. One may question whether at this stage of our knowledge it is worthwhile to add all these complications. After all, a model with unit capability prices identical for all capability levels generates a linear earnings equation in which differences in earnings are explained from differences in capability levels, evaluated at given capability prices. A more general analysis would indeed generalize the earnings equation and add earnings differences that arise from differences in unit capability prices. Such differences may confidently be expected to be of a secondary magnitude relative to the former differences. They will therefore be ignored in the present stage of the analyses, and the required model will not be developed. Naturally, however, the linearity of the earnings equation is a worthy target for empirical analysis.

Unit prices equal for all capability levels can be guaranteed by a model that will allow arbitrage: if unit prices differ in some jobs, individuals will make job combinations to obtain the highest returns and, in so doing, will exert pressure to eliminate the price differential. Job divisibility is an essential assumption for such arbitrage. Assume that jobs in given circumstances have given required capability levels. An individual taking a job performs at that given capability level. Suppose also that within a given period of time (the standard period), the individual's preferences only relate to average (or total) capability supply over that period, not to its composition. Then consider three jobs that demand capability levels c_1, c_2, and c_3, respectively. The individual's desired capability supply is c_2. Now suppose the unit capability price is higher in a c_1 job than in any other job. Call the unit capability price in a c_1 job w_1 and the unit price in other jobs w_0; hence $w_1 > w_0$. The individual will then benefit by spending a proportion h_1 of his time in job 1, where h_1 is set so that $h_1 c_1 + (1 - h_1)c_3 = c_2$. In other words, the job combination is utility equivalent to working in job 2 only. In that case, the individual would earn $w_0 c_2$ in job 2, but by combining jobs 1 and 3, he would earn $h_1 w_1 c_1 + (1 - h_1)w_0 c_3$, and (from $w_1 > w_0$):

$$h_1 w_1 c_1 + (1 - h_1)w_0 c_3 > h_1 w_0 c_1 + (1 - h_1) w_0 c_3 = w_0 c_2.$$

By working at least some time in the higher-paying job, the individual can increase earnings without utility loss from changed job content. The generated excess supply of labor in job 1 will then eliminate the price differential $w_1 - w_0$.

The assumption of job divisibility thus guarantees the emergence of an equilibrium capability price that is independent of the level of the capability supply or demand. Now, in fact, a sufficient condition for equilibrium in the labor market is equality of aggregate capability supply and aggregate capability demand. The distribution of supply and demand over bundles of various sizes is no longer of any relevance. The result for a general model with more than one capability will be demonstrated in the next section.

4.2 DIVISIBILITY AND EQUILIBRIUM

In a perfect market for ordinary economic commodities, equality of aggregate supply and aggregate demand is a sufficient (and necessary) condition for equilibrium. The size of individual bundles supplied and demanded is entirely irrelevant. This result is crucially dependent on homogeneity of the commodity (i.e., on each unit being identical to any other) and on divisibility of lot sizes (i.e., on suppliers and demanders being indifferent between one lot of size q and n lots of size q/n each; in other words, they are perfect substitutes). Homogeneity and divisibility guarantee that arbitrage can eliminate any differences among unit prices. As mentioned above, there are clear analytical advantages in dealing with divisible and homogeneous commodities. How can such a situation be modeled for a multicapability world?

Individual i's supply of capability m, which was analyzed in Chapter 2, may for present purposes be written as

$$s_{im} = s_{im}(\mathbf{w}) \qquad m = 1,2,\ldots,M; i = 1,2,\ldots,I \tag{4.8}$$

where

$$\mathbf{w} = \{w_n, n = 1,2,\ldots,M\}.$$

Now allow the individual to combine jobs j in proportions of a standard working period h_{ij}. If he works in job j, he has to supply the capability combination that is also required of the full-time worker, and total capability m supplied per standard working period should equal his preferred capability supply:

$$\sum_{j=1}^{J} h_{ij} v_{mj} = s_{im}(\mathbf{w}) \qquad m = 1,2,\ldots,M; j = 1,2,\ldots,J, \tag{4.9}$$

with v_{mj} the amount of capability that a full-time worker has to supply in a standard working period. As to the proportions h_{ij}, it is required that

$$\sum_{j=1}^{J} h_{ij} = 1 \qquad i = 1,2,\ldots,I, \tag{4.10}$$

$$h_{ij} \geqslant 0 \qquad j = 1,2,\ldots,J; i = 1,2,\ldots,I. \tag{4.11}$$

The labor demand relationships derived in Chapter 3 for total capability m demanded in job j (ℓ_{jm}), for total number of workers in job j (A_j), and for capability m per worker j can be written as

$$\ell_{jm} = \ell_{jm}(\mathbf{w}) \qquad m = 1,2,\ldots,M; j = 1,2,\ldots,J; \tag{4.12}$$

$$A_j = A_j(\mathbf{w}) \qquad j = 1,2,\ldots,J; \tag{4.13}$$

$$v_{mj} = \ell_{jm}/A_j \qquad m = 1,2,\ldots,M; j = 1,2,\ldots,J. \tag{4.14}$$

The equilibrium conditions have two components. First, aggregates should be equal:

$$\sum_i s_{im}(\mathbf{w}) = \sum_j \ell_{jm}(\mathbf{w}) \qquad m = 1,2,\ldots,M. \tag{4.15}$$

Second, the decomposition through job combination should be feasible. This means, as already stated in Equations (4.9), (4.10), and (4.11), that

$$\sum_{j=1}^{J} h_{ij}\ell_{jm}/A_j = s_{im}(\mathbf{w}) \qquad m = 1,2,\ldots,M; i = 1,2,\ldots,I;$$

$$\sum_{j=1}^{J} h_{ij} = 1 \qquad i = 1,2,\ldots,I;$$

$$h_{ij} \geqslant 0 \qquad j = 1,2,\ldots,J; i = 1,2,\ldots,I.$$

The job combinations should also satisfy demand. Thus,

$$\sum_{i=1}^{I} h_{ij}\ell_{jm}/A_j = \ell_{jm}(\mathbf{w})$$

or

$$\sum_{i=1}^{I} h_{ij} = A_j \qquad j = 1,2,\ldots,J. \tag{4.16}$$

Now, assuming the equations to be consistent, a necessary condition for a solution requires that there are at least as many variables as equations. The equilibrium conditions are decomposable in two groups. Equations (4.15) can be solved to obtain the M capability prices w_m. This also yields the supplies s_{im}, the demands ℓ_{jm}, the demand for workers A_j (from [4.13]), and hence $v_{mj} = \ell_{jm}/A_j$. That leaves Equations (4.9), (4.10), and (4.16) to solve for the job combination variables h_{ij}. Thus, there are $MI + I + J$ equations and IJ variables. Feasibility therefore requires that

$$IJ \geqslant MI + J + I$$

or

$$J \geq M + 1 + \frac{J}{I}.\qquad(4.17)$$

Thus, if $J \geq M$, a situation with more jobs than capabilities, it is possible to find a set of job combination variables h_{ij} so that equality of aggregate supply and aggregate demand (condition [4.15]) is sufficient for equilibrium. Individuals can always realize their desired capability supply by job combinations, and job demands will also be satisfied. Since it is quite reasonable to assume that J will be much larger than M, many variables h_{ij} can be set equal to zero. In fact, one could imagine pressures that try to minimize the number of nonzero h_{ij} for each individual—for example, by including some costs that were neglected here. Note that conditions (4.11) were also neglected; it is simply assumed that nonnegative solutions are feasible.

It is important to realize the nature of the present assumptions. Equality of aggregate supply and aggregate demand is sufficient for equilibrium if both individuals and employers are indifferent with respect to the individual's job combination. The individual's utility level is only affected by the average level of effort during the standard working period, not by the composition,[1] and employers are willing to take on any part-time worker in a job as long as he works at the capability levels that were set for that job. Unit prices for capabilities are now guaranteed, since any deviation would be wiped out by arbitrage. Individuals can supply the capability levels per standard working period in any combination of jobs, and, naturally, they take the combination with highest rewards. Thus, if a job is overpaid (compared to the capability requirements and capability prices paid elsewhere), individuals gain by increasing the share of that job in their "portfolio." Similarly, if a job is underpaid, they will decrease its share. Such adjustments in supply will then eliminate price differentials. For example, if garbage collection is overpaid, intelligent individuals will be willing to collect garbage one day a week, and they will compensate the underutilization of their intelligence by taking a job that overutilizes their intelligence to the same extent (compared to preferred utilization) for another day in the week.

In evaluating these assumptions, two aspects should be kept in mind. First, modest degrees of arbitrage activity can maintain an implicit set of unit prices. The possibility of arbitrage in itself goes a long way in barring deviations, and there is usually no need for massive job combination schemes as sketched above; minor shifts usually will do. Second, the assumptions are selected, not for their reliability in depicting the real world as such, but as instruments to generate a useful and consistent model. Here, they guarantee that the labor market can be analyzed *as if* capabilities are divisible and separable and carry equilibrium unit prices. This means that comparative statics can employ the usual market framework. What is lost is the possible variation of the unit price with the level and kind of combination of capabilities. This is certainly a secondary effect. In the present approach, wage differences are explained as differences in required capability levels, evaluated at a standard set of capability prices. Indivisibility and inseparability might add variations in income because of variations in implicit capability prices. It is claimed that the latter are negligible. However, this is clearly a testable statement, and testing will indeed be taken up in Chapter 8.

4.3 COMPARATIVE STATICS

4.3.1 A Single Market

Because of the assumption of job divisibility, capabilities have become commodities in the traditional economic sense, and the conventional approach to problems of comparative statics (the comparison of equilibrium situations) can therefore be applied. This will be done first for a single market with only one capability.

Let L^s and L^d indicate aggregate labor supply and aggregate labor demand, measured in capability units. The effect on equilibrium prices of a shift in some parameter z can then be found from the condition that after the disturbance, the market should return to equilibrium:

$$dL^s = dL^d. \tag{4.18}$$

Writing out these total differentials yields

$$\left\{ \frac{\partial L^s}{\partial z} + \frac{\partial L^s}{\partial w} \frac{dw}{dz} \right\} dz = \left\{ \frac{\partial L^d}{\partial z} + \frac{\partial L^d}{\partial w} \frac{dw}{dz} \right\} dz. \tag{4.19}$$

Obviously, then,

$$\frac{dw}{dz} = -\left\{ \frac{\partial L^d}{\partial z} - \frac{\partial L^s}{\partial z} \right\} \left\{ \frac{\partial L^d}{\partial w} - \frac{\partial L^s}{\partial w} \right\}^{-1}. \tag{4.20}$$

The equilibrium-restoring change in w is the product of the initial effect of a change in z on excess demand and of the inverse of the sensitivity of excess demand to the price w.

Comparative statics commonly employs the assumption of market stability: following some disturbance, the market will reestablish an equilibrium price. Stability is guaranteed if excess demand reacts negatively to price changes (i.e., if the second bracketed term in Equation [4.20] is negative). Proceeding on this assumption, it is immediately clear that a change in z that causes excess demand to rise will increase the equilibrium wage rate. This leads to the prediction that the market wage rate will increase if labor demand increases (due, e.g., to an increase in commodity demand or a change in technology or organization requiring more labor) of if labor supply decreases (due, e.g., to a shift in leisure preferences or to an increase in income tax rate parameters). These results are, of course, evident from any good textbook.

The method may be applied to study the effect of a change in income tax rate parameters in more detail. This produces the following:

$$\frac{dw}{d\Theta_1} = \frac{\partial L^s}{\partial \widetilde{w}} \frac{\partial \widetilde{w}}{\partial \Theta_1} D; \tag{4.21}$$

$$\frac{d\widetilde{w}}{d\Theta_1} = \frac{\partial L^d}{\partial w} \frac{\partial \widetilde{w}}{\partial \Theta_1} D; \tag{4.22}$$

$$\frac{dw}{d\Theta_0} = \frac{\partial L^s}{\partial \Theta} D; \tag{4.23}$$

$$\frac{d\widetilde{w}}{d\Theta_0} = \frac{\partial L^s}{\partial \Theta_0} \frac{\partial \widetilde{w}}{\partial w} D, \tag{4.24}$$

where

$$D = \left\{ \frac{\partial L^d}{\partial w} - \frac{\partial L^s}{\partial \widetilde{w}} \frac{\partial \widetilde{w}}{\partial w} \right\}^{-1} \tag{4.25}$$

and

$$\widetilde{w} = (1 - \Theta_1) w. \tag{4.26}$$

Note that the effects on w result from two parts:

$$\frac{d\widetilde{w}}{d\Theta_i} = \frac{\partial \widetilde{w}}{\partial \Theta_i} + \frac{\partial \widetilde{w}}{\partial w} \frac{dw}{d\Theta_i}. \tag{4.27}$$

The first part, $\partial \widetilde{w}/\partial \Theta_i$, may be called the *initial effect*—the impact of the tax rate parameter change if market prices have not yet adjusted. The second part, $(\partial \widetilde{w}/\partial w)(dw/d\Theta_i)$, reflects the market adjustment and may be called the *shifting effect*. If $i = 0$, the initial effect is zero.

Under the assumption of market stability, that is,

$$D < 0, \tag{4.28}$$

and using $\partial \widetilde{w}/\partial \Theta_1 < 0$, the following results emerge:

$$\text{sign}\left(\frac{dw}{d\Theta_1}\right) = \text{sign}\left(\frac{\partial L^s}{\partial \widetilde{w}}\right); \tag{4.29}$$

$$\text{sign}\left(\frac{d\widetilde{w}}{d\Theta_1}\right) = \text{sign}\left(\frac{\partial L^d}{\partial w}\right); \qquad\qquad (4.30)$$

$$\text{sign}\left(\frac{dw}{d\Theta_0}\right) = -\text{sign}\left(\frac{\partial L^s}{\partial\Theta_0}\right); \qquad\qquad (4.31)$$

$$\text{sign}\left(\frac{d\widetilde{w}}{d\Theta_0}\right) = -\text{sign}\left(\frac{\partial L^s}{\partial\Theta_0}\right) \qquad\qquad (4.32)$$

The results may be illustrated by some particular cases of a change in the marginal tax rate:

1. If labor supply does not respond to prices, labor bears the tax (no "shifting"):

$$\frac{\partial L^s}{\partial\widetilde{w}} = 0 \text{ implies } \frac{dw}{d\Theta_1} = 0\left(\text{and } \frac{d\widetilde{w}}{d\Theta_1} = \frac{\partial\widetilde{w}}{\partial\Theta_1}\right).$$

2. If labor demand does not respond to prices, there is full shifting of the tax:

$$\frac{\partial L^d}{\partial w} = 0 \text{ implies } \frac{d\widetilde{w}}{d\Theta_1} = 0\left(\text{and } \frac{dw}{d\Theta_1} = \frac{w}{1-\Theta_1}\right).$$

3. If labor supply dictates the net wage rate, there is full shifting:

$$\frac{\partial L^s}{\partial\widetilde{w}} \to -\infty \text{ implies } \frac{d\widetilde{w}}{d\Theta_1} \to 0.$$

4. If labor demand dictates the gross wage rate, there will be no shifting:

$$\frac{\partial L^d}{\partial w} \to -\infty \text{ implies } \frac{dw}{d\Theta_1} \to 0.$$

So far, these results are standard textbook cases. They can be applied, however, to obtain some unambiguous predictions on effects of changes in income tax parameters when the multicapability theory is reduced to a one-capability model, the single market. Information obtained in the analyses of individual supply and individual demand will therefore be added to the above results. Considering labor demand, recall from Chapter 3 the implication that $\partial L^d/\partial w \leqslant 0$ (Equation 3.32, summed over j). Looking at labor supply, the sensitivity of L^s to Θ_0 and to $\widetilde{w}$ has the sign of the sensitivity of effort $(1-f)$. These sensitivities are (using [2.20], [2.31], the definition of R, resp. [2.27] with $M = 1$):

$$\frac{\partial (1 - f)}{\partial \widetilde{w}} = -\frac{1}{\widetilde{w}}\frac{f}{R}\{(1 - s_0)\widetilde{y} + \Theta_0\}; \tag{4.33}$$

$$\frac{\partial (1 - f)}{\partial \Theta_0} = \frac{f}{R} \geqslant 0. \tag{4.34}$$

From (4.34), the conclusion follows that $\partial L^s/\partial \Theta_0 \geqslant 0$. With $\Theta_0 < 0$, (4.33) implies that $\partial L^s/\partial \widetilde{w} > 0$ if $s_0 \geqslant 1$. If $0 < s_0 < 1$, the sign may switch if different values of s_0 are considered. Since the critical value of s_0 (where the derivative switches sign) depends on the individually determined value of $\widetilde{y}$ relative to Θ_0, results can only be derived with further restrictions on the distribution of parameters across individuals. Such an attempt will not be made here.

Combining the results obtained so far, predictions can be made on the effects of changes in income tax rate parameters in a single capability market:

$$\frac{dw}{d\Theta_1} \geqslant 0 \text{ (provided } s_0 \geqslant 1); \tag{4.35}$$

$$\frac{d\widetilde{w}}{d\Theta_1} \leqslant 0; \tag{4.36}$$

$$\frac{dw}{d\Theta_0} \leqslant 0; \tag{4.37}$$

$$\frac{d\widetilde{w}}{d\Theta_0} \leqslant 0. \tag{4.38}$$

4.3.2 A Multimarket System

On the assumption of separability of capabilities, the working of the labor market can be studied as a multimarket system. Suppose there are M capability markets. In each such market, equilibrium values are determined for quantities supplied and demanded and for prices. Let these markets be in equilibrium; let there then be a change in parameter z. The change in equilibrium prices can then be found by equating the changes in supply to the changes in demand for each capability and solving for the prices. The approach is the straightforward generalization of the single-market case.

Consider the market for capability 1. The equilibrium-restoring equation after a change in parameter z may be written as

$$\frac{\partial L_1^d}{\partial z} + \sum_m \frac{\partial L_1^d}{\partial w_m}\frac{dw_m}{dz} = \frac{\partial L_1^s}{\partial z} + \sum_m \frac{\partial L_1^s}{\partial \widetilde{w}_m}\frac{\partial \widetilde{w}_m}{\partial w_m}\frac{dw_m}{dz}. \tag{4.39}$$

L_1^s, L_1^d indicate aggregate market supply and market demand for capability 1. Equation (4.39) postulates equality between total change in demand and total change in supply. As before, the change in demand consists of a primary impulse $\partial L_1^d/\partial z$ (i.e., an immediate impact of a change in z on L_1^d) and an indirect effect through the change in equilibrium prices w_m. Similarly, the change in supply consists of a primary impulse $\partial L_1^s/\partial z$ and an impulse working through prices, where the change in market prices has to be translated into a change in net, after-tax prices.

Rearranging Equation (4.39) yields

$$\sum_m \left\{ \frac{\partial L_1^d}{\partial w_m} - \frac{\partial L_1^s}{\partial \widetilde{w}_m} \frac{\partial \widetilde{w}_m}{\partial w_m} \right\} \frac{dw_m}{dz} = -\left(\frac{\partial L_1^d}{dz} - \frac{\partial L_1^s}{\partial z} \right). \tag{4.40}$$

This equation contains the changes in all equilibrium prices dw_m/dz. A solution for the price changes requires restoration of equilibrium in all markets simultaneously. It is now straightforward to apply the above reasoning to all these markets. Using matrix notation, the solution then equals

$$\frac{d\mathbf{w}}{dz} = -\mathbf{E}^{-1} \mathbf{e} \tag{4.41}$$

where

$$\frac{d\mathbf{w}}{dz} = \left[\frac{dw_1}{dz}, \frac{dw_2}{dz} \cdots \frac{dw_M}{dz} \right]', \text{ the solution vector;} \tag{4.42}$$

$$\mathbf{E} = \left[\frac{\partial L_i^d}{\partial w_j} - \frac{\partial L_i^s}{\partial \widetilde{w}_j} \frac{\partial \widetilde{w}_j}{\partial w_j} \right], i, j = 1, 2, \ldots, M, \text{ the multiplier matrix;} \tag{4.43}$$

$$\mathbf{e} = \left[\frac{\partial L_1^d}{\partial z} - \frac{\partial L_1^s}{\partial z} \cdots \frac{\partial L_M^d}{\partial z} - \frac{\partial L_M^s}{\partial z} \right]', \text{ the primary impulse vector.} \tag{4.44}$$

The result is immediately comparable to the single-market result of Section 4.3.1: the effect on market prices depends on the initial effect on excess demands (e) and on the sensitivity of excess demands to prices (E). In the single-market case, results can be derived from the assumption of market stability. A similar assumption should now apply to all markets simultaneously (i.e., to E). The assumption often adopted for this purpose in general equilibrium theory is *diagonal dominance* (Malinvaud, 1972, p. 115), and this approach will also be used here. Diagonal dominance entails:

1. For all i,

$$\frac{\partial (L_i^d - L_i^s)}{\partial w_i} < 0.$$

2. For all j,

$$\left| \frac{\partial (L_j^d - L_j^s)}{\partial w_j} \right| > \sum_{i \neq j} \left| \frac{\partial (L_i^d - L_i^s)}{\partial w_j} \right|.$$

3. For all i, j,

$$\frac{\partial (L_i^d - L_i^s)}{\partial w_j} \geqslant 0.$$

These restrictions on the wage rate sensitivities of excess demands mean negative own effects (1) (just as in the single-market case), positive cross effects (3), and dominating effect on the own market (2). On these assumptions, the matrix of excess-demand sensitivities $\mathbf{E}$ has an inverse with all elements nonpositive (Arrow, 1960, p. 7; McKenzie, 1960, p. 49).

Returning to Equation (4.41), it is clear that diagonal dominance is insufficient for unambiguous predictions on dw/dz. This is because the initial changes in excess demands may have different signs. However, if these signs are identical, predictions are unambiguous, and all wage rates will move in the same direction. All wage rates w_i will increase if all initial excess demands e_i are positive and will fall if all initial excess demands are negative. These results also apply if only one initial excess demand is positive (or negative), while all other excess demands remain zero.[2] Restating the examples given in the single-market case, a technological change reducing demand for at least one capability will reduce wage rates; a preference shift reducing supply for at least one capability will increase wage rates. Because of the assumption of diagonal dominance, a positive excess demand in one market can never stimulate a reshuffling of supply and demand that causes the wage rate in another market to fall.

Again, the method may be used to study the impact of changes in income tax rate parameters.[3] This requires investigation of the initial excess demand caused by the change. Obviously, this originates only in labor supply. Market supply of a capability is the result of the aggregate of individual supplies. If all supplies move in a particular direction, so will the aggregate supply. With given capability stocks, the direction of changes at the level of the individual is completely determined from the direction of change of effort $(1 - f_m)$. With respect to tax rate changes, the relevant derivatives are (similarly to [4.33] and [4.34]):

$$\frac{\partial (1 - f_m)}{\partial \Theta_0} = \frac{f_m}{R} \geqslant 0; \tag{4.45}$$

$$\frac{\partial (1 - f_m)}{\partial \Theta_1} = \frac{f_m}{1 - \Theta_1} \frac{1}{R} \{(1 - s_0)\widetilde{y} + \Theta_0\}. \tag{4.46}$$

The results are completely similar to the single-market case. This is not surprising since a linear income tax does not discriminate among incomes from different capabilities; hence, relative capability prices are not affected, and substitution does not occur. The remarks and the assumptions made in the single-market case will be applied again ($\Theta_0 < 0$, $s_0 \geqslant 1$ for all individuals). The initial excess demands can then be derived.

$$e(\Theta_0) = \left[\frac{\partial (L_i^d - L_i^s)}{\partial \Theta_0} \right] \leqslant 0; \tag{4.47}$$

$$e(\Theta_1) = \left[\frac{\partial (L_i^d - L_i^s)}{\partial \Theta_1} \right] \geqslant 0. \tag{4.48}$$

The prediction on equilibrium wage rates then follows immediately:[4]

$$\frac{d\mathbf{w}}{d\Theta_0} \leqslant 0; \tag{4.49}$$

$$\frac{d\widetilde{\mathbf{w}}}{d\Theta_0} = \frac{\partial \widetilde{\mathbf{w}}}{\partial \Theta_0} + \frac{\partial \widetilde{\mathbf{w}}}{\partial \Theta_0} \frac{d\mathbf{w}}{d\Theta_0} \leqslant 0; \tag{4.50}$$

$$\frac{d\mathbf{w}}{d\Theta_1} \geqslant 0; \tag{4.51}$$

$$\frac{d\widetilde{\mathbf{w}}}{d\Theta_1} = \frac{\partial \widetilde{\mathbf{w}}}{\partial \Theta_1} + \frac{\partial \widetilde{\mathbf{w}}}{\partial \mathbf{w}} \frac{d\mathbf{w}}{d\Theta_1}. \tag{4.52}$$

Note that these results do not require the explicit aggregation of supply and demand functions for single agents. It is sufficient to know the direction of the effects on initial excess demand at the individual level and to impose some general restrictions on the market adjustments (such as diagonal dominance).

5 THE INCOME DENSITY FUNCTION

Any one of intellectual capacity who consorts with the average persons of the "superior" classes, and observes their narrowness, their dullness, their fatuous self-content, their essential vulgarity, must hesitate before believing that they and their descendants achieve success solely because of unusual gifts.

—F.W. Taussig (1915)

The previous chapters specified the microeconomic foundations of labor supply and labor demand in terms of capabilities. They also described the conditions required for market equilibrium and made some necessary assumptions. This chapter will use these elements to analyze the shape of the income density function.

Empirically, such income density functions show a remarkable stability over time and place in their gross appearance (see, e.g., Lydall, 1968, Chap. 3). The outstanding feature, which has received wide attention, is the deviation from the normal or Gaussian curve. The upper tail is too fat; the distribution has positive skew. Although the deviation from normality is an accepted fact, there is no consensus on the proper alternative mathematical specification. The attempts to find one functional form, limited in parameters and yet sufficiently flexible to describe empirical distributions at different times and places, started with Pareto. Later, the lognormal curve was added as a candidate to cover the entire distribution, rather than just the upper tail. Although the issue has been taken up recently by a number of researchers, the debate has not yet reached consensus on the proper mathematical specification of the income density function (see, e.g., Salem and Mount, 1974; Bartels and van Metelen, 1975; Bartels, 1977; Singh and Maddala, 1976; Kloek and van Dijk, 1978).

Lacking the emergence of a generally accepted specification, the theoretical analysis cannot move in the straightforward direction of a fixed target. However, it can aim at the general features of the distribution: unimodal, skewed to the right. Moreover, the purpose of the present analysis is not just explanation of the empirically observed shape of the income distribution; it will also investigate consequences of assumptions that seem interesting enough to warrant examination. This can produce valuable analytical insights. The focus will be on studying the impact of tastes and the impact of talents. Income distribution is shaped both by individuals' endowments and by the choices they make regarding the use of their endowments. The theory developed here permits analysis of each of these elements.

The analysis will start from the individual earnings function as specified in Chapter 2. Since income distribution deals with comparison of individual positions, starting from the labor supply model seems only natural.[1] This means that labor demand has only an indirect impact through the determination of equilibrium prices; it is important for the relative scarcity of each capability. The indirect role of labor demand in shaping the distribution of income is a consequence of the assumption of divisibility.

This chapter attempts to investigate the consequences of assumptions on the distribution of characteristics with respect to the personal income distribution. A straightforward approach would be to specify some general features of a joint distribution of all the relevant characteristics across the labor force and then derive implications with respect to the income distribution. The complexity of the labor supply model (which is the medium of transformation) prohibits such an all-encompassing approach. Instead, a number of simplified models, obtained by adding restrictions to the general labor supply model, will be studied. These models yield a number of valuable insights, uncovering piece by piece what a more general model might produce in one stroke. Necessary results on transformations of distributions are collected in Appendix 3.

5.1 THE EARNINGS FUNCTION

The general earnings function has two specifications, individual income before income tax deduction (y) and after $(\tilde{y})$:

$$y = \sum_m (1 - f_m)\, w_m\, x_m;\tag{5.1}$$

$$\tilde{y} = \sum_m (1 - f_m)\,(1 - \Theta_1)\, w_m\, x_m - \Theta_0.\tag{5.2}$$

The symbols have the same meaning as before—that is, $(1 - f_m)$ measures the individual's effort (the proportion of his stock of capability m offered in the labor market); f_m is the proportion of the stock not offered for work (his "leisure component m"); w_m is the market wage rate per unit of capability m; and x_m indicates the individual's stock of capability m.

Equation (5.2) specifies after-tax income. The income tax function was supposed to be linear:

$$\text{tax} = \Theta_1 y + \Theta_0 \qquad 0 \leqslant \Theta_1 < 1.\tag{5.3}$$

Linearity of the tax function was chosen because of analytical tractability. The development of the average income tax rate with income depends on Θ_0. If $\Theta_0 < 0$, the income tax schedule is progressive in the sense of exhibiting an increasing average tax rate (not in the sense of increasing marginal tax rate). $\Theta_0 < 0$ reflects the fact (in many tax schedules, such as the Dutch one) that tax is only levied at incomes surpassing an exemption level (equal to $-\Theta_0/\Theta_1$).

The linearity of the income tax function has an immediate consequence for the relationship between the distributions of income before taxes and income after taxes: they are linear transformations of each other, implying, for example,[2] that $\sigma^2_{\tilde{y}} = (1 - \Theta_1)^2\, \sigma^2_y$. Also, since a linear transformation of a distribution preserves the general shape, analysis of this shape can focus on either y or $\tilde{y}$, whichever is most convenient.

Note the generality of the earnings equation, where capability stocks, capability prices, and efforts distinguished by capability type determine the individual's income. Each element represents an important component of the distribution problem: differences in individual efforts and the impact of the labor market.

Some conclusions can be drawn from this earnings function without employing the model of individual labor supply. In particular, (5.1) allows consideration of an *effort or talent* specification. If either talents x_m or efforts $(1 - f_m)$ are assumed to be identical across individuals, income distribution will result as the linear combination of either the distribution of efforts or the distribution of talents. For example, assume that the efforts of all individuals are equal. Assume also that capability stocks are distributed independently. In that case, the first three moments of the income distribution follow as the linear combination of the corresponding moments of the distribution of each capability (see Section M.1, Appendix 3). The distribution of income will have positive skew if at least one capability has a positively skewed distribution, while none has negative skew. Also, with efforts fixed, if the capabilities are each independently distributed as a two-parameter gamma function (with identical scale parameter; cf. Section M.2, Appendix 3), the income distribution has this same distribution.[3]

5.2 OPTIMAL EFFORTS

From Chapter 2 it is known that the individual's decisions on the supply of his capabilities are interrelated; in fact, he makes a simultaneous choice. Further analysis should therefore reflect this. Substituting for f_m the optimum values derived in Chapter 2 yields, using (2.8), (2.11), (2.12), and the definition of R,

$$\tilde{y} = \Pi R \tag{5.4}$$

where

$$\Pi = \left\{ 1 + \frac{\alpha_L}{\alpha_c} \left(\frac{P_L}{p}\right)^{1-s_0} \right\}^{-1} = \left[1 + \frac{\alpha_L}{\alpha_c} \left\{ \sum_m \alpha_{Lm} \left(\frac{P_{Lm}}{p}\right)^{1-s_1} \right\}^{\frac{1-s_0}{1-s_1}} \right]^{-1} . \tag{5.5}$$

Hence, net income is a proportion Π of resources R. R, the individual's maximum after-tax income, represents his talents—that is, the capability stocks, summed after multiplication by the market value of each capability. Π equals the optimal proportion of resources R turned into income. It is determined by the individual's preferences and therefore serves as an index of his tastes. Income distribution is now shaped by tastes and talents. The following results are immediate:

1. *Taste or Talent.* The distribution of income may originate in either the distribution of tastes (Π) or in the distribution of talents (R); any skewness in these distributions would show up unrestrictedly in the income distribution. Conversely, explaining the positive skew in the earnings distribution requires a skewed distribution of either tastes or talents.
2. *Taste and Talent.* If Π and R are each normally distributed across the population, the income distribution has positive skew, provided the co-

efficient of correlation between Π and R exceeds some critical level r^*, $-1 < r^* < 0$ (see Section M.3, Appendix 3). Thus, the income distribution has positive skew even if tastes and talents are independent. Note that the normal distribution of R may result from the summation over M capability stocks that follow a normal distribution.

If tastes and talents are independently lognormally distributed, the income distribution is lognormal.

An interesting model is obtained if one further assumption is adopted — namely, that $s_0 = 1$. The basic equations then reduce to (cf. [5.5]):

$$f_m = \alpha_L \, \alpha_{Lm} \, \frac{R}{P_L} \left(\frac{P_L}{P_{Lm}} \right)^{s_1} ; \tag{5.6}$$

$$y = (1 - \Theta_1)^{-1} \, \{\alpha_L \, R + \Theta_0\}; \tag{5.7}$$

$$\tilde{y} = \alpha_c \, R. \tag{5.8}$$

Under this assumption, individuals will take care that their net income always equals a constant proportion of their resources (of course, the proportion may vary across individuals). The shape of the income density function can therefore be predicted from restrictions on this proportion α_c and resources R only ($\Pi = \alpha_c$).

Tastes are thus reflected by α_c, and the three conclusions summarized above immediately carry over to the present specification. Restrictions on "lower-level" parameters α_{Lm} and s_1 are not required; they are irrelevant for the shape of the density function of income. Hence, a multicapability model, allowing explanation and analysis of individual labor supply, labor demand, and occupational wage rates, can also explain the shape of the density function with some simple assumptions. The implication on the irrelevance of α_{Lm} and s_1 is also important: a given shape of the density function (from α_L and R) is compatible with quite different structures of labor supply and occupational wage rates. This is particularly interesting in view of the similarity in shape of income distributions at different times and different places.

5.3 AGE DISTRIBUTION AND INCOME DISTRIBUTION

The methods and models used here can also be used to investigate the impact of the age distribution of the labor force on the distribution of income. Interesting conclusions can be obtained since direct observations on the age distribution are usually available.

Again, the analysis will begin with some general observations. Write income as a general function of age:

$$y = y(t). \tag{5.9}$$

Obviously, then, if the age-income profile (5.9) were linear, the income distribution could only have positive skew if the age distribution were also positively skewed. If the profile is increasing, but nonlinear, a positive second derivative pushes the income distribution toward positive asymmetry, as compared with the age distribution, while a negative second derivative pulls it toward negative asymmetry (for asymmetry, see Section U.4, Appendix 3). Empirically, age-income profiles are characterized by a negative second derivative.

The shape of the age distribution may vary in time and place, depending on demographic and economic conditions. Population birth rates, rates and ages of entry into the labor force, and rates of departure from the labor force (retirements, deaths) will shape the appearance of the age distribution. In other words, the age distribution may be skewed both to the right and to the left. The age distribution of the Dutch labor force exhibits rapid density increase at early ages and slow regress after the mode —that is, positive skew.

The typical age-income profile with negative second derivative can turn such a positively skewed age distribution into a negatively skewed earnings distribution. Positive skew in the earnings distribution will remain if the second derivative of the age-income profile is rather small in absolute value.[4]

The profile presented in (5.9) postulates a unique relationship between age and earnings. However, empirically, earnings are not identical for individuals of equal age. This feature can be acknowledged by considering the distribution of income conditional on age. In general, the latter distribution can be obtained by methods similar to the ones used above. Changes in this distribution with changing age then follow from the effect of age on determining parameters.

Consider the following model. Let capability endowments vary across individuals and let tastes be identical. Indicate the individual's capability stock at age t as the product $z_m x_{mt}$, where x_{mt} is used to describe the age-capability profile and z_m governs the differences in capability stocks among individuals. Capability development follows the assumption employed in Section 2.3:

$$x_{mt} = x_{om} + x_{dm} (1 - e^{-t\gamma_m}). \tag{5.10}$$

Each capability m has a typical profile of its own. Individual differences in capabilities are supposed to apply to such an entire profile (5.10); the profile holds for an individual with weight z_m. This implies that the ratio between initial endowment x_{om} and maximum level $x_{om} + x_{dm}$ is identical for all individuals. Note that the individual weights will generally differ by capability.

Under these assumptions and assuming $s_0 = 1$, income distribution is a linear transformation of the joint distribution of capability weights z_m across individuals, since

$$\widetilde{y}_t = \alpha_c \sum_m \widetilde{w}_m z_m x_{mt} - \alpha_c \Theta_0. \tag{5.11}$$

It is assumed that the α_c are identical for all individuals and that the $\widetilde{w}_m$ are equilibrium capability prices that apply throughout, irrespective of age. The z_m are supposed to be distributed independently of each other and also independently of age. In other words, all age cohorts have the same z distribution. This means that entries into the labor force, as well as departures, are not related to z. All income distributions for given age groups then have a similar shape, determined by the shape of the z distribution. But some parameters change for successive cohorts. Because of the assumed capability development according to (5.10), the following results emerge (where $E[.]$ denotes the mean and σ^2 the variance):

$$E(\widetilde{y}_t) = \alpha_c \sum_m \widetilde{w}_m x_{mt} E(z_m) - \Theta_0; \tag{5.12}$$

$$\frac{d E(\widetilde{y}_t)}{dt} = \alpha_c \sum_m \widetilde{w}_m E(z_m) \frac{d x_{mt}}{dt} > 0; \tag{5.13}$$

$$\frac{d^2 E(\widetilde{y}_t)}{dt^2} = \alpha_c \sum_m \widetilde{w}_m E(z_m) \frac{d^2 x_{mt}}{dt^2} < 0; \tag{5.14}$$

$$\sigma^2_{\widetilde{y}t} = \alpha_c^2 \sum_m \widetilde{w}_m^2 x_{mt}^2 \sigma^2_{z_m}; \tag{5.15}$$

$$\frac{d\sigma^2_{\widetilde{y}t}}{dt} = \alpha_c^2 \sum_m 2 \widetilde{w}_m^2 \sigma^2_{z_m} x_{mt} \frac{d x_{mt}}{dt} > 0; \tag{5.16}$$

$$\frac{d^2 \sigma^2_{\widetilde{y}t}}{dt^2} = \alpha_c^2 \sum_m 2 \widetilde{w}_m^2 \sigma^2_{z_m} \left\{ \left(\frac{d x_{mt}}{dt} \right)^2 + x_{mt} \frac{d^2 x_{mt}}{dt} \right\}. \tag{5.17}$$

Mean income increases at a decreasing rate, reproducing the empirically observed earnings profile from assumed capability development. The variance of earnings also increases with age, but this may be at a decreasing or an increasing rate, depending on the parameter values for the capability profiles. Empirically, variance usually increases with age, and so this would set restrictions on admitted parameter values.

5.4   INCOME DISTRIBUTION AND INCOME TAX RATE CHANGES

This section presents some attempts to derive predictions on changes in the income distribution if the tax rate parameters Θ_1 and Θ_0 change. It will be assumed that $s_0 = 1$.[5] The earnings functions then reduce to

$$y = (1 - \alpha_L) \sum_m w_m x_m + \alpha_L \frac{\Theta_0}{1 - \Theta_1} \; ; \qquad (5.18)$$

$$\widetilde{y} = (1 - \alpha_L) \sum_m \widetilde{w}_m x_m - (1 - \alpha_L) \Theta_0. \qquad (5.19)$$

As before, two types of models will be studied, the *taste or talent* model and the *taste and talent* model. In both cases, changes in income tax parameters will affect the capability wage rates w (and $\widetilde{w}$), and this in turn will have an impact on the income distribution. Effects on the wage rates were already studied in Section 4.3.2. For convenience, they will be reviewed:

$$\left. \begin{array}{cc} \dfrac{dw_m}{d\Theta_1} \geqslant 0 & \dfrac{d\widetilde{w}_m}{d\Theta_1} \leqslant 0 \\[3mm] & \\[1mm] \dfrac{dw_m}{d\Theta_0} \leqslant 0 & \dfrac{d\widetilde{w}_m}{d\Theta_0} \leqslant 0 \end{array} \right\} \text{all } m. \qquad (5.20)$$

The result $d\widetilde{w}_m/d\Theta_1 \leqslant 0$ does not follow from Section 4.3.2. There, the sign could not be determined a priori and appeared to depend on the opposing forces of a negative initial effect through the increase in Θ_1 and of a positive shifting effect through the increase in the market wage rate w_m. The outcome depends on parameter values, but it will be assumed here that an increase in a net wage rate $\widetilde{w}_m$ after an increase in the marginal tax rate ("overshifting") is so unlikely that it can be ruled out. With these unambiguous results on wage rates, the changes in the income distribution can also be predicted for each type of model mentioned above.

1. *Only Tastes Differ.* This model is represented by allowing $\alpha_c = 1 - \alpha_L$ to vary across the population and by assuming all other parameters to be identical; α_c is assumed to have a positively skewed distribution. For convenience, write the earnings equations as

$$\tilde{y} = \alpha_c R; \tag{5.21}$$

$$y = \alpha_c R/(1 - \Theta_1) + \Theta_0/(1 - \Theta_1). \tag{5.22}$$

The income distributions are linear transformations of the α_c distribution. Hence, moments of the income distribution are easily derived (see Appendix 3), and differentiation to wage rates then produces the results. For example, (5.21) implies (if σ_z^2 represents the variance in z):

$$\sigma_{\tilde{y}}^2 = \sigma_\alpha^2 \left\{ \sum_m \tilde{w}_m \, x_m - \Theta_0 \right\}^2. \tag{5.23}$$

Thus, using (5.20),

$$\frac{d\sigma_{\tilde{y}}^2}{d\Theta_1} = \sigma_\alpha^2 \, 2R \sum_m x_m \frac{d\tilde{w}_m}{d\Theta_1} \leqslant 0. \tag{5.24}$$

Other results on gross income and skew (third moment about the mean) are obtained similarly. Derivations are given in Appendix 4, while results are collected in Table 5.1.

2. *Only Capabilities Differ.* This case is shaped by the assumption that capability endowments x_m vary across the population, with all other parameters identical; x_m, $m = 1, 2, \ldots, M$ are assumed to have a stochastically independent distribution, with nonnegative skew for each and positive skew for at least one capability. This implies that the income distribution is also positively skewed (see Section M.1 in Appendix 3). The calculation of tax rate sensitivities is similar to the above model, and, again, results are shown in Table 5.1, with details of the calculation appearing in Appendix 4.

3. *Both Tastes and Capabilities Differ.* In this case, it will be assumed that capabilities x_m, $m = 1, 2, \ldots, M$ are independently, normally distributed (implying a normal distribution for a linear combination of capabilities, such as R); α_c is also supposed to be distributed normally, independent of capabilities. From Haldane (1942), it follows that the income distribution has positive skew (see Section M.3, Appendix 3). The analysis of tax rate changes is slightly more complicated now (see Appendix 4), but since moments of the α_c distribution are

Table 5.1. Income Distribution and Tax Rate Changes

	Income before Taxes, y	Income after Taxes, $\tilde{y}$

1. *Taste: Only the taste parameter α_c differs.*

	Income before Taxes, y	Income after Taxes, $\tilde{y}$
$\dfrac{d\sigma_y^2}{d\Theta_0}$	$\leqslant 0$	$\leqslant 0$
$\dfrac{d\sigma_y^2}{d\Theta_1}$	$\geqslant 0$	$\leqslant 0$
$\dfrac{dsk_y}{d\Theta_0}$	$\leqslant 0$	$\leqslant 0$
$\dfrac{dsk_y}{d\Theta_1}$	$\geqslant 0$	$\leqslant 0$

2. *Talent: Only capability endowments x_m differ.*

	Income before Taxes, y	Income after Taxes, $\tilde{y}$
$\dfrac{d\sigma_y^2}{d\Theta_0}$	$\leqslant 0$	$\leqslant 0$
$\dfrac{d\sigma_y^2}{d\Theta_1}$	$\geqslant 0$	$\leqslant 0$
$\dfrac{dsk_y}{d\Theta_0}$	$\leqslant 0$	$\leqslant 0$
$\dfrac{dsk_y}{d\Theta_1}$	$\geqslant 0$	$\leqslant 0$

3. *Taste and Talent: Capability endowments x_m and tastes α_c differ.*

	Income before Taxes, y	Income after Taxes, $\tilde{y}$
$\dfrac{d\sigma_y^2}{d\Theta_0}$	$\leqslant 0$	$\leqslant 0$
$\dfrac{d\sigma_y^2}{d\Theta_1}$	$\geqslant 0$	$\leqslant 0$
$\dfrac{dsk_y}{d\Theta_0}$	$\leqslant 0$	$\leqslant 0$
$\dfrac{dsk_y}{d\Theta_1}$	$\geqslant 0$	$\leqslant 0$

unaffected, the analysis only involves the moments of the R distribution. Results are also collected in Table 5.1.

Interestingly, according to Table 5.1, the three models lead to identical results. This provides some confidence in the generality of the outcome. The results are also identical for variance and skew and can thus be summarized by referring to inequality. It appears, then, that both an increase in the marginal tax rate Θ_1 and an increase in the intercept Θ_0 (reducing the exemption level $-\Theta_0/\Theta_1$) reduce after-tax inequality. Before-tax inequality is affected differently by these parameters: Θ_1 has a positive effect, and Θ_0 has a negative effect. This follows from the differential effect on efforts (see Sections 2.1.3 and 4.3.2): increasing taxes through the marginal tax rate reduces efforts and increases market wage rates; increasing tax rates through the intercept Θ_0 increases efforts and thereby reduces capability wage rates. Thus, to summarize again by instrument: increasing Θ_0 reduces gross and net inequality; increasing Θ_1 increases gross and reduces net inequality.

5.5 CONCLUDING REMARKS

This chapter presented an exploration of inequality. Starting from the model of individual labor supply and combining it with results obtained from the analysis of market equilibrium, the shape of the income density function was investigated. Empirically, the density function is positively skewed, and this chapter has demonstrated that the multicapability theory can cope with this observation.

The analysis stressed the role of tastes and of talents in shaping the income distribution. There can be no doubt that these concepts are essential for the most interesting questions. If the concept of tastes is taken in the broad sense of reflecting the proportion of endowments that are used for earning an income, the models can be put in an interesting historical perspective:

> In the eighteenth century, the common belief was that men were endowed by nature with the same mental and moral gifts. "The difference between the most dissimilar characters, between a philosopher and a common street porter, seems to arise not so much from nature, as from habit, custom, education". (Adam Smith, *Wealth of Nations*, Book I, Chapter II.) Rousseau believed that with proper education he could shape men's capacities at will; and Robert Owen rested his optimistic social experiments on the belief that, given favoring conditions, all men would prove equally industrious and equally virtuous. During the nineteenth century, the effect of biological investigation and the leadership of Darwin, was to turn opinion the other way, it laid stress on the inborn differences between individuals of the same species, the transmission of variations from ancestor to descendant, the close association of physical and mental traits. [Taussig, 1915, Vol. 2, p. 130]

In Taussig's view, opinions have alternated between the two specifications of the *taste or talent* models. However, it would seem that both taste and talent have an impact, and that models that allow both taste and talent to vary across the population therefore have an advantage over models that allow only taste *or* talent to vary. In particular, the multicapability specification with unit elasticity of substitution between leisure and consumption is very attractive. Rather unrestrictive hypotheses can then produce the proper shape of the income distribution. One of the interesting features of this model is that the restrictions from which the conclusions on the income distribution shape are derived barely affect the more detailed choice of labor market position of the individual (his actual job).

The relative importance of tastes and of talents in shaping the distribution of income can only be established empirically.[6] It is hoped that the concepts defined and used in the above models will prove their usefulness in guiding such empirical research.

6 A TWO-CAPABILITY ILLUSTRATION

But people earn incomes by means of several different sorts of capacity, among which the principal division is between manual capacity and mental capacity. From the point of view of income-getting, therefore, it cannot properly be assumed that we are dealing with a single homogenous group.

—A.C. Pigou (1924)

The theory developed so far is completely general. Relevance requires operational specification, in particular of capabilities and of a number of essential parameters, such as elasticities of substitution. Such operational specification will be initiated in Chapters 7 and 8. In this chapter, the nature of the theory and its implications will be brought out by adding some restrictions on the parameters in a two-capability specification. While these restrictions are made only to illustrate what may be accomplished with the theory, it is nevertheless believed that they are sufficiently close to reality to claim some degree of validity for real-world problems.

The two capabilities will be referred to as manual capability and mental (or intellectual) capability. The restriction to two capabilities in itself enhances analytical insight. However, further assumptions on the magnitude of certain parameters also allow some predictions on the effects of experience accumulation and on effects of changes in the marginal income tax rate.

6.1 LABOR SUPPLY

The labor supply model follows Chapter 2. Assume labor services to originate in two capabilities, indicated by x_1 and x_2, with x_1 referring to manual capability and x_2 to mental capability. These stocks will develop with age according to

$$x_{it} = x_{oi} + x_{di}(1 - e^{-t\gamma_i}),$$ (6.1)

where t indicates age. It will be assumed that

$$\gamma_2 > \gamma_1;$$ (6.2)

$$\frac{x_{o2} + x_{d2}}{x_{o2}} > \frac{x_{o1} + x_{d1}}{x_{o1}};$$ (6.3)

that is, mental capability grows faster and over a larger relative distance. The assumptions express the view that learning is a more important feature for mental capability than for manual capability.

As in Section 5.3, an individual is described by endowments $(z_1 \, x_{1t}, z_2 \, x_{2t})$, with the z_i being individually determined parameters. Endowments change with age (due to changes in x_{it}, since the z_i are assumed to be constant over age). The individual is supposed to offer a proportion $(1 - f_i)$ of his stock of capability i $(z_i \, x_{it})$ for employment. Hence, his job choice is given as the bundle of capabilities:

$$\{(1 - f_1) z_1 \, x_{1t}, (1 - f_2) z_2 \, x_{2t}\}.$$ (6.4)

Substituting the solutions for f_i from Chapter 2 shows that relative leisure choice is given by (cf. [2.19]):

$$\frac{f_1 \, z_1 \, x_{1t}}{f_2 \, z_2 \, x_{2t}} = \frac{\alpha_{L1}}{\alpha_{L2}} \left(\frac{\tilde{w}_2}{\tilde{w}_1}\right)^{s_1} \left(\frac{z_1 \, x_{1t}}{z_2 \, x_{2t}}\right)^{1-s_1}.$$ (6.5)

The model has some immediate implications:

1. At any age, the individual's job choice is restricted to the feasible area $\{z_1 \, x_{1t}, z_2 \, x_{1t}\}$. A job with high intellectual requirements is not within the reach of individuals with a low endowment of that capability.
2. The individual's feasible area will expand with age. Due to the assumptions

on capability development, the area expands most in the direction of mental capability (see [6.2] and [6.3]).

3. The individual's job choice is determined primarily by preference weights (α_{Li}); wage rates $(\widetilde{w}_i)$; capability endowments $(z_i\, x_{it})$; and elasticity of substitution (s_1). Individuals with identical capability endowments and elasticity of substitution will choose different jobs according to their different values of α_{Li}. If capability endowments differ, but all individuals have $s_1 = 1$, the effect of capability endowments on relative job choice is eliminated. In case $0 < s_1 < 1$, individuals will seek a leisure composition with high relative content of the capability with which they are most gifted. This tendency is reinforced if α_{Li} is positively correlated with z_i. If $s_1 > 1$, relative leisure choice will respond inversely to relative capability endowments. This response is strengthened if α_{Li} correlates negatively with z_i. This means that job choice responds positively to capability endowments: individuals whose talents are mainly mental will also choose to supply more of this capability than of their manual capability. If $\alpha_{Li} = \alpha_{L2}$ and $s_1 > 1$, individuals will follow their capability endowments in choosing a job.

4. Assuming the individual's preference parameters to be stable over age, his response to a change in capability endowments with age depends on s_1. By assumption, an individual's endowments over age shift in favor of capability 2 (the mental capability). The leisure ratio (6.5) will then move toward greater weight of capability 1 (the manual capability) if $s_1 > 1$. Hence, with $s_1 \geqslant 1$, individuals will tend to move toward jobs with greater relative weight of the mental ability. Conversely, the empirical observation that with increasing age individuals move toward "mental," rather than "manual," jobs may be taken as evidence that $s_1 > 1$.

5. The age-income profile follows from the development of capabilities and the individual's response to it. The profile is analyzed most conveniently on the assumption that $s_0 = 1$. Then, after-tax income $\widetilde{y}$ is given by (cf. [5.8]):

$$\widetilde{y} = \alpha_c R; \tag{6.6}$$

$$\frac{d\widetilde{y}}{dt} = \alpha_c (1 - \Theta_1) \left\{ w_1\, z_1 \frac{dx_{1t}}{dt} + w_2\, z_2 \frac{dx_{2t}}{dt} \right\}. \tag{6.7}$$

According to (6.7) and the assumptions on capability development, income growth with age is faster the greater the individual's mental capability weight z_2.

If $s_0 \neq 1, \widetilde{y}/R \neq \alpha_c$, the proportion is also influenced by relative prices. Again, resources R increase faster with age the higher the individual's value of z_2. But he may substitute leisure for consumption when the price of leisure increases. A decrease in income is ruled out, however (see Chapter 2).

6.2 LABOR DEMAND

The analysis of labor demand follows Chapter 3. There, a nested CES type of production function was introduced. In that function, capabilities combine to labor types; labor types, types of capital equipment, and intermediate goods combine to production units; and production units combine to the firm's output of commodities. From cost minimization, the firm's demand for capability i in labor type j, ℓ_{ji}, is given by (cf. [3.10]):

$$\ell_{ji} = \beta_{ji}\,\beta_{aj}\,\beta_j \left(\frac{P_Q}{P_{ej}}\right)^{s_q} \left(\frac{P_{ej}}{P_{aj}}\right)^{s_{ej}} \left(\frac{P_{aj}}{w_i}\right)^{s_{aj}} \frac{O}{P_Q}. \tag{6.8}$$

As mentioned in Chapter 3, the β's and s's are technology parameters; the P's are price indexes; P_Q is the firm's overall price index; P_{ej} is the price index of production unit j; P_{aj} is the price index of labor type j; and O indicates the total cost of optimally producing the firm's fixed output Q.

The following implications are immediate:

$$\frac{\ell_{j1}}{\ell_{j2}} = \frac{\beta_{j1}}{\beta_{j2}} \left(\frac{w_2}{w_1}\right)^{s_{aj}}. \tag{6.9}$$

Relative capability demand at given prices in each firm is governed by the distribution parameters β_{ji} and the elasticity of substitution s_{aj}:

$$\frac{\ell_{ji}}{A_j} = \beta_{ji} \left(\frac{P_{aj}}{w_i}\right)^{s_{aj}}. \tag{6.10}$$

A_j measures the units of labor of type j. Hence, the capability composition of labor type j depends on the distribution parameter β_{ji} and relative prices, as weighted by s_{aj}. A change in capability prices will lead to a change in the capability composition of labor. If $s_{aj} = 0$, the capability composition of labor has a Leontief structure, and $\ell_{ji}/A_j = \beta_{ji}$. This means that for each job, the manual and the mental requirements are fixed. If $s_{aj} = 1$, the production function is Cobb-Douglas, and (6.10) yields $\ell_{ji}\,w_i/A_j\,P_{aj} = \beta_{ji}$.

The cost index of labor type j, in the firm's optimum position, is a weighted average of capability prices w_i:

$$P_{aj} = \{\beta_{j1}\,w_1^{1-s_{aj}} + \beta_{j2}\,w_2^{1-s_{aj}}\}^{\frac{1}{1-s_{aj}}}. \tag{6.11}$$

If it is assumed that $s_{aj} = 0$, this index reduces to a linear combination of capability wages:

$$P_{aj} = \beta_{j1} w_1 + \beta_{j2} w_2 .$$ (6.12)

At the same time, $s_{aj} = 0$ reduces (6.10) to

$$\ell_{ji}/A_j = \beta_{ji} .$$ (6.13)

Hence, under a Leontief production structure, the optimum cost index is linear.

6.3 THE DISTRIBUTION OF INCOME

Assume that for all individuals, $s_0 = 1$. The distribution of income can then easily be derived from Equation (6.6). Let the distribution of capability stocks ($z_1 x_{1t}$, $z_2 x_{2t}$) be normal, with coefficient of correlation r. Resources R are also then normally distributed, with the following moments:

$$R = \tilde{w}_1 z_1 x_{1t} + \tilde{w}_2 z_2 x_{2t} - \Theta_0;$$ (6.14)

$$\mu_R = \tilde{w}_1 \mu_1 + \tilde{w}_2 \mu_2 - \Theta_0;$$ (6.15)

$$\sigma_R^2 = \tilde{w}_1^2 \sigma_1^2 + \tilde{w}_2^2 \sigma_2^2 + 2r \tilde{w}_1 \tilde{w}_2 \sigma_1 \sigma_2$$ (6.16)

where μ_i and σ_i^2 are the mean and the variance of $z_i x_{it}$ and where the subscript i in μ_i and σ_i refers to the first and the second capability. Assuming α_c to be distributed normally, with mean μ_α and variance σ_α^2, independent of R, the distribution of net income $\tilde{y}$ is positively skewed (see Section M.3, Appendix 3), with moments

$$\mu_{\tilde{y}} = \mu_\alpha \mu_R;$$ (6.17)

$$\sigma_{\tilde{y}}^2 = \sigma_\alpha^2 \mu_R^2 + \mu_\alpha^2 \sigma_R^2 + \sigma_\alpha^2 \sigma_R^2 ;$$ (6.18)

$$sk_{\tilde{y}} = 6 \mu_\alpha \mu_R \sigma_\alpha^2 \sigma_R^2 .$$ (6.19)

6.4 THE DISTRIBUTION OF JOB WAGE RATES

Up to now, when the size distribution of labor incomes has been studied, the behavior of the individual supplier of labor has been the point of departure. This is a natural thing to do if one is interested in the relationship between differences among individuals and the impact of such differences on the distribution of income. However, one might also start from the other end of the labor market — the individual firm. In such an approach, the frequency function of job wage rates would be the focus of analysis. This seems most appropriate if one wishes to stress the role of technology in shaping the frequency function.

The distribution of individuals according to the size of their labor incomes and the distribution of job positions according to the job wage rate are generally not identical. They will only be identical if there is exact correspondence between one worker and one job. Deviations will occur if individuals combine (parts of) jobs. Empirically, this appears to be the case, in particular among high-income earners (who combine, e.g., some salaried work with some self-employment).

The present theory does not assume identity of the two distributions. This relates to the hypothesis of job divisibility. This section derives a frequency function of job positions by job wage rates in the two-capability specification. Equation (6.11) is instrumental in deriving this size distribution: it gives the cost index of jobs, which, in the firm's optimum, equals the market wage rate of that job (see also Section 3.3). Assuming the number of labor types j is so great that approximation by a continuous density function is warranted, the distribution of the technology parameters β_{ji} over the entire labor market can be represented by a bivariate density function. Let this joint density function of (β_1, β_2), where the subscript j is now suppressed, be given by the bivariate exponential

$$f(\beta_1, \beta_2) = \lambda_1 \, \lambda_2 \, e^{-\lambda_1 \, \beta_1 - \lambda_2 \, \beta_2}, 0 \leqslant \beta_1, \beta_2. \tag{6.20}$$

According to (6.12), if $s_{aj} = 0$, the job wage rate is given by

$$P_a = \beta_1 \, w_1 + \beta_2 \, w_2. \tag{6.21}$$

The density function of job wage rates P_a can now be found by transforming the density function (6.20) through Equation (6.21). This yields[1]

$$\Phi(P_a) = \frac{\lambda_1' \, \lambda_2'}{\lambda_1' - \lambda_2'} \, e^{-\lambda_2' \, P_a} \, \{1 - e^{(\lambda_2' - \lambda_1')P_a}\} \tag{6.22}$$

where

$$\lambda_i' = \lambda_i/w_i, \, i = 1, 2.$$

This function is unimodal, with rapid density increase below the mode, slow density regress thereafter (positive skew), and modal job wage $\hat{P}_a$ occurring at

$$\hat{P}_a = \frac{ln\lambda_1' - ln\lambda_2'}{\lambda_1' - \lambda_2'}. \tag{6.23}$$

6.5 EFFECTS OF INCOME TAX RATE CHANGES

Chapter 4 gave the general formulation for finding effects of tax rate changes on wage rates. Suppliers of labor respond to net (after-tax) wage rates and demanders to gross (market) wage rates. The incidence of the tax is determined by relative price sensitivities (including cross effects) of aggregate supply and aggregate demand. Only empirical estimation can produce definite answers here, although some general restrictions were sufficient to predict the direction of effects on income inequality (Chapter 5). Again for the sake of illustration, consequences of changes in the marginal income tax rate Θ_1 will be investigated on the basis of the following hypothesis:

$$\frac{dw_i}{d\Theta_1}\frac{1}{w_i} = b_i, i = 1,2; \tag{6.24}$$

$$\frac{d\widetilde{w}_i}{d\Theta_1}\frac{1}{\widetilde{w}_i} = -\frac{1-b_i}{1-\Theta_1}, i = 1,2; \tag{6.25}$$

$$0 \leqslant b_i \leqslant 1; \tag{6.26}$$

$$b_1 < b_2. \tag{6.27}$$

Hence, it is assumed that a percentage-point change in the marginal tax rate Θ_1 leads to a relative change in the market wage rate b_i ([6.25] is implied by the assumption of [6.24]). If $b_i = 0$, labor suppliers bear the tax change completely; if $b_i = 1$, labor suppliers bear no part at all, and the after-tax wage rate is unchanged. Also, "shifting" is assumed greater for mental capability than for manual capability. Thus, in this illustration, the market position for mental capability supply is assumed stronger than that for manual capability, which may not be a poor approximation of the real world. Returning to individual incomes, analyzed from the model of labor supply, the following effects are predicted:

1. Income differentials between "mental" jobs and "manual" jobs will increase. This applies to both gross and net incomes (assuming that $0 < [b_1, b_2] < 1$).
2. Effects on income variance and skew can be predicted in a *taste and talent* model. Still assuming $s_0 = 1$, let individuals differ in consumption preference parameter α_c and in capability stocks $z_1 x_{1t}, z_2 x_{2t}$. Let α_c be uncorrelated with capability stocks, but allow some negative correlation between mental and manual capability stocks. The distribution of net income is then the one spelled out in Section 6.3, and the distribution of gross income is a linear transformation of it. Now, increasing the marginal

tax rate Θ_1 increases variance and skew of gross incomes and reduces variance and skew of net incomes (the results on variance require the correlation between mental and manual capability stocks to be modest).[2]

3. Still assuming $s_0 = 1$, the slope of the age profile of gross income will increase (as long as $b_i > 0$ for at least one i), while the slope of the net-income profile will decrease (as long as $b_i < 1$ for at least one i).

4. With $s_0 = 1$, the absolute age-income profile differences between mental and manual jobs will be enlarged since the relative wage of the faster-growing mental capability will increase.

6.6 CONCLUDING REMARKS

This chapter was intended as an illustration of the theory. Within the general framework of the approach, a few specific assumptions on the nature of "manual" and "mental" capability were sufficient to bring out a number of interesting predictions on age-income profiles, income distribution, and job design. These predictions do not seem at variance with reality, but solid testing of the theory remains to be done.

Although this chapter primarily illustrated results already obtained, one element emerged clearer than before: the distinction between the distribution of income and the distribution of job wage rates. The latter distribution was derived explicitly from assumptions on the joint density function of technology parameters, and it also appeared to be positively skewed. This demonstrates that the demand side of the labor market can be analyzed in the same way as the supply side—that is, by studying the transformation of the distribution of technology parameters into a distribution of job wage rates at equilibrium capability prices.

7 ON TESTING

As we learn from our mistakes our knowledge grows, even though we may never know — that is, know for certain. Since our knowledge can grow, there can be no reason for despair of reason. And since we can never know for certain, there can be no authority here for any claim to authority, for conceit over our knowledge, or for our smugness.

—Karl R. Popper (1963)

A theory is an agenda for empirical work. With the foregoing chapters having presented the theoretical developments, it is now time to turn to the empirical aspects. The word *agenda* has been used deliberately. The theory that has been developed yields a number of assertions that are amenable to testing, and it demands measurement of its crucial variables. Such measurement will take much time and effort and cannot be dealt with exhaustively in this book. In fact, the remainder of the book will deal only with the initial empirical steps. These steps consist of enumerating important predictions and examining them in the light of empirical results obtained by others. Chapter 8 will present original evidence from data available in the United States.

7.1 MAIN HYPOTHESES AND THEIR TESTING

This section enumerates important, refutable predictions of the theory and describes how they can be tested.

1. *Capabilities are operational variables.* They distinguish among jobs and among individuals. The hypothesis that capabilities can be made operational can be tested by defining a collection of such capabilities, stating how they can be measured, and investigating whether these variables discriminate among jobs and among workers. Section 7.2 presents the results of an inquiry into this topic in the literature. Operationality is certainly not considered self-evident among economists.

2. *Individuals supply proportions of their capability stocks.* The essential feature of individual adjustment to the labor market is the choice of parts of capability stocks for work activity. The hypothesis can be tested directly by comparing the individual's capability stocks and the capability requirements of his job, in the process measuring the values of f_m. The test can also be indirect—for example, through examining the implication that individual income is predicted better from required capability levels than from capability stocks. Some evidence on these matters is presented in Section 7.3.

3. *Job wage rates can be explained from capability requirements.* Testing demands data on job wage rates and on capability requirements. Section 7.4 provides some initial results drawn from the work of others, while Chapter 8 is entirely devoted to this prediction.

4. *Job wage rates are linear in capability requirements.* This prediction is intimately related to the assumption that capabilities are separable and divisible, as was discussed at some length in Chapter 4. Testing occurs through comparison with alternative specifications. A linear regression of job wages on capability requirements should not be significantly outperformed by a nonlinear, nonadditive relation. Section 7.4 cites some evidence on the matter, while Chapter 8 further explores the issue.

5. *Age-income profiles have an asymptotic shape, similar to that of capability profiles.* The first part of the hypothesis can be tested with data on individual income by age, the second with data on capability development over age. Section 7.5 is devoted to this issue.

6. *The individual's feasible job area expands with age.* At given capability stocks, the individual's job choice is restricted to jobs that require no more than the size of his stocks. Since these stocks are assumed to increase with age, the feasible job area should also expand. The hypothesis might be tested by determining whether the number of jobs for which

individuals qualify increases with age. If an ordering of jobs in terms of capability requirements has been obtained, the hypothesis can also be tested through exploring the prediction that as the individual ages, the level of the highest position open to him increases.

7. *Tax rate changes have predictable effects on income distribution.* Increasing the intercept (and reducing the exemption level) in a linear income tax schedule reduces variance and skew of the distribution of gross and net income; increasing the marginal income tax rate increases variance and skew of the gross income distribution and reduces variance and skew of the net income distribution. Testing can be accomplished on time-series observations of the variables.

7.2 CAPABILITIES AS OPERATIONAL VARIABLES

This section presents evidence for the claim that hypothesis 1, which states that capabilities can be made operational, does not have to be rejected. The evidence is found in the work that has been done in the fields of occupational psychology, vocational and educational counseling, and classification of work.

Empirical work on individual abilities started with the measurement of general intelligence, or IQ, at the beginning of this century. Stimulated in both world wars by the need for large scale recruitment and allocation, much work was accomplished and many data collected. The findings generated by military experience were applied to civilian populations, and IQ standards were set for many occupations. The standards were obtained by establishing median test scores for members of particular occupations. Researchers found it possible to rank occupations in terms of IQ and established, in the early 1920s, four to five primary occupational levels (professional, technical, skilled, semiskilled, and unskilled), and detailed levels were set for finer breakdowns.[1] Later work also emphasized the variance of scores within an occupation, and it became clear that there is a great deal of overlap of intelligence levels among occupations. This fact is illustrated quite well in Figure 7.1.

Quite early during the process of developing and validating occupational aptitude tests, the single-minded concentration on IQ was given up in favor of a multidimensional approach. Emphasis differs in the two methods that have been used. One method may be said to stress *job content,* while the other stresses *worker content.* The difference in focus reflects the distinction made in Chapter 1 between differences in tasks and in individuals. If one stresses job content, one concentrates on the activities that have to be performed in the job. The complex of job tasks is decomposed into a number of elementary activities, which are the building blocks of the job performances. Alternatively, stressing worker content

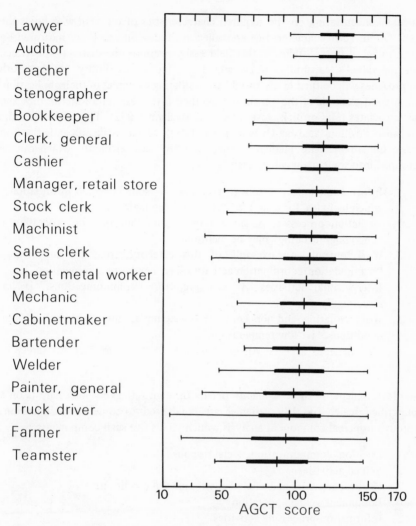

Figure 7.1. Intelligence by Occupation: AGCT Means, Standard Deviations, and Ranges for Enlisted Men from 20 Civilian Occupations. (AGCT is a measure of general intelligence.)

Source: A. Roe, *The Psychology of Occupations* (New York: Wiley, 1956), p. 72. Reprinted by permission of the publisher, John Wiley & Sons, Inc.

means concentrating on the required characteristics of the man who holds the job. Often, such characteristics are called aptitudes, and they are measured by psychological tests. Studies in this field easily overlook the distinction between an individual's capability stock and his effective capability supply. Both approaches will be further discussed by considering examples of their application.

A good example of the job-content method is the research of McCormick and his associates (McCormick, Jeanneret, and Mecham, 1972). They developed the so-called Position Analysis Questionnaire (PAQ), which breaks job activities into basic human behavior elements. There are 189 such elements, which can be grouped into some main categories:

1. Information input. A subcategory here is "sources of job information," which includes, for example, "use of written materials."
2. Mediation processes. As an example (from "information processing"), "encoding/decoding" may be mentioned.
3. Work output. An example of this category, from the subcategory "manipulation/coordination activities," is "hand-arm manipulation."
4. Interpersonal activities. An example, from "communications," is "instructing."
5. Work situation and job context. An example, from "physical working conditions," is "low temperature."
6. Miscellaneous aspects. An example here is "responsibility for safety of others."

Measurement of these elements occurs through ratings by job analysts on a prescribed scale. The 189 variables are condensed to some basic dimensions through principal component analysis, which yields five such components:

1. Decision, communication, social responsibilities
2. Skilled activities
3. Physical activities and related environmental conditions
4. Equipment/vehicle operation
5. Information-processing activities

McCormick and his associates concluded that "the results lend further support to the thesis that it is possible to analyze human work in terms of meaningful 'units' or job-elements of a worker-oriented nature and that this analysis can be carried out with acceptable reliability. Further, there is evidence that such job elements tend to form reasonably stable job dimensions [from principal component analysis] that characterize the 'structure' of human work" (1972, p. 367). The authors use their results for further work along the lines of the worker-content approach.

Another application of the job-content method was developed by the Dutch Government Employment Office (Direktoraat-Generaal voor de Arbeidsvoorziening, 1973), which uses a method of job analysis as a tool for vocational counseling and for providing information on occupations. Two types of variables are distinguished, "job requirements" and the worker's "physical requirements." The job requirements involve such qualifications as quantitative, technical, organizing, verbal, artistic, and manual skills, as well as contact, exactness, coordination, attention, and memory. An attempt has been made to define the variables in such a way that disjunct categories are obtained. Admittedly, however, this has not always been accomplished (Direktoraat-Generaal voor de Arbeidsvoorziening, 1973, p. 39). Measurement is obtained by grading on a zero to four scale and is done by job analysts. The results have been used to devise a classification of jobs and job families (see Rijksarbeidsbureau, 1952). In his study, ten Cate (1977) applied factor analysis to a number of samples drawn from these data; the samples were not representative of the entire job structure. (The original observations were limited to a small sector of the labor market, and the need for observations on wage rates caused further truncation.) In his analyses, the samples pointed to a limited number of factors, some of which were easily interpreted, while others were more difficult to understand. Important factors were a social-organizational factor, dexterity, motor coordination, punctuality, some dimensions of observing, and some dimensions of understanding and applying engineering principles.

In the formulation known as the "normalized method" (NM), job content is also the basis for the classification of work, which is used to determine wages. NM was developed in conjunction with the centralized wage determination applied in the Netherlands in the postwar period. It is called the normalized method because it involves a normalization of a number of classification-of-work systems already in use in industries or particular firms. NM distinguishes ten aspects (knowledge, independence, contact, authority, expression, motor ability, feeling for machines and material, unfavorable working conditions, special demands, and potential loss). Each aspect is measured through grading by a job analyst. Weights are attached to each aspect, and the product of grade and weight is added across aspects to obtain a total score for a job. Wages are then determined in relation to the total score. NM was developed in the context of close cooperation among the parties engaged in the centralized wage determinations and has been widely applied for blue-collar workers. It appears to have worked to the satisfaction of labor market participants.

In its implementation, NM has been made to fit the existing wage structure, in particular through the choice of the weights of the aspects (see Lijftogt, 1966, p. 81). Introduction of the method has not been accompanied by systematic research into the question of whether the aspects are sufficient to bring out the relevant differences or whether a smaller number of aspects might do as well. However, an analysis by Sandee and Ruiter (1957) has demonstrated a high degree of intercorrelation between some aspects, indicating that a combination of knowledge, independence, and potential loss would absorb the greater part of the variance in grades between jobs (in a factor analysis). Wiegersma (1958) reached this same conclusion in an analysis of a different sample of the same data.

Next, consider capabilities derived from stressing worker content. The basic approach here is to distinguish among people engaged in different jobs through psychological differences measured in aptitude tests. Thorndike and Hagen (1959) used this approach in their follow-up study on more than ten thousand men who were tested in the U.S. Air Force on their suitability for specific tasks (as pilots, navigators, or bombardiers). These men had passed a general army classification test and had to have met the standards for admission to the Air Force training program (for which they had volunteered). Thus, in accordance with the standards, they were single, between the ages of eighteen and twenty-six, in good health, and had passed a scholastic aptitude test; the qualifying score was set at a level that could be reached by at least half the high school graduates nationwide. The mental-ability level of those in the sample was therefore above average. Thorndike and Hagen collected additional data on occupation and occupational success some twelve years after the tests were taken and then compared capability stocks of men in different occupations. The test battery yielded scores on twenty testing instruments, which could be grouped into five main categories:

1. General intellectual ability, or scholastic aptitude
2. Numerical fluency
3. Speed and accuracy of visual perception
4. Mechanical knowledge and experience
5. Psychomotor coordination

Test scores were analyzed by occupation. On the basis of the five composite test scores, the following conclusions were reached:

1. Some occupations call for distinctive ability patterns, whereas a number of other occupations have no outstanding ability requirements. For example, architects have distinctively high scores on visual perception, while clergymen are about average on all test composites.
2. The general level of performance differs markedly by occupation. For example, engineers and physicians score above average on all test composites, while painters and production assemblers score below average.
3. The intellectual composite shows greater variation among occupations

than any other (i.e., discriminates most); the range is smallest for the psychomotor composite.

McCormick and his associates (1972) also considered psychological aptitudes. They devised a list of sixty-eight potentially relevant attributes (such as verbal comprehension, memory, acuity, dexterity, coordination), which were rated by psychologists on a scale of zero to five, according to their relevance for the job elements measured through the Position Analysis Questionnaire. Hence, after breaking up jobs into basic human behavior elements, McCormick, Jeanneret, and Mecham related these elements to required aptitudes. Again, principal components analysis on the aptitude scores yielded stable job dimensions. In fact, these researchers concluded that the dimensions based on the aptitudes "are somewhat more manifest" than those based on the behavioral elements (1972, p. 357).

The worker-content method has been applied extensively in personnel selection. This application has generated an enormous amount of data. Ghiselli (1966) has drawn on this information to summarize knowledge on the "validity of occupational aptitude tests"—that is, on their performance in predicting occupational success. Ghiselli's data consist of validity studies undertaken between 1919 and 1964. (Samples covering less than 100 cases were excluded; some samples were as large as 10,000 cases.) Ghiselli concluded:

> Two properties of the organization and grouping of jobs seem clear. First of all, in terms of their requirements jobs are not organized into clear-cut and separate groups. Rather, there is a continuous variation among jobs, and they form clusters which do not have distinct boundaries. Second, jobs which superficially appear to be similar in terms of nature of work may have quite different ability requirements, and jobs which appear to be quite different may have very similar requirements. [1966, p. 111]

The first conclusion, in particular, provides clear support for the general approach adopted in this book.

Some of Ghiselli's particular results on validity may also be mentioned. Validity is measured by the (squared) correlation coefficient between a measure of "success" in the job (physically measurable output or supervisor rating) and test score (reflecting the individual's capability stocks). Test batteries usually include a number of different tests, but validity is measured on the different tests separately. The combined information yielded by the test battery is therefore seldom used. It appears that aptitude tests have a validity with a central tendency of .30 to .40 if training success is to be predicted and .15 to .30 in the case of job proficiency.

Although training performance is therefore generally better predicted than job proficiency, the results differ a little by type of aptitude. With perceptual and motor abilities, training and job proficiency are about equally well (or poorly) predicted; with intellectual and spatial/mechanical aptitudes, training performance is better predicted than job performance.

An impressive amount of research on worker content has been undertaken by the United States Employment Service. In research initiated in the 1930s, this agency developed and validated the General Aptitude Test Battery (GATB). The GATB consists of a number of test instruments, which measure the following aptitudes:

G: Intelligence
V: Verbal aptitude
N: Numerical aptitude
S: Spatial aptitude
P: Form perception
Q: Clerical perception
K: Motor coordination
F: Finger dexterity
M: Manual dexterity

Scoring norms on the separate aptitudes have been established for a large number of occupations. The GATB appears to cover most existing knowledge about the relevance of various aptitudes (Super and Crites, 1965, p. 332–33). Many detailed studies on the performance of the GATB have been undertaken, and some interesting results may be mentioned.

Bemis (1968) summarized 424 validity studies on the GATB, involving over 25,000 tested persons. He found that median validity is approximately equal for training and for job proficiency. However, median validity is greatest for training for the cognitive variables G, V, N, and S and greatest for job proficiency for the manipulative variables K, F, and M.

Fozard and Nuttall (1971) described a sample of 1,146 men who were given the GATB. Table 7.1, which indicates the occupational distinction of the GATB aptitudes, is based on their data. The table clearly indicates different scores by occupational level. Standard deviations of the scores by level are on the order of 10 to 15 percent of the corresponding mean scores, thus indicating a fair degree of overlap between the levels. Note that from level 5–7 to level 1–2, there is a monotonic increase of scores for the aptitudes G, V, N, Q, P, S, and K and that there is a break in this pattern for F and M. Variables that seem particularly relevant for blue-collar work thus show a different pattern.

Thus, the hypothesis that was mentioned at the beginning of this section appears to have been substantiated. Capabilities have apparently been defined and measured in such a way that they discriminate between jobs and/or between

Table 7.1. GATB Aptitudes: Mean Score by Occupational Level, Men Aged 36-40

Occupational Level[a]	GATB Aptitude								
	G	V	N	Q	F	M	P	S	K
1-2	123.9	120.8	122.2	125.8	89.3	102.5	115.5	113.7	117.8
3	119.3	115.2	118.7	123.6	91.2	108.3	109.8	110.8	116.6
4	108.5	107.2	106.5	114.8	89.8	103.5	109.4	105.5	106.4
5-7	102.8	101.3	102.5	108.1	85.1	98.9	98.7	99.2	104.0

Source: Fozard and Nuttall (1971).
[a]Measured by the Warner index, an index of socioeconomic level in which level 1 is the highest occupational class and level 7 is the least-skilled level.

the individuals holding the jobs. The most thorough analysis of job-content variables, which was made by McCormick and his colleagues, yields a limited number
of job dimensions with which the variety of jobs can be structured. Worker content has been analyzed in depth in research that has focused on the GATB. The
aptitudes distinguished in this test battery are representative of the worker-
content approach. There appears to be a slight tendency in the GATB to sub-
stantiate the distinction that is often made between blue-collar and white-collar
work. This distinction has also been found in an application of McCormick's
methods to Dutch data (Simmelink, 1975). The GATB data are considered so
attractive that they will be used for further analysis in Chapter 8.

7.3 THE DISTINCTION BETWEEN CAPABILITY STOCKS AND
CAPABILITY SUPPLY

A key element in the multicapability theory is the distinction between individuals' capability stocks and their effective supply of these stocks in the labor
market. Testing of this feature can be accomplished indirectly by determining
whether job wage rates will correlate better with effective capability supply
(i.e., required capability levels) than with individuals' capability stocks (see Section 7.4). A direct test can be made if data are available on capability requirements of jobs and on capability stocks of individuals holding those jobs. A study
using such observations was conducted by Trattner, Fine, and Kubis (1955).
Their observations concerned the aptitudes measured through the GATB (see
Section 7.2) for ten jobs. Requirements were determined by job analysts, while
capability stocks were determined by administering the GATB to typical groups
of about sixty workers in each of these ten jobs. Since the data were not published in any detail, they cannot be used for tailor-made testing, but one of the
conclusions can be reproduced. The researchers found that the capability requirements as specified by the job analysts had a significantly lower mean than the
test scores of the individuals, which is precisely what the multicapability theory
predicts: individuals supply proportions of their stocks. The researchers also
found a higher coefficient of correlation between requirements and test scores
for "mental" (G, V, N) and "perceptual" (S, P, Q) aptitudes than for "physical"
aptitudes (K, F, M). This result can be interpreted to mean that the variance
across individuals in efforts $(1 - f_m)$ is smaller for mental and perceptual aptitudes than for physical aptitudes. (If efforts are constant, the correlation coefficient equals unity.)

It should be noted, however, that this interpretation is correct only if the
measurements of capability requirements and capability stocks are correct.
Although Trattner and his associates expressed some concern about the problems involved in measuring job requirements, it is reassuring that job require-

ments based on job analysts' readings of the job descriptions do not differ markedly from those based on job analysts' direct observations of the jobs involved (the researchers interpreted this as a reflection of a common system of concepts used by job analysts).

The distinction between capability stocks and capability supply is also compatible with insights gained in the field of occupational counseling, as recorded by Bailey and Stadt (1973). Judged by their account of historical developments, the multicapability theory, as presented in this book, fits in with the older views held in occupational counseling. These views (the "trait theory") distinguished supply and demand of labor in terms of capabilities, in much the same way as the multicapability theory assumes. In addition, however, it was assumed that through occupational choice, individuals would gravitate toward the jobs for which they were most suited. Vocational guidance, which could help in this process by providing better information (both about the worker and about the labor market), was based on the assumption that individuals were suited for only one or a few jobs. By implication, then, knowledge of individual abilities would allow a prediction of later occupational position.

The trait theory was discredited in the 1950s when it was found that occupational choice is a more complicated process and that such choices cannot be explained solely from knowledge of individual capabilities. Bailey and Stadt (1973) used the study by Thorndike and Hagen (1959) as evidence that the trait theory was unsuccessful. Thorndike and Hagen, as well as other researchers, found that members of particular occupations show large variations in their test scores; they therefore concluded that capability measurement is not sufficient to predict later occupational positions.

All these developments are perfectly in line with the multicapability theory as long as it is assumed that efforts $(1 - f_m)$ are not constant across individuals. In fact, the findings are evidence that the distinction made in Chapter 5 between "tastes and talents" is empirically relevant. The implication is also that a good deal of variation in earnings will be associated with differences in efforts $(1 - f_m)$ rather than with endowments x_m (cf. Figure 7.1). Note, however, that this deviation between capability stock and capability requirement—that is, $(1 - f_m)$—does not necessarily reflect only differences in tastes (the coefficients of the utility function). This applies under the ideal conditions of the foregoing chapters, but in reality deviations may also occur because some of these conditions do not hold: information, as well as mobility (entrance), may be less than perfect.

7.4 CAPABILITIES AND WAGES

A few analyses have related capabilitylike variables to wages. For example, McCormick and his associates used their material to investigate just this type of relationship. In a sample of 340 jobs from forty-five different organizations, covering a wide range of occupations and earnings (from about \$375 to \$1,525 a month), they obtained multiple correlation coefficients, in a linear regression, ranging from .83 to .90. Their explanatory variables were taken from the job elements as measured through the PAQ. In particular, correlation of wage rates with the five dimensions obtained from principal component analysis of the scores on the basic human behavior elements yielded a correlation coefficient of .85. Although other functional forms were not tried, the magnitude of this coefficient implies some support for the hypothesis that the reward scale is linear in the capabilities (McCormick, Jeanneret, and Mecham, 1972, p. 364).

Thurow and Lucas (1972) related earnings of a job to its characteristics, as those characteristics are defined in the *Dictionary of Occupational Titles* (U.S. Department of Labor, 1965). These include, with minor deviations, required scores on the GATB. As their explanatory variable, these researchers used the probability that the job requires the level of aptitude possessed by the top 20 percent of the population. This peculiar specification is the result of data problems and is not in line with what the theory developed here requires. Nevertheless, Thurow and Lucas obtained aptitude prices, which can be compared between males and females and whites and nonwhites. Some of the "prices" so obtained are negative; their results will be further discussed in Section 8.2.4.

Somermeijer (1947) used a job-content method to explain wages in forty-five construction trades in the Netherlands. He found that 40 percent of wage differences could be explained from a linear regression of wages on two variables: scores on a scale for the level of skill and scores on a scale for level of physical requirements. Also, multiplicative combination of both variables raised the degree of explanation to 50 percent.

In the analysis of Dutch data mentioned earlier, ten Cate (1977) also used the factors obtained from factor analysis on the requirements of the job to explain job wage rates. A particularly relevant factor in his samples was the social capability. Other factors with a significant effect on wage rates included quality observation, applied engineering, and punctuality. Explained variance ranged between 30 and 60 percent. Interestingly, in one sample, the capabilities as measured through factor analysis gave a better explanation of wages than did length of required education.

In many empirical studies on individual incomes, the role of intellectual ability is acknowledged. Typically, in one favored approach, there is a long list of ad hoc variables, such as length of schooling, age, occupational variables, socioeconomic background, and region, that are thought to explain earnings differentials. In these regression equations, ability is included as an IQ measure. The conclusion almost invariably is that controlling for ability reduces the coefficient of schooling, but its contribution in explaining earnings differentials is very modest, if not negligible (see, e.g., Olneck, 1976, or Gintis, 1971). Gintis's inference that firms do not reward cognitive characteristics but do reward affective ones seems too easily drawn. Rather, one might expect that ability is instrumental in achieving an education and therefore that the effect of ability is subsumed in that of schooling (Bowles and Nelson, 1974). As mentioned in Chapter 2, this is the line of thought that would be adopted if schooling were to be incorporated into the present model. Note that the modest contributions of IQ can also be understood from the large degree of overlap in individual capability levels between occupations and from the fact that these regressions are invariably based on available, rather than required, levels.

Thorndike and Hagen (1959) made an unsuccessful attempt to explain earnings from their capability measurement. They studied partial correlation coefficients of income with test scores (on single tests or on the composites; see Section 7.2) for separate occupational groups (five types of engineers), but did not find significant relations. It seems likely that their failure was due to two causes: the nature of their data and the nature of their approach. As to their data, it should be realized that the sample had been truncated to contain only individuals with above-average abilities (cf. Section 7.2); also, the data they used related to capability stocks, not to effective capability supply. As to their approach, they seem to have asked too much by taking correlations only for very specific groups, rather than across their entire sample.

The Thorndike and Hagen data have been updated and analyzed extensively by Taubman (1975). The result is a very rich data set with information on education, ability, biographical history, personal interest, and so on, and two observations on earnings, in 1955 and in 1969.[2] It appears to be very difficult to explain earnings differentials, with only a modest part of the variance associated with the observed variables. The ability measures are those from the Air Force selection tests (see Section 7.2), which were subjected to a factor analysis. Taubman scales them as fifths of the ability distribution and represents them with a set of dummies. Only mathematical ability obtains a significant coefficient. The rewards appear to differ by occupation, yielding the highest levels for independent workers (owners). One should interpret those findings cautiously. Not only is the sample atypical for the U.S. population (being better educated, of higher ability, and in better physical condition), but also the battery of tests is limited since it is geared to the purpose of selecting men for Air Force tasks. This emerges in the problems of identifying the composites in factor analysis. What Taubman calls mathematical ability would be called general intelligence by Thorndike (Taubman, 1975, p. 224). The tests aim predominantly at such abilities as mathematics, mechanical principles, spatial orientation, and motor coordination.

Another rich data set in the United States is Project Talent, a follow-up on twelfth-grade students. Welland (1976) analyzed the eleven-year follow-up, with a special emphasis on the role of abilities. He concluded that cognitive earnings capacity is multidimensional: "A single summary measure of ability is not adequate to characterize cognitive earnings capacity for different schooling levels" (1976, p. 153). However, Welland did not support the linear specification. In his view, best results are obtained with the natural logarithm of earnings as the dependent. Note that this study, like the majority of empirical work, deals with capability stocks, not capability requirements. If available capability were all that mattered, the returns should not differ by occupation, as they do in Taubman's findings (1975).

7.5 CAPABILITY DEVELOPMENT

According to the fifth hypothesis of Section 7.1, the asymptotic age-income profile originates in a shape similar to that of the development of capability stocks. Is there any empirical evidence to support this claim?

First, some of Hartog's (1976a) conclusions may be restated. There have been studies investigating the relation between general intelligence and age. Cross-sectionally, these relations exhibit a rapid increase of IQ between the ages of twelve and twenty, a peak somewhere in the range from twenty to thirty-two, and a decline thereafter. Clearly, this profile is not in conformity with that required by the fifth hypothesis. The period of growth and the time of the peak come far too early.

Certain physical abilities appear significantly related to age: maximum dexterity, manual strength, and so on. However, this relation is negative: there is a decline with increasing age. Mental abilities (such as concentration, perceptual speed, and memory capacity) are also negatively related to age, but only weakly. Hartog (1976a) reaches the general conclusion that all the measurable abilities considered in his study gradually decline after the age of thirty, but that this decline only becomes marked well after age fifty.

Similar results have been obtained with the ability components that are measured in the GATB. Fozard and Nuttall (1971) reported on a sample in which the general pattern of development, for all GATB aptitudes, was a decline in average score with increasing age; the decrease was more manifest at higher ages (beyond forty-five to fifty) than at lower ages. Increases in mean score with rising age did occur (in particular for the aptitudes N, V, Q, K, and G), but this may have been attributable to sampling variation. According to Droege (1967), all aptitudes except V (verbal) decline with age.

Although capability growth over age therefore cannot be established from the studies cited above, the growth of productivity cannot be denied. First, consider Mincer's observations:

Casual observation suggests that patterns of age-changes in productive performance differ among occupations as well as among individuals. The exploration of such differences is a well-established subject of study in developmental psychology. A survey of broad, rather tentative findings in this field indicates that (a) growth in productive performance is more pronounced and prolonged in jobs of higher levels of skill and complexity; (b) growth is less pronounced and decline sets in earlier in manual work than in other pursuits; and (c) the more capable and the more educated individuals tend to grow faster and longer than others in the performance of the same task. [1958, p. 173]

Next, recall the evidence about the learning curve given in Chapter 2. This curve brings out a typical, asymptotic profile of productivity growth with experience. The limited direct evidence on capabilities and careers thus points to observed productivity growth with experience, but fails to establish observations of capability growth. For one thing, this may mean that the proper capabilities have not yet been identified. For another, it may indicate that the link between capability, experience, and performance is more complicated than assumed in the simple life-cycle model of Chapter 2. Perhaps capabilities should be viewed as determinants of learning curve parameters—that is, initial and final performance levels and rates of convergence. The shortcut applied in Chapter 2, in which capabilities are supposed to develop themselves, cannot then be validated, although it still reproduces the observed age-income profiles and job mobility. Further work on this topic undoubtedly will pay off, as not much is known on the processes that determine individual careers.[3]

7.6 CONCLUDING REMARKS

This chapter has drawn from the literature to get an initial feel for the relevance of the theory when confronted with the facts. The search through published empirical studies led mainly to fields outside of economics as a science, in particular to the field of occupational psychology.

The lessons from the search are encouraging. Capabilities appear to have been given clear operational content, and two basic approaches have been encountered: the job-content method and the worker-content method. Capabilities were found to discriminate among jobs and/or the individuals holding the jobs. The search also yielded some evidence regarding the linearity of job wages in relation to capabilities. In addition, it found some apparent support for the relevance of the distinction between capability stocks and capability supply. Similarly, the distinction between "tastes and talents" described in Chapter 5 proved meaningful; in particular, the impression emerged that the variance in efforts $(1 - f_m)$ may have substantial effect on the distribution of income.

Obviously, however, a search in empirical work already accomplished cannot yield adequate testing since this work is not tailor-made to the particular needs of the theories developed here. Thus, further attention needs to be devoted to the development of such tailor-made testing.

8 MEASUREMENT AND TESTING ON AMERICAN DATA

Grant, oh God, Thy benedictions on my theory's predictions.

— R.L. Weber and E. Mendoza (1973)

This chapter reports on original empirical work on the relation between income and capabilities. In doing so, it presents the first direct attempt to measure and test relevant elements of the multicapability theory.[1] The analysis aims at the first three predictions mentioned in Chapter 7: that capabilities can be made operational, that job wage rates can be explained from capability requirements, and that capabilities are separable and divisible. The data apply to the United States and were taken from two different sources: income was derived from the *Census of Population* (U.S. Bureau of the Census, 1950, 1960, 1970), and capabilities from the *Dictionary of Occupational Titles* (DOT) (U.S. Department of Labor, 1965).

The capabilities that have been measured are capability requirements as selected and measured by job analysts working for the U.S. Employment Service (Department of Labor). The data set is unique for its systematic organization and huge coverage of the labor market. Two separate data sets are analyzed, one merging DOT data with incomes from the 1970 census and one merging them with incomes from the 1950 and the 1960 census. Because of differences in the census breakdown of occupations, the 1970 data set is more limited than the 1950–1960 data set. Therefore, the 1970 data set will be considered first, for initial exploration and for some first tests of hypotheses. Part of the analysis is then repeated for the 1950–1960 data set; the latter also allows a comparison of relative capability prices at different points in time. Owing to its larger coverage of the labor force, it is also more suited for some additional analyses. Details of the variables and the matching of the data sources will be given in the subsequent sections.

8.1 THE DATA

8.1.1 Description

The research reported here uses two data sets that have been merged as a set of observations on job characteristics and income. Incomes have been taken from the U.S. *Census of Population*; these data are well known and do not require special explanation. The precise description of the variables that were used is given at the presentation of the analysis (Sections 8.2 and 8.3).

The job characteristics are taken from the *Dictionary of Occupational Titles* (DOT). The DOT is an enormous accomplishment of the U.S. Employment Service. It contains information based on 45,000 individual job studies, collected over many years and regularly updated. The information describes the job content, indicates to which family a job belongs, and gives a qualifications profile of the workers in the job. The DOT was primarily developed for use in job counseling by government agencies.

For present purposes, the *3-digit code* and the *qualifications profile* are the most interesting elements. Appendix 5 reproduces the explanations given in the DOT. Since details can be found there, only a brief overview will be given here.[2]

The *3-digit code*, which is actually the second part of a 6-digit code,[3] classifies the job according to its place in three hierarchies: DATA, PEOPLE, and THINGS. The hierarchies are arranged "from the relatively simple to the complex in such a manner that each successive relationship includes those that are simpler and excludes the more complex." The 3-digit code identifies the highest level of complexity at which the job requires the worker to function, as reflected by the following list:

DATA (4th digit)	*PEOPLE (5th digit)*	*THINGS (6th digit)*
0. Synthesizing	0. Mentoring	0. Setting up
1. Coordinating	1. Negotiating	1. Precision working
2. Analyzing	2. Instructing	2. Operating-controlling
3. Compiling	3. Supervising	3. Driving-operating
4. Computing	4. Diverting	4. Manipulating
5. Copying	5. Persuading	5. Tending
6. Comparing	6. Speaking-signalling	6. Feeding-offbearing
7.⎫ No significant	7. Serving	7. Handling
8.⎭ relationship	8. No significant relationship	8. No significant relationship

The *qualifications profile* (the "worker-trait components") has five components.[4]

1. Training time
2. Aptitudes
3. Interests
4. Temperaments
5. Physical demands

Training time covers general educational development (GED) and specific vocational preparation (SVP). GED is best explained by a quotation from the appendix:

> [GED] embraces those aspects of education (formal and informal) which contribute to the worker's (a) reasoning development and ability to follow instructions, and (b) acquisition of "tool" knowledges, such as language and mathematical skills. It is education of a general nature which does not have a recognized, fairly specific, occupational objective. Ordinarily such education is obtained in elementary school, high school or college. It also derives from experience and individual study.

Six levels have been distinguished, with 1 identifying the lowest level and 6 the highest level.

SVP (specific vocational preparation) indicates "the amount of time required to learn the techniques, acquire information, and develop the facility needed for average performance in a specific job-worker situation. This training may be

acquired in a school, work, military, institutional, or a vocational environment."
Nine levels are distinguished, according to the following list:

1. Short demonstration only
2. Anything beyond short demonstration up to and including thirty days
3. Thirty days to three months
4. Three to six months
5. Six months to one year
6. One to two years
7. Two to four years
8. Four to ten years
9. Over ten years

Aptitudes are "specific capacities and abilities required of an individual in
order to learn or perform adequately a task or job duty." Eleven aptitudes have
been distinguished:

G: Intelligence (general learning ability)
V: Verbal ability
N: Numerical ability
S: Spatial perception
P: Form perception
Q: Clerical perception
K: Motor coordination
F: Finger dexterity
M: Manual dexterity
E: Eye-hand-foot coordination
C: Color discrimination

Five levels have been distinguished:

1. The top 10 percent of the (general working) population
2. The highest third, exclusive of the top 10 percent of the population
3. The middle third of the population
4. The lowest third, exclusive of the bottom 10 percent of the population
5. The lowest 10 percent of the population

Note that the aptitudes distinguished here are those measured by the GATB
(General Aptitude Test Battery), which was discussed in Chapter 7.[5]
    The component interests identify preferences for certain types of work activi-
ties or experiences. This information has not been used since it is not relevant to

the theory that is put to test—that is, that capabilities will be rewarded, not interests.

Temperaments are "different types of occupational situations to which workers must adjust." Twelve types of situations have been distinguished, each in the form of a dichotomy (the job involves the situation or it does not). Some of the temperament variables have been included in the data set because they were thought to reflect a capability required of the worker:

1. "Situations involving the direction, control and planning of an entire activity or the activities of others"; this was included as an indication of leadership.
2. "Situations involving influencing people in their opinions, attitudes or judgments about ideas or things"; this was included as a variable that reflects the ability to convince people, as required in commerical jobs. It is indicated as salesmanship.

Both variables are measured with a dummy—1 if the job involves the situation, 0 if it does not.

Physical demands are the physical activities required of a worker in a job. Most of the demands distinguished were not deemed relevant to the present theory (e.g., the information that a job requires climbing, reaching, or talking and hearing was not considered information linked to a capability that should be included). One dummy variable was created, however, from these demands: if a job required heavy work (H) or very heavy work (V), this dummy was set to unity. The dummy was included to test for the "compensatory" argument that was given in its classical form by Adam Smith.

Finally, a dummy variable was defined for independence. In the data, some occupations in the management sector are included twice: as a salaried function and as an independent one. The latter has been identified by setting the independence dummy to unity. It may be noted here that the multicapability theory developed above is also considered relevant for the self-employed; their positions are thought to be characterized by the same set of capabilities, but of course with different values (e.g., a high value on such capabilities as responsibility or independence, or whichever may prove relevant).

The variables that have been derived from the DOT information are summarized in Table 8.1. They will henceforth be referred to by the symbols used in that table. As the table shows, the numbers attached to the variables are sometimes positively related to the levels and sometimes negatively. This should be kept in mind when interpreting the results presented later in this chapter.

In creating a data set, the starting point was the *Census of Population,* which gives income statistics for detailed occupational groups. An occupation was

Table 8.1. DOT Job Characteristics

Symbol	Definition	Value, Lowest Level	Value, Highest Level	Number of Intervals
DATA	Relation to data (4th digit, DOT code)	8	0	9
PEOPLE	Relation to people (5th digit, DOT code)	8	0	9
THINGS	Relation to things (6th digit, DOT code)	8	0	9
GED	General educational development	1	6	6
SVP	Specific vocational preparation	1	9	9
G	Intelligence	5	1	5
V	Verbal ability	5	1	5
N	Numerical ability	5	1	5
S	Spatial perception	5	1	5
P	Form perception	5	1	5
Q	Clerical perception	5	1	5
K	Motor coordination	5	1	5
F	Finger dexterity	5	1	5
M	Manual dexterity	5	1	5
E	Eye-hand-foot coordination	5	1	5
C	Color discrimination	5	1	5
LEAD	Leadership	0	1	2
SALES	Salesmanship	0	1	2
HEAVY	Heavy/very heavy work	0	1	2
INDEP	Independence	0	1	2

included in the sample if it could be identified in the DOT without intolerable uncertainty. For example, both the DOT and the *Census of Population* include carpenters, and one may be reasonably confident that both mean the same job (the same applies to bakers, bookkeepers, bank tellers, blacksmiths, etc.). However, categories "not elsewhere classified" (n.e.c.), such as certain entertainers and clerical workers and unpaid family farm workers, could not be retrieved in the DOT and hence had to be omitted. Admittedly, the selection and the matching are made on rather untuitive grounds, but it does not seem to lead to important mismatching.

8.1.2 Some Qualifications

The data do not perfectly match the requirements of the multicapability theory.[6] A first gap consists in the nature of the measurement. The theory assumes continuous variables, of which the level in general will be different for each particular job. The DOT measurements consist of intervals of fairly large size. This means that the DOT measurement is rather crude when compared with the very detailed and fine-scaled measurement employed in the theory.

The problem is related to the question of the grouping of job positions into jobs or occupations. Which positions are lumped together? For example, architects constitute one occupation; there is no distinction by experience, and such a position as a "senior architect" has not been defined or classified by requirements. On the other hand, foremen in the metal industry constitute a separate group, while normally such a foreman is an experienced metal worker. This poses the question of the criteria for defining a job or occupation, easily answered in the multicapability theory, not so easily in practice. Generally, it seems that industrial labor has been classified into finer categories than has intellectual labor. It is doubtful whether this is warranted in terms of the requirements of the jobs. Averaging will not bias the estimates, however.

There is a more important point involved in the nature of measurement. The multicapability theory assumes cardinal capability measurement (measurement with fixed origin that allows the calculation of ratios of requirements, such as, e.g., job 1 requiring twice as much of capability i as job 2).

As discussed in Chapter 1, there are some good reasons for this assumption. Some hypotheses can now only be tested if the data match the requirement of cardinal measurement. Neither the first hypothesis (operationality) nor the second (wage rates depend on capability requirements) is affected, but the third is: testing of divisibility and separability only makes sense for cardinally measured variables (ordinal measurement always allows such rescaling that the wage function becomes linear in the capabilities). The DOT data do not meet this condition unequivocally. But the scaling employed there will not be completely arbitrary either. Consider the scale used for the GATB variables (which are prominent in the analyses that follow). The lowest level distinguished is a "negligible degree of the aptitude." Such a formulation can logically be extended to a zero degree of the aptitude (i.e., the scale has a fixed origin). As to the distinction of the different levels, one may apply the reasoning of van Praag (1968): one may assume that the scale has been devised to yield maximum information and that the intervals have been chosen to represent distances of equal relevance with respect to the description of the structure of work. With this interpretation, the data can also be used to investigate the third hypothesis, on divisibility and separability. Only separability will be studied, since this is by far the most important aspect.

The present data set does not allow analysis of career development or job ladders (common sequences of jobs). To some extent, such careers are subsumed in the data: consecutive jobs are entered here separately, each with its own capability requirements and earnings.[7] But the data from the 1970 *Census of Population* distinguish earnings by age even for jobs that are entered as a single entry in the DOT. Hence, the DOT does not follow the age profile of capabilities; it gives the characteristics "required of a worker in order to achieve average successful job performance." This calls for income data corresponding to such average successful performance. The 1970 *Census* gives both mean and median incomes, distinguished by some age categories, and all these data will be used, thus allowing a comparison of results. The 1950 and the 1960 *Census* give only median income, not distinguished by age.

In this data set, the same capability requirements are used to explain wage rates in different years (1949, 1959, and 1969). Lack of data prohibited the matching in time of earnings and capability requirements. This implies that the assumption of a Leontief capability structure for each job has to be adopted: jobs have fixed capability requirements, which do not respond to changes in relative capability prices. However, even with fixed capability requirements for each job, demand for capabilities may change. This occurs if the job structure changes. Technological and organizational changes or changes in the product composition of aggregate demand may then lead to different labor demands.

The assumption of a Leontief capability structure for each job is not a bad one. The period covered is certainly long enough for changes in the requirements of jobs to take place, but it would seem that the bulk of changes in the structure of the labor market actually take place along the lines mentioned above, and the assumption therefore does not appear to be really binding.

The DOT usually specifies more than one value for the required aptitudes. The sequence of these values is not always the algebraic one (e.g., from low to high, or vice versa). Only the first-mentioned value was used; this value was taken to represent the ordinary requirement level.

8.2 RECONNAISSANCE: THE 1970 CENSUS DATA

8.2.1 Data

The empirical research was started with a sample of eighty-eight observations for which characteristics according to the DOT and incomes according to the *Census* were matched. The income data, which were taken from the 1970 *Census* and are in U.S. dollars, are the 1969 earnings of white males in the experienced civilian labor force who worked fifty to fifty-two weeks in 1969. Earnings include wage or salary income, nonfarm net self-employment income, and farm net self-employment income. Both mean and median earnings were used for different age groups. Most analyses used the incomes of those 25 to 64 years old and of those 25 to 34; a separate analysis was made for the other two age groups (35 to 54 and 55 to 64).

The sample consists of forty jobs in the professional category, eight jobs in management and administration, four sales jobs, seven clerical jobs, eighteen jobs among craftsmen, four among operatives, three among farmers and farm workers, and four among service workers. The representation of the professional category is relatively high, but the method of sample construction did not allow a larger selection of jobs in the other categories, and it was deemed unnecessary to delete observations.

The 1970 sample does not contain all the variables available in the DOT; the empirical analysis started with the variables that seemed closest to individual capabilities and that were found in Chapter 7 to be valuable: the GATB variables. GED was included as a closely related variable and SVP as one that seems important in its own right.

A characterization of the data set (means, variances, frequencies) is given in Appendix 6. The information given there makes it clear that the observations tend to concentrate in the higher levels of the intellectual variables (such as G, V, N) and in the median to lower levels of the manual variables (K, F, M). In a number of cases, empty cells occur, in particular at the lowest levels of the GATB variables (level 5). The variables GED and SVP tend to the higher values; in particular, SVP has a large concentration at the highest levels (7 and 8).

Table 8.2 presents the intercorrelation of the explanatory variables. Inspection of this matrix brings out a notable structure of the dependence between these variables. In the discussion of this dependence, positive correlation will mean that high levels of one variable tend to be associated with high levels of the other variable, thus ignoring the fact that for some variables the highest level may score the lower value on the scale (which is the case with all GATB variables).

The following groups of variables are related through the positive correlations of the variables within a group:

GED, G, V (N)
K, F, M
S, P
P, K, F, M

Table 8.2. Intercorrelations of Explanatory Variables

	GED	SVP	G	V	N	S	P	Q	K	F	M
GED											
SVP	.696										
G	-.831	-.639									
V	-.848	-.594	.943								
N	-.696	-.570	.771	.794							
S	-.426	-.431	.260	.297	.537						
P	-.274	-.224	.219	.233	.451	.741					
Q	-.386	-.160	.507	.526	.615	.308	.378				
K	.135	.086	-.110	-.099	.104	.464	.709	.288			
F	.040	.012	-.041	-.016	.183	.479	.753	.362	.964		
M	.158	.101	-.179	-.161	.066	.519	.741	.215	.854	.846	

The intercorrelations (across the groups) are negative for variables taken from two groups of variables: {K, F, M} versus G, V. The following groups of variables are more or less independent of each other:

GED versus {K, F, M}
SVP versus {K, F, M}
{G, V} versus {K, F, M}

According to the intercorrelation matrix, then, the following structure emerges: two subsets of variables {GED, G, V, N} and {K, F, M} with high correlations within the groups and (near) independence between the groups. S, P, and Q are rather separate variables, although S relates to P and P relates to {K, F, M}.

The results show that GED is typically an intellectual variable (see the intercorrelation with G, V, N and the virtual independence of K, F, M). The information content of GED after knowing G (or G, V, N) is therefore very small. One would prefer education to have been measured as required type of school or length of education, but unfortunately this is not the case.

Another interesting conclusion relates to SVP. Apparently, long training associates more with the intellectual variables G, V, N than with manual variables K, F, M: jobs requiring long training are the jobs that require high intellectual levels.

8.2.2 Explaining Income

This section will present results of regressions run on the available capability variables. The theory developed earlier states that income is derived from the reward to capabilities supplied in the labor market and from nothing else. Hence, the income-generating function will have a zero intercept if all relevant capabilities have been included and if they are measured properly (starting at the true origin). The specification used here allows nonzero intercept to represent the value of omitted capabilities.

Table 8.3 presents the result of regressions run on all variables available in this sample.[8] Two measures of location—the mean and the median—were used for income. Both were available in the *Census,* and there is not much a priori reason to select between them. Also, two age classifications were used, one covering the ages 25 to 64 and the other the ages 25 to 34. Since capability requirements are measured as average requirements, the income concept should also be an average. As far as the capability requirements indicate levels needed for entry in the particular job, it is reasonable to match the requirements with income measured at an early stage in the career; therefore, incomes at ages 25 to 34 were also used.

The results in Table 8.3 indicate that about 40 percent of income variance

Table 8.3 Regressions of 1969 Income on Capability Requirements

	Intercept	GED	SVP	G	V	N	S	P	Q	K	F	M	$\bar{R}$	F	$\hat{S}_e$
Median 25–64	19,815	−352 (.51)	92 (.36)	−2,165 (1.96)	−806 (.83)	463 (.75)	−1,336 (2.52)	1,828 (2.31)	264 (.61)	3,768 (1.90)	−3,526 (1.74)	−1,955 (1.79)	.648	6.55	2,930
Mean 25–64	22,124	−306 (.37)	−13 (.04)	−2,672 (2.03)	−1,185 (1.03)	929 (1.27)	−1,368 (2.17)	2,170 (2.31)	290 (.57)	4,078 (1.73)	−3,779 (1.56)	−2,493 (1.92)	.621	5.78	3,485
Median 25–34	12,736	42 (.09)	52 (.30)	−1,157 (1.58)	−97 (.15)	11 (.02)	−891 (2.55)	938 (1.80)	254 (.90)	3,088 (2.37)	−2,797 (2.09)	−950 (1.32)	.625	5.89	1,932
Mean 25–34	13,797	154 (.31)	−48 (.26)	−1,569 (1.97)	−190 (.27)	464 (1.05)	−997 (2.61)	1,158 (2.04)	212 (.69)	3,267 (2.29)	−2,958 (2.02)	−1,283 (1.64)	.604	5.38	2,113

can be explained with the available capability data, and the F-test indicates that the hypothesis that all coefficients are simultaneously zero can be rejected at the 1 percent confidence level.[9] Comparing regressions for mean income with those for median income, the results on estimated parameter values and on their t-values are quite similar, while explained variance is greater for median than for mean income. Looking at the signs of the coefficients (which should be positive for GED and SVP and negative for the GATB variables in order to read them as prices), some wrong signs turn up. However, recalling the structure of the variables found in Section 8.2.1, it appears that in each group of related variables, at least one correct sign emerges. (This applies to the groupings GED, SVP, G, V, N; S, P; and K, F, M. Only Q, which is rather independent, remains with a wrong sign, but its coefficient is not significant.) Looking at significance levels,[10] there is again at least one significant variable for each of the groups that have been detected (significant variables are G, S, P, K, and F). Finally, comparing age groups, the results do not differ very much, although the relative magnitude of coefficients varies somewhat. Income of males aged 25 to 64 is explained better than income of those 25 to 34, however. If GED and SVP are set equal to 0 and the GATB variables equal to 6, which yields a situation with no supply of any of these variables, income in the first equation (median 25–64) is predicted at –975. This is interpreted as evidence that the present data set does not leave out important capabilities.

The results obtained in those regressions underscore the view that there is some structure in the set of explanatory variables and that it is not necessary to use all these variables simultaneously. An attractive method of reduction of the number of variables is stepwise regression, where the data determine the selection of variables. Stepwise regression starts from the variable that has the highest partial correlation coefficient with the dependent variable and then adds variables to the equation according to their contribution in the reduction of the remaining variance (after allowance has been made for the variables selected in earlier steps). The process can be terminated if the reduction in variance is smaller than a predetermined level. Here 1 percent was used as a cut-off level.[11] Results are presented in Table 8.4.

Roughly the same level of explanation can be obtained with only four variables instead of eleven. The selection of these four varies between specifications, but not in the representation of the different groups. Q is not represented in any specification, K, F, M in only one. Most signs are correct now, leaving only P as a variable with a wrong coefficient that differs significantly from zero. The elimination of the "manual" variables K, F, and M is remarkable. Apparently, earnings relate more to the intellectual variables than to these manual ones. G and S come out as important single variables.

For comparison, stepwise regression analysis was also applied to a semilog specification. The selection of variables changes somewhat, but they are drawn

Table 8.4 Stepwise Regression of 1969 Income

	Intercept	GED	SVP	G	V	N	S	P	M	Sequence	$\bar{R}$	F	$\bar{S}_e$
Median 25–64	19,215			−2,479 (6.52)			−1,128 (2.84)	1,687 (2.37)	−1,613 (1.97)	G, S, P, M	.654	16.78	2,786
Mean 25–64	17,799			−1,837 (1.57)	−1,302 (1.24)	1,068 (1.60)	−853 (2.16)			G, S, N, V	.607	13.29	3,379
Median 25–34	10,952	325 (.87)		−896 (2.30)			−781 (2.70)	436 (1.24)		GED, S, G, P	.616	13.90	1,864
Mean 25–34	11,197	412 (1.01)		−1,257 (2.37)		458 (1.17)	−600 (2.32)			GED, G, S, N	.587	12.04	2,053
ln Median 25–64	9.435		.036 (2.05)		−.133 (4.54)		−.042 (1.65)			V, SVP, S	.668	23.76	.242[a]
ln Mean 25–64	9.854			−.209 (7.12)			−.044 (1.81)			G, S	.654	32.64	.249[b]
ln Median 25–34	8.808	.066 (2.10)	.028 (1.92)			−.047 (1.72)				GED, SVP, N	.624	18.96	.192[c]
ln Mean 25–34	9.145	.065 (1.72)		−.072 (1.82)			−.037 (1.83)			GED, S, G	.618	18.35	.191[d]

Note: Q, K, F were also included, but never obtained a significant coefficient.
The product of $\bar{S}_e$ and geometric mean of the dependent equals:
[a] 2,496;
[b] 3,713;
[c] 1,796;
[d] 1,835.

114

from the same sets. S is still important, but the role of G is sometimes taken over by related variables (such as V or N). Also, SVP enters the picture in some specifications. The goodness of fit does not differ very much, although it should be admitted that the semilog specification performs somewhat better. This can be seen from the coefficients of correlation, but they are not completely comparable since they relate to variables measured in different units (one to the variance of income, the other to the variance of log income). A proper comparison can be made with a likelihood ratio in the way spelled out by Sargan (1964). The procedure he outlines entails comparing the standard error of estimate in the linear model with the standard error of estimate in the semilogarithmic model multiplied by the geometric mean of the dependent variable. This measure also shows some advantage for the semilog specification; it parallels the information obtained by comparing the values of $\bar{R}$ (this parallel reappears in all results presented in this chapter).

It may seem remarkable that SVP does not come out strongly, since it might be considered a very relevant variable. So far, SVP has been used in the specification given in the DOT. The scaling in nine intervals was accepted, and this is justified by interpreting SVP as an index of required trainability. In this view, SVP indicates a capability required from individuals (the capability to be successfully trainable). There is an alternative, however. In the human capital theory, education and training length are important for their time dimension. Training time involves an opportunity cost, and this cost of foregone earnings is the largest component of total training cost. According to this theory, then, earnings should be related to the training length. To investigate the relevance of this view, the scaling of SVP has been adjusted to a time-equivalent scale. This is accomplished by valuating an interval by the approximate midpoint of the length of training covered by the interval. The adjustment leads to the following scale:

SVP Value	Training Time		Adjusted Scale
1	Short demonstration		1
2		< 30 days	15
3	30 days	- < 3 months	60
4	3 months	- < 6 months	135
5	6 months	- < 1 year	270
6	1 year	- < 2 year	540
7	2 year	- < 4 year	1,080
8	4 year	- < 10 year	2,520
9		> 10 year	4,320

Table 8.5 presents the results. The change in fit is small, and the modified SVP variable does not come out as a strong, significant variable. Only the equation for median earnings for the 25–34 age group is affected: SVP now replaces S as an explanatory variable. Both equations containing the modified SVP vari-

Table 8.5 Stepwise Regression: Modified SVP Scale

	Intercept	GED	SVP	G	V	N	S	P	M	Sequence	$\bar{R}$	F	$\hat{s}_e$
Median 25–64	18,162		.964 (1.81)	−2,076 (4.76)			−809 (1.88)	1,686 (2.40)	−2,140 (2.50)	G, S, P, M, SVP	.665	14.44	2,765
Mean[a] 25–64													
Median 25–34	10,725	319 (.79)	.93 (2.69)		−528 (1.55)				−712 (2.20)	GED, SVP, M, V	.622	14.27	1,854
Mean[b] 25–34													

Note: Q, K, F were also included, but never obtained a significant coefficient.
[a]SVP enters in the 7th step, beyond the cutoff level, with coefficient .912 (1.42).
[b]SVP enters in the 5th step, beyond the cutoff level, with coefficient .40 (1.06).

able indicate the same magnitude of the coefficient, however; the return to an additional day of training is slightly less than one dollar a year.[12]

An important restriction in the theory developed earlier states that the earnings function is linear in the capabilities, so that the coefficients in regression equations can be interpreted as prices. This means that in each job all capabilities are separately and independently rewarded according to the market price of that capability. There should be no reward for the possible interaction among variables that would make combined levels count. This hypothesis may be put to a test in the following way: one may introduce a dummy variable that can be set to unity only if all of a number of particular capabilities are required beyond a certain critical level. The coefficient then measures the contribution to earnings that originates in the fact that some capabilities are simultaneously required at a high level. With the data available here, interaction was tested for the variables G, S, and K. They were selected for two reasons. In the first place, they each represent different groups identified in the correlation matrix. Second, their intercorrelations are low. Testing for interaction on highly collinear variables would be meaningless since it would be impossible to identify the separate prices of each of the capabilities, and such identification has to precede testing for interaction. The dummy variable GSK was defined so that it was equal to unity if each of the variables G, S, and K was required at level 1 or 2 (i.e., at a level possessed by the highest third of the population). The following jobs score 1 on GSK: six types of physical scientists, dentists, physicians, draftsmen, and electrical engineering technicians.

Table 8.6. presents the results. Clearly, in this data set, interaction as defined above cannot be neglected. The coefficient is large, has the proper sign, and is significantly different from zero. This means that the hypothesis used in the theory above is not supported here. Of course, one such observation is not sufficient to embrace the opposite hypothesis. More testing on different material is required, and clear insight into the relevance and magnitude of interaction with respect to the total wage structure and labor market is needed. In this respect, it may be pointed out that including the interaction term does not systematically improve the fit ($\bar{R}$ even decreases in one specification) and that the variable is relevant for ten out of eighty-eight observations. Thus, these results support the claim made in Chapter 4 that inseparability is at best responsible for some secondary effect on income differentials; this secondary effect turns out to be very modest indeed. Interaction will be studied again in Section 8.3.

8.2.3 Factor Analysis

The previous sections have made it clear that the explanatory variables can be structured into some groups of variables. It therefore seems only natural to

Table 8.6. Stepwise Regression: Interaction

	Intercept	GED	SVP	G	V	N	S	P	Q	M	GSK	Sequence	$\bar{R}$	F	$\bar{S}_e$
Median 25-64	11,456			-981 (1.02)	-1,078 (1.27)		-986 (2.48)	1,329 (2.30)	650 (1.65)		4,040 (2.82)	G, S, P, GSK, Q, V	.667	12.29	2,777
Mean 25-64	13,984			-1,258 (1.08)	-1,518 (1.52)		-788 (1.69)	2,194 (2.65)	861 (1.86)	-1,316 (1.23)	4,549 (2.46)	G, GSK, Q, V, P, S, M	.652	9.93	3,283
Median 25-34	4,292	833 (3.14)	264 (1.83)								1,447 (2.29)	GED, GSK, SVP	.609	17.56	1,866
Mean 25-34	5,017	805 (1.80)		-595 (1.22)			-519 (1.62)	828 (1.96)	401 (1.43)		2,772 (2.45)	GED, GSK, P, S, Q, G	.613	9.44	2,029

Note: K, F were also included, but never obtained a significant coefficient.

118

attempt a systematic, or factor, analysis of such latent structure. In this way, the dimensions of the problem can be reduced, and repeated measurement of essentially the same (latent) variable can be circumvented.[13]

The GATB variables would seem particularly relevant for applying a factor analysis. Although apparently in the judgment of the analysts of the U.S. Employment Service, all these variables are needed for adequate description of the labor market, one may still ask whether a smaller number of variables might not do equally well with respect to the measurement and the testing of the theory developed here. Table 8.7 presents the results of the factor analysis of the GATB variables.[14] Two factors jointly account for 81 percent of the variance. The factors can be identified fairly easily. Factor 1 has high loadings on K, F, and M, a fairly high loading on P, and very low loadings on G, V, and N. It will be called the manual factor since it combines the variables that seem particularly relevant for manual (or perhaps blue-collar) jobs. The second factor clearly indicates intellectual capabilities: G, V, and N score high, and S, P, K, F, M score quite low. Note the impact of the way that the GATB variables have been measured: since the lowest level received the highest number, measurement is inverse. Negative factor loadings correct this inversion (so that the highest level again gets the highest number); positive loadings do not.

It is interesting to see if these results change very much if GED and SVP are included in the factor analysis. Table 8.8 presents the results from this analysis. Neither GED nor SVP appear to remain as separate factors; they are simply included in the intellectual factor. The factor loadings on the GATB variables are barely affected. Note the reversal of the ordering of the factors. With GATB

Table 8.7. Factor Matrix (after Rotation): GATB Variables

Variable	Factor 1	Factor 2
G	.095	–.941
V	.075	–.954
N	–.206	–.901
S	–.674	–.386
P	–.853	–.318
Q	–.334	–.650
K	–.943	.048
F	–.945	–.037
M	–.944	.100
Cum. percentage of eigenvalues	.491	.814
Identification	"Manual"	"Intellectual"

Table 8.8.   Factor Matrix (after Rotation): GED, SVP, and GATB

Variable	Factor 1	Factor 2
GED	.912	−.017
SVP	.748	.003
G	−.941	.048
V	−.944	.027
N	−.860	−.255
S	−.413	−.680
P	−.294	−.863
Q	−.530	−.385
K	.104	−.941
F	.012	−.947
M	.143	−.937
Cum. percentage of eigenvalues	.449	.779
Identification	"Intellectual"	"Manual"

only, the manual factor catches 48 percent of the variance. With GED, SVP, and GATB, it is the intellectual variable that catches the bulk of the variance (about 45 percent).

The fact that GED and SVP can be subsumed so well into the factor analysis does not, of course, imply that they do not deserve a place as a separate variable; this is something that factor analysis can never determine. But considering the definition and measurement of GED, it seems natural to include it with the intellectual factor. Including SVP might be equally well defended, since in practice distinguishing training programs by their duration seems tantamount to a distinction according to the required intellectual level. However, as mentioned earlier, others have pointed out the special relevance of the time dimension of training because of the cost and the required return that it involves (Becker, 1964). That approach is different from the one adopted in this book, but its basic ideas can easily be incorporated in the present theory (see Section 2.5). Although the stress here is on identifying capabilities, it nonetheless seems warranted to keep an eye on this alternative and to allow for it in the empirical analyses. (The point will be taken up again in Section 8.3.)

The factors can be used to explain incomes.[15] Regressions to this effect are presented in Tables 8.9 and 8.10. In Table 8.9, factors are measured using GED, SVP, and the GATB variables. The intellectual factor stands out as the best explanatory variable. Its coefficient is highly significant and of large magnitude. (Note that factor scores are standardized variables with mean 0 and variance 1,

Table 8.9. Regression on Factor Scores (GED, SVP, GATB): 1969 Income

	Intercept	Factor 1 ("Intellectual")	Factor 2 ("Manual")	$\bar{R}$	F	$\bar{s}_e$
Median 25-64	10,781	2,181 (6.93)	339 (1.10)	.597	24.07	2,892
Mean 25-64	11,457	2,381 (6.29)	244 (.66)	.560	19.88	3,479
Median 25-34	9,573	1,361 (6.66)	209 (1.05)	.582	22.24	1,878
Mean 25-35	9,846	1,384 (6.09)	199 (.90)	.546	18.58	2,088

implying immediate comparability of regression coefficients.) The manual factor contributes very little; it does have the proper sign, however.

Table 8.10 presents results for the case in which GED and SVP have been maintained as separate variables. The insignificance of the manual variable reappears, but the strength of the intellectual factor is diminished. The effect of the intellectual factor is now spread out over three variables: GED, SVP, and intellectual. After all, they can be interpreted as different measures of essentially the same variable. This view is corroborated by the intercorrelations between the three variables: r (GED, intellectual) = .83; r (SVP, intellectual) = .61. For the sake of comparison, regressions were also run with log earnings as the dependent variable. The fit improves, but the nature of the conclusions given above is not affected.

Finally, the effect of age has been studied more extensively. In the analyses presented above, only one age group was studied separately, apart from the aggregate over all age groups. The results were not very sensitive to the specification of the age group. To check this in greater detail, regressions were run for all the age groups mentioned in the *Census of Population*. The results are not qualitatively different by age. Correlation coefficient and significance levels do not vary much, and neither does the ranking of variables in order of importance. But, of course, the coefficients vary with age, reflecting changing income levels. Relative magnitudes may also vary somewhat with age. Consider the results presented in Table 8.11. Only median income is reported. These results illustrate the remarks made above quite well. The regression for the overall age group comes out neatly between the extremes of the three composing age groups. Relative prices do seem to vary with age, however. The price of the intellectual capa-

Table 8.10. Regression on GED, SVP, and Factor Scores (GATB): 1969 Income

	Intercept	GED	SVP	Factor 1 ("Manual")	Factor 2 ("Intellectual")	$\bar{R}$	F	$\bar{s}_e$
Median 25–64	7,050	392 (.65)	340 (1.49)	317 (1.01)	1,309 (2.31)	.588	11.95	2,952
Mean 25–64	7,338	653 (.89)	222 (.80)	190 (.50)	1,447 (2.11)	.545	9.69	3,565
Median 25–34	6,104	454 (1.17)	254 (1.73)	229 (1.13)	553 (1.51)	.581	11.58	1,901
Mean 25–34	5,911	717 (1.65)	147 (.89)	209 (.92)	480 (1.18)	.542	9.58	2,121
ln Median 25–64	8.828	.042 (.84)	.037 (1.94)	.022 (.84)	.115 (2.41)	.643	15.72	.248[a]
ln Mean 25–64	8.870	.066 (1.25)	.023 (1.16)	.006 (.23)	.116 (2.35)	.630	14.68	.259[b]
ln Median 25–34	8.740	.049 (1.25)	.031 (2.07)	.021 (1.04)	.055 (1.49)	.611	13.40	.194[c]
ln Mean 25–34	8.728	.075 (1.87)	.019 (1.29)	.016 (.78)	.043 (1.16)	.593	12.27	.196[d]

The product of $\bar{s}_e$ and geometric mean of the dependent equals:
[a] 2,558;
[b] 2,822;
[c] 1,815;
[d] 1,883.

122

Table 8.11. Effect of Age: Regression on Factor Scores (GED, SVP, GATB); 1969 Income

	Intercept	Factor 1 ("Intellectual")	Factor 2 ("Manual")	$\bar{R}$	F	$\bar{s}_e$
Median 25–64	10,781	2,181 (6.93)	339 (1.10)	.597	24.07	2,892
Median 25–34	9,573	1,361 (6.66)	209 (1.05)	.582	22.24	1,878
Median 35–54	11,587	2,525 (7.15)	245 (.71)	.610	25.72	3,245
Median 55–64	11,001	2,734 (7.25)	322 (.87)	.615	26.33	3,468

bility relative to the manual factor peaks in the 35–54 age group (the ratio equals 6.4 for the aggregate and 6.5, 10.3, and 8.5 for the successive age groups). Judging by the coefficient of correlation, the capability requirements are (slightly) more relevant for incomes of those above age 35. In light of the attempt in the DOT to specify requirements for "achieving average successful performance," this would imply that only at ages above 35 has the worker really mastered his job. That seems an acceptable implication.

8.2.4 Conclusions

The analysis of the data presented in the foregoing sections warrants the following conclusions:

1. The concept of multidimensional capability can be made operational in a meaningful way, allowing interpretations. This conclusion was already obtained in the search of the literature reported in Chapter 7; it is now reestablished through detailed analysis of a data source mentioned there, the *Dictionary of Occupational Titles*.
2. Capability requirements as defined and measured here are relevant in explaining earnings differentials. The correlation coefficient hovers about values of .60 to .65, implying that roughly 40 percent of the earnings variance can be explained with the capability variables that have been

employed. This may seem low, but the very crude nature of the data should not be forgotten.

3. Generally, median earnings are explained better than are mean earnings (judged by $\bar{R}^2$)—weakly, but consistently. One could argue, therefore, that the DOT specification aims at median requirements rather than at mean requirements.

4. The intercorrelation matrix indicates some structure of capability requirements in the labor force. The famous division between mental-manual capabilities seems illustrated in the occurrence of capability subsets: {G, V, N} versus {K, F, M}. However, some other capabilities, which hesitate between these subsets, also exist: S, P, Q. This view is corroborated by factor analysis. Two main factors emerge, catching 80 percent of the variance: intellectual and manual capability. The educational variables GED and SVP are submerged in the intellectual factor.

5. It seems that the DOT employs more variables than are needed to describe differences among jobs. However, this conclusion has to be considered with caution, considering the relatively small sample.

6. Mental and manual capabilities are not of equal importance when it comes to explaining earnings differentials; the intellectual factor is far more important than the manual one.

7. There is evidence of interaction in this sample: simultaneous high scores on G, S, and K yield a significant reward. This is in conflict with an important hypothesis of the theory developed above.

8. There is no problem with the signs of the estimated coefficients. Wrong signs can be ignored because of insignificance, and hence the coefficients can be interpreted as positive prices. Thus, the problem that confronted and puzzled Thurow and Lucas (1972) does not occur in the present specification.

9. Analyzing incomes of separate age groups does not affect any of these conclusions. However, relative capability prices may change with age. In particular, there is evidence that the price of the intellectual capability relative to the manual capability peaks in the middle age group. The DOT requirements predict incomes at ages above 35 better than incomes at ages below 35.

With these conclusions in mind, a few words may be said about the study by Thurow and Lucas (1972). They matched the DOT data with income observations from the Survey of Economic Opportunity by applying a matrix that cross-classified the occupations in the two data sets. They used a long list of variables from the DOT and a number of personal characteristics and regressed earnings on them. A most remarkable result is the negative price for a number of characteristics.

Thurow and Lucas's study differs from the present one in a number of aspects. First, they did not structure the variables (as the present study did with factor analysis), but used them all simultaneously in a multiple regression; thus, there may be a serious problem of multicollinearity. In this respect, it is relevant to mention their results with respect to some of the subsets of the variables as determined here on the basis of intercorrelation (and factor analysis). Intelligence (G) obtains a negative coefficient in most of their regressions, but numerical ability (N) a positive; also, in the one case in which G has a positive coefficient, N has a negative one. This points to the interdependence of the estimates and serves as a warning of multicollinearity. A similar effect occurs with the variables K, F, and M, which in the sample analyzed in this book appeared highly correlated and factor-analytically related to one and the same latent factor. In Thurow and Lucas's sample, negative coefficients occur on the variables K, F, and M, but never on all three variables simultaneously.

Second, as far as the GATB aptitudes are concerned, Thurow and Lucas's measurement did not specify the required level as given in the DOT; rather, it specified the probability of the job requiring the level of ability possessed by the top 20 percent of the population. This specification means that only top-level requirement can produce earnings, which is at variance with the assumptions made (and tested) in the present approach.

8.3 FURTHER ANALYSIS: THE 1950 AND 1960 CENSUS DATA

8.3.1 Data

The experience with the 1970 *Census of Population* data warrants a further exploration of similar data from 1950 and 1960. The latter provide information on a large number of jobs for which incomes have been observed in both years. Moreover, there is more detail in the occupational breakdown than in the 1970 *Census*. This means that it is possible to construct a large sample (in fact, 239 jobs were chosen) on which to make two income observations. The DOT characteristics were only observed once. This entails the assumptions of a Leontief production function for labor types, as mentioned and discussed in the introduction.

Comparability of the income data with 1970 is weak. The set of jobs differs, and, most important, the income concept differs. Even the income concepts for 1950 and 1960 differ. The 1950 *Census* was the source of data on the median income in 1949 of the experienced male civilian labor force who worked fifty to fifty-two weeks in 1949. The 1950 and the 1960 *Census* give only median income, not the mean, but, as Section 8.2 indicated, median income better matches the DOT qualifications. The income concept used in 1949 was income before deductions, excluding income in kind and including wages and salary income, net farm income, net income from rents and boarding houses, royalties, interests, dividends, pensions, alimony, and so on. The 1960 *Census* provides data on the median earnings in 1959 of the experienced male civilian labor force who worked fifty to fifty-two weeks in 1959. Earnings include wages or salary income and self-employment income. Recipients are restricted to those 25–64 years old.

The differences in income concept make the 1949 and 1959 data imperfectly comparable. The 1959 concept comes closest to the required concept of labor income, but it still includes some income from capital through its inclusion of self-employment income. The 1949 income concept is too broad, explicitly including capital income and transfers, such as pensions and royalties. One might hope, however, that the disturbances are small and evenly distributed over all jobs. It would seem that such payments as alimony, pensions, and income from rents and boarding houses would not have a large disturbing effect; they would be minor among job holders and would not affect relative earnings very much. Income from royalties, interests, and dividends is potentially more dangerous since it would tend to concentrate among the higher-income jobs and might produce a bias in the estimations whose magnitude could not be detected.

As was already mentioned, the sample consisted of 239 jobs for which matching between the *Census* and the DOT appeared acceptable. Observations focused on 40 professional and technical workers, 49 managers, 9 sales workers, 16 clerical workers, 61 craftsmen, 32 operatives, 6 laborers, 2 farmers, 2 farm laborers, and 22 service workers. Table 8.12 indicates the representation of the labor force and its occupational families. For each job included in the sample, the number of job holders in 1949 and 1959 is known, and the number of workers so represented in the sample has been expressed as a proportion of the actual number of workers in the relevant category. The coverage on the whole is quite good (two-thirds of the workers covered), but some occupations are underrepresented, particularly laborers. This is an unfortunate consequence of the matching procedure. It will have an impact on some of the tabulations presented later on, but will not necessarily bias the estimated regression coefficients.

Table 8.13 reveals some very interesting features of the structure of the labor market. It gives the relative frequencies (derived from the number of job holders) of capability requirements as specified in the DOT.[16] Most revealing are the zero frequencies. It appears that in this sample there are no workers in jobs that require intellectual capabilities (G and V) of level 5; in other words, there are no jobs for people who belong to the bottom 10 percent of the population in this respect. The same applies to many other GATB capabilities: S, P, K, F, and M. Clerical aptitude Q, however, seems a capability that is particularly relevant to

Table 8.12. Proportions and Numbers of Workers in Jobs Included in the Sample

| | Workers Covered in the Sample | | | |
| | Absolute Number | | Relative Number | |
Occupation	1959	1949	1959	1949
Professional workers	2 443 879	1 556 700	.71	.78
Managers	3 753 350	2 958 990	.93	.94
Sales workers	984 400	646 620	.44	.37
Clerical workers	816 184	734 310	.37	.39
Craftsmen	4 713 052	3 876 960	.78	.83
Operatives	2 779 130	2 297 250	.49	.49
Laborers	198 068	204 780	.14	.13
Farmers	1 750 974	2 662 140	1.00	1.00
Farm laborers	442 504	596 910	.94	.81
Service workers	1 621 641	1 427 670	.93	.94
Total	19 503 182	16 962 330	.64	.68

some jobs and not to others: belonging to the bottom 10 percent does not preclude finding a job. Top-level requirements (top 10 percent) occur only in the intellectual sector (G, V, N) and in the spatial aptitude S. The typically manual capabilities K, F, and M are never required at high levels. In fact, these capabilities are medium-level requirements: the bulk of the demand is in the middle third and in the 20 percent below it.

As might be expected, C is not a discriminating capability. Two-thirds of the workers hold jobs that can be performed with the level of color discrimination possessed by the bottom 10 percent of the population. Eye-hand-foot coordination E is also not usually required, but there are still a fair number of workers in jobs requiring at least some average level of this capability. There is, however, no demand for more than average levels.

The 3-digit DOT code has also been tabulated. With respect to DATA, the distribution is bimodal: concentration at the extremes, low frequencies in the middle. One mode occurs at synthesizing, coordinating, and analyzing, the other at "no significant relationship." Data handling therefore is required at high levels for a great number of workers. Relationships with people are not commonly demanded at a high level of complexity: the bulk of demand does not require more than speaking or serving. Relationship to things again shows bimodality in its

128

Table 8.13. Frequency Distributions of the DOT Capabilities, 1949 and 1959 (Percentage of Workers in Jobs with Specified Level)

Interval		1	2	3	4	5
G	(1959)	15.12	18.52	63.38	3.97	.00
	(1949)	11.05	16.96	66.21	5.78	.00
V	(1959)	13.09	18.49	43.05	25.36	.00
	(1949)	9.38	17.67	47.63	25.32	.00
N	(1959)	5.67	8.85	53.00	28.82	3.66
	(1949)	4.00	6.41	57.60	26.68	5.31
S	(1959)	5.55	16.27	33.84	44.34	.00
	(1949)	3.87	16.09	37.55	42.49	.00
P	(1959)	.46	9.58	48.38	41.57	.00
	(1949)	.41	8.10	52.39	39.10	.00
Q	(1959)	.49	17.42	7.11	56.99	17.99
	(1949)	.43	16.88	6.28	58.60	17.80
K	(1959)	.00	4.19	62.66	33.15	.00
	(1949)	.00	3.92	66.01	30.07	.00
F	(1959)	.00	4.28	52.69	43.02	.00
	(1949)	.00	3.61	56.31	40.07	.00
M	(1959)	.00	4.87	63.61	31.52	.00
	(1949)	.00	4.61	65.67	29.73	.00
E	(1959)	.00	.14	18.35	1.14	80.37
	(1949)	.00	.10	24.09	1.14	74.67
C	(1959)	.24	6.03	12.29	12.90	68.54
	(1949)	.18	5.02	18.70	10.27	65.83

Table 8.13—Continued

Interval		0	1	2	3	4	5	6	7	8	9
DATA	(1959)	4.61	38.50	13.34	12.22	1.38	.13	.03	4.69	25.09	
	(1949)	3.29	40.83	12.17	13.07	1.45	.17	.09	4.51	24.41	
PEOPLE	(1959)	3.29	5.37	.45	5.20	.18	5.79	17.68	3.52	58.52	
	(1949)	2.64	3.84	.32	3.82	.18	4.31	17.72	3.87	63.29	
THINGS	(1959)	2.80	29.81	6.32	9.01	7.02	.51	.00	4.60	39.93	
	(1949)	2.74	35.27	5.16	8.14	6.60	.68	.00	6.23	35.18	
GED	(1959)		3.14	7.69	20.85	51.06	14.23	3.02			
	(1949)		4.63	7.48	20.17	55.00	10.79	1.92			
SVP	(1959)		.00	11.98	12.52	8.20	3.59	22.14	27.51	14.05	.00
	(1949)		.00	12.77	12.48	6.94	3.85	28.73	25.41	10.12	.00
LEAD	(1959)	59.90	40.10								
	(1949)	58.41	41.59								
SALES	(1959)	92.98	7.02								
	(1949)	94.69	5.31								
HEAVY	(1959)	49.24	50.76								
	(1949)	43.78	56.22								
INDEP	(1959)	93.28	6.72								
	(1949)	91.61	8.39								

129

frequency distribution, with about a third requiring the worker to operate at relatively high levels of complexity and almost half of the workers having no significant relationship to things.

Educational requirements are unimodally distributed across the work force. More than half of the workers hold jobs that require level 4, which indeed seems to be some intermediate level of knowledge. But the definition and scaling of this variable are not very lucid, and implications are hard to derive. SVP is a better variable in this respect. There is some concentration of demands about level 3, indicating a training length of one to three months, and a concentration at levels beyond 6, indicating specific training length of more than one year; the latter concentration entails roughly two-thirds of the labor force.

Finally, the four dummy variables have been tabulated. SALES and INDEP would seem to be dummies that identify a particular set of jobs. LEAD seems to identify too many jobs to deserve its name. It seems wise to keep its complete description in mind (directing, controlling, and planning an entire activity or the activity of others) and to stress the first part of its definition rather than the second. For convenience, the name is maintained, however. The frequency of HEAVY is probably higher than anticipated, but the variable has been defined in a way that leaves little scope for doubt. Apparently, then, half of the workers hold jobs that require them to do heavy or very heavy work.[17]

Interesting results also obtain from tabulation of requirements by broad occupational categories, such as those applied in the *Census* (with eleven main groups; one of them—private household workers—is not represented here). The tabulation is given in Appendix 7, but the conclusions are condensed here in Tables 8.14 and 8.15. Some of the results are remarkable and perhaps unexpected. It appears that the required level of general learning ability G, a variable quite close to IQ, is never low. Level 3, associated with the middle third of the population, is a predominant minimum level. Level 4, associated with the 23 percent of the population below the middle third is rarely an acceptable minimum level. (It has some acceptability in clerical work and for operatives and service workers.)

Another remarkable result is that blue-collar workers (craftsmen, operatives, and laborers) do not score high on K, F, or M: requirements on the typical manual capabilities are about average for these groups of workers. Instead, S and P are far more important in shaping the capability profiles: blue-collar workers stand out on the requirements of spatial orientation and form perception.

Finally, note the predominance of the professions in shaping the high-level requirement occupations. With respect to each capability, the professions stand out as the occupations that require levels surpassing those of the middle third of the population. Remarkably, even in the typical blue-collar capabilities of S, P, K, F, and M, the professions contain most of the top-level requirement occupations.

Table 8.14. Capability Requirements, by Occupational Group

	Capability Requirements	
Occupation[a]	High	Low
Professionals	G, V	
Managers	G, V, Q	S, P, K, F, M
Sales workers[b]		
Clerical workers		S
Craftsmen	S	Q
Operatives		V, N, Q
Laborers		V, N, S, Q
Service workers		V, N, S, P, Q, K, F

Note: Table based on the frequencies given in Appendix 7.
[a]Occupations of farmer and farm laborers have too few observations to be included here.
[b]Requirements about average on all capabilities.

Table 8.15. Occupations with High Requirements, by Capability

Capability	Occupation with Large Contribution to Total Frequency of Capability Level 1 or 2	
	(1)	(2)
G	Professionals, managers	Professionals, managers, clerical workers
V	Professionals, managers	Professionals, managers, clerical workers
N	Professionals	Professionals, managers
S	Professionals	Craftsmen
P	Professionals	Professionals
Q	Professionals	Managers
K		Professionals
F		Professionals
M		Professionals (craftsmen)

Note: Table based on the frequencies given in Appendix 7.

8.3.2 Income Distribution by Capability Level

The data that have been collected permit derivation of crude income distributions by capability level. For each level of a capability, a frequency distribution of median incomes can be given. Frequencies are counted as the number of workers in jobs for which the given capability level applies. For any capability

level, jobs that require this level can be identified, and for these jobs, both number of workers and median income level are given. The frequency distribution so
obtained is a frequency distribution of median incomes.[18]

Table 8.16 presents the results. The income intervals have been measured in
1959 dollars; 1949 interval boundaries were calculated by applying the ratio of
the mean of the income observations in 1959 to 1949. Because of the crude
measurement, interpretation should be cautious; one should remember that this
is a frequency distribution of median incomes. Recall also from Table 8.13 that
some capability levels have quite low frequencies, which affects the reliability of
the estimated income distribution.

The general picture emerging from Table 8.16 entails a positive association
between level of required capability and level of income. This shows up as an
increase in frequencies of higher income intervals when higher level of capability requirements are considered. (The picture is somewhat clearer in a tabulation with a finer income interval.) G and GED, in particular, provide illustrations
of this association.

Deviations from this general effect also occur. At higher capability levels, the
dispersion sometimes tends to increase, and, in particular, the frequency of the
lowest income interval may rise with rising capability levels. This is illustrated by
V, S, and other capabilities. In some cases, the dispersion first diminishes and
then increases (as occurs in the intervals of DATA and THINGS).

Considering the changes between 1949 and 1959, it appears that in most cases
there is a rather strong reduction in the frequencies of the lowest income interval
and a rather weak increase in the frequencies of the highest income intervals.
Frequency reductions are predominant in the $3,000-$6,000 income interval,
while frequency increases dominate the $6,000-$9,000 interval. Such generalizations about changes over time based on a small number of intervals are dangerous, however, since the intervals are sufficiently wide to conceal quite different
patterns of movement at a finer breakdown.

Although these results are very interesting, the information they yield is still
too complex to draw precise inferences about capability prices. This requires
different techniques, which will be applied in the next section.

8.3.3 Factor Analysis

As with the 1970 *Census of Population* data set, the 1950 and 1960 data set can
be used for testing and measurement of elements of the multicapability theory.
Results obtained earlier will be used to guide this investigation. The available
data set now contains twenty variables (see Table 8.1). Some of these variables
are immediately recognized as capabilities, while others may be interpreted as

Table 8.16. Income Distribution, by Capability Level (Income in Thousands of 1959 Dollars)

Level	Year	G <3	3-<6	6-<9	≥9	N <3	3-<6	6-<9	≥9	S <3	3-<6	6-<9	≥9
5	1949	67.5	27.0	5.5		70.8	24.9	4.3					
	1959	61.5	38.5			64.4	35.6						
4	1949	24.0	61.3	14.6	.1	.7	81.6	17.7		9.9	53.3	29.7	7.2
	1959	15.8	57.3	26.7	.2	2.0	73.1	24.8		7.7	50.8	32.4	9.1
3	1949	46.3	53.7			27.5	46.5	24.7	1.3	41.4	36.5	21.9	.2
	1959	39.7	60.3			17.7	42.4	38.0	1.9	26.3	39.1	34.3	.3
2	1949					16.7	32.1	51.2		87.5	12.5		
	1959					10.6	40.6	48.8		61.9	38.1		
1	1949	8.9	54.2	36.9		2.5	95.2	2.3		15.3	58.1	26.6	
	1959	8.5	53.5	38.0		2.3	88.1	9.6		2.3	66.7	31.0	

Level	Year	V <3	3-<6	6-<9	≥9	K <3	3-<6	6-<9	≥9	F <3	3-<6	6-<9	≥9
5	1949	15.0	77.8	7.2									
	1959	11.3	78.6	10.2									
4	1949	33.5	48.1	18.2	.1	1.5	46.9	41.5	10.1	10.5	50.5	31.4	7.6
	1959	21.9	41.2	36.6	.3	3.2	40.6	44.0	12.2	7.9	48.8	33.9	9.4
3	1949	42.0	58.0			29.2	52.3	18.2	.2	27.6	51.3	20.9	.3
	1959	37.7	62.3			17.9	49.1	31.9	1.1	16.9	44.4	37.5	1.3
2	1949						61.4	14.6	24.0		53.1	20.9	26.0
	1959						41.0	31.0	28.0		36.6	36.0	27.4
1	1949	10.5	46.1	43.4									
	1959	9.8	46.3	43.9									

Level	Year	P <3	3-<6	6-<9	≥9	Q <3	3-<6	6-<9	≥9
5	1949					21.1	75.9	3.0	
	1959					13.1	85.4	1.5	
4	1949	10.1	51.3	30.8	7.8	27.3	44.2	23.1	5.5
	1959	7.1	50.2	33.0	9.7	17.5	35.7	38.6	8.2
3	1949	30.2	50.4	19.3	.1	76.1	23.9		
	1959	19.3	44.4	36.0	.2	60.1	39.9		
2	1949	54.9	32.4	12.7		39.9	54.5	5.6	
	1959	36.0	46.1	17.9		33.4	59.9	6.7	
1	1949	24.1	75.9			22.6	77.4		
	1959	27.7	72.3			26.0	74.0		

133

Table 8.16—Continued

		M				E				C			
		<3	3-<6	6-<9	≥9	<3	3-<6	6-<9	≥9	<3	3-<6	6-<9	≥9
5	1949					5.7	56.7	32.2	5.5	6.0	66.2	28.2	4.6
	1959					4.3	45.0	43.5	7.2	4.3	57.2	32.6	5.9
4	1949	13.1	35.2	41.4	10.2		83.9	16.1			45.4	53.1	1.5
	1959	7.8	34.2	45.3	12.8		78.5	21.5		.1	34.7	60.1	5.1
3	1949	24.2	57.3	18.3	.2	64.5	32.1	3.1	.2	84.6	7.1	3.2	5.0
	1959	15.5	50.6	32.9	1.0	48.4	47.3	3.7	.6	76.0	10.4	4.0	9.5
2	1949		63.2	16.4	20.4		100.0				28.9	71.1	
	1959		61.6	14.3	24.1						15.8	84.2	
1	1949							100.0				100.0	
	1959											100.0	

		DATA				PEOPLE				THINGS			
		<3	3-<6	6-<9	≥9	<3	3-<6	6-<9	≥9	<3	3-<6	6-<9	≥9
8	1949	17.3	75.3	7.4		30.5	55.9	13.4	.2	1.3	42.7	44.7	11.3
	1959	13.6	76.1	10.3		19.2	54.4	25.3	1.1	2.7	35.3	49.1	13.0
7	1949		73.1	26.9		1.7	98.3			60.4	32.0	7.6	
	1959		50.8	49.2		14.6	85.4			51.5	48.5		
6	1949			100.0		.6	55.0	44.4					
	1959		100.0			.4	51.2	48.4					
5	1949		100.0			6.5	12.1	31.4			100.0		
	1959		100.0			8.2	2.3	89.5			100.0		

134

SVP

	Year							
4	1949	100.0			100.0		95.5	4.5
	1959	100.0			100.0		96.2	3.8
3	1949	81.4	18.6		12.7	87.3	98.8	5.5
	1959	64.5	35.5	.2	7.4	92.4	95.0	3.7 · 1.3
2	1949	79.5	20.0		13.1	86.9	29.6	70.3
	1959	61.4	37.7 · .5		45.5	54.5 · .9	21.1	78.9
1	1949	17.0	35.2 · 9.8		.5 · 38.6 · 60.9	44.1	38.1	43.5 · 12.1 · .3
	1959	16.4	47.0 · 13.5		.7 · 40.8 · 58.8	29.8	23.1	33.6 · 34.8 · 1.8
0	1949	13.8	83.4 · 2.8		32.7 · 5.2 · 62.1		91.6	8.4
	1959	10.9	77.3 · 11.9		33.9 · 3.6 · 62.5		87.0	13.0

GED

	Year	SVP			GED			
1	1949	33.0	40.2	26.8	81.1	13.9	5.0	
	1959	28.5	33.8	37.6	75.0	25.0		
2	1949		97.6	2.4	1.9	93.0	5.1	
	1959		97.9	2.1	1.1	95.4	3.4	
3	1949				1.6	91.1	7.3	
	1959				4.7	84.2	11.1	
4	1949		100.0		28.3	41.8	29.8	.1
	1959		100.0		17.4	34.4	48.0	.2
5	1949		56.5	43.5	19.1	44.0	36.9	
	1959		50.5	49.5	18.9	44.6	36.6	
6	1949	54.1	19.2	26.7	95.2	4.8		
	1959	40.1	20.9	39.0	81.9	18.1		
7	1949		73.4	22.6	3.9			
	1959		52.0	43.3	4.7			
8	1949	.1	6.0	63.1	31.0			
	1959		4.8	62.6	32.6			
9	1949							
	1959							

135

such. It seems unlikely that all twenty of these variables measure independent and relevant capabilities. Results obtained with the 1970 data set provide sufficient motivation to apply factor analysis.

Factor analysis has been applied to the GATB variables and to two larger selections, one including GED and SVP and one also covering the 3-digit code and E and C. The motivation for including these variables requires that they be discussed separately.

The motivation for including GED and SVP was already given in Section 8.2.3. GED, by definition, is a variable that comes very close to the intellectual GATB variables, such as G, V, or N, and therefore cannot be taken as a really different capability. Although SVP will also be used as a separate variable (in relation to the human capital view that the time dimension of it is predominant), it could equally well be argued that SVP indicates a particular capability—namely, the capability of being trainable. In that case, it is quite acceptable to include it in the set of variables to be subjected to factor analysis.

The 3-digit DOT code, according to its authors, is a ranking of job requirements according to the level of complexity at which the job holder must perform in relation to data, to people, and to things. It is not hard to interpret these variables as measuring the capability to deal with data, people, and things at increasing levels of complexity. The variables have also been included in a data set to which factor analysis was applied in order to investigate their role within a set of other variables. The question was, Would they merge with these variables to capabilities already discovered within this set, or would they bring out new relevant capabilities?[19]

The results of factor analysis on these alternative selections of variables are presented in Table 8.17. The outcome is unexpectedly pleasing. As was the case with the data set employed in Section 8.2, the explanatory variables can be divided quite clearly into two distinct factors: the intellectual capability and the manual capability. The intellectual factor is composed of high loadings of G, V, N, and Q, while the manual factor is composed of high loadings of K, F, M, and of S and P. This latter factor therefore embraces more than just physical dexterity: it also has a dimension of understanding, as reflected through S and P.

Comparison of the three alternative analyses brings out the stability of the structure: the loadings of previously included variables are barely affected, and the new variables harmoniously merge into the dichotomy. GED and SVP join the intellectual factor, underscoring the interpretation of their character given above. The 3-digit code divides itself between the two factors. The capability to deal with data at increasing levels of complexity may be viewed as just another dimension of the intellectual factor, while the capability to deal with things may be viewed as another manifestation of the manual factor.

The only disturbance arises from factor 3 in the third factor analysis. It is highly loaded with color discrimination, and, at a lower level, the loading on

Table 8.17. Three Alternative Factor Analyses (Rotated Factor Scores)

Variables	Factor 1	Factor 2	Factor 1	Factor 2	Factor 1	Factor 2	Factor 3
DATA					-.915	-.039	-.019
PEOPLE					-.526	.390	.437
THINGS					.168	-.862	-.340
GED			.930	.163	.929	.179	.003
SVP			.790	.229	.790	.318	.319
G	-.015	-.923	-.917	.040	-.906	.076	.086
V	.045	-.950	-.931	.105	-.937	.143	.104
N	-.262	-.893	-.903	-.208	-.886	-.227	-.030
S	-.834	-.232	-.310	-.823	-.302	-.862	-.007
P	-.915	-.143	-.180	-.902	-.177	-.879	.207
Q	.183	-.706	-.636	.233	-.633	.275	.103
K	-.892	.182	.150	-.899	.135	-.810	.364
F	-.936	.011	-.030	-.933	-.047	-.846	.368
M	-.883	.196	.146	-.892	.139	-.813	.378
E					.100	-.157	.375
C					-.222	-.309	.771
Cum. percentage of eigenvalues	.455	.810	.440	.796	.365	.674	.764
Identification	"Manual"	"Intellectual"	"Intellectual"	"Manual"	"Intellectual"	"Manual"	?

PEOPLE stands out. One should conclude that the third factor does not indicate a meaningful capability. It identifies an apparent combination of required capabilities, which do not appear to stem from a meaningful latent variable. The third factor will therefore be ignored in the analyses that follow.

The results are almost identical to the factor analysis applied to the 1970 *Census* data set, although they cover 88 observations rather than 239. In comparing factor loadings, only two differences appear, both rather minor. Comparing the factors found from GATB variables only, it appears that the loading of manual on Q has been reduced, from .334 to .183, thus strengthening the manual character of that factor. Comparing the factors found from GATB, GED, and SVP, the loadings of manual on GED and SVP appear to have increased, thus slightly weakening the interpretation of "manual."

Before turning to an explanation of income differences, it may be repeated that factor analysis is only a formalized way of interpreting relations between variables. It does not prove the existence or nonexistence of particular capabilities. For example, that SVP or the variables of DATA and THINGS merge very well with factor analyses on a reduced data set that does not include these variables does not prove that the variables do not measure something that is relevant on its own. The only conclusion from such a factor analysis is that the observations do not conflict with the hypothesis that there exist two basic, latent factors, which are independent of each other and which can generate the correlations between the variables actually observed.

8.3.4 Explaining Income Differentials

Factor analysis has clearly brought out the relevance of two main factors for structuring the labor market. Are these factors also relevant when it comes to structuring the income distribution? To answer this question, multiple regressions were run in various alternative combinations of explanatory variables. A number of results are collected in Appendix 8, but the main conclusions will be discussed and documented here.

Most adequate for investigating the question seems the specification that employs 1959 income as the dependent variable (it being the superior income concept since 1949 income contains more transfer elements) and that measures intellectual and manual capabilities from the GATB variables only, thus leaving room to study the other variables separately.

The regressions start from a specification using the intellectual and manual factors only (Table 8.18). The equation explains 36 percent of the income variance; both variables have the proper positive sign; both are significant; and the price of the intellectual factor is about three times that of the manual. This

Table 8.18. Regressions for 1959 Income: Factor Scores from GATB Variables

Intercept	Intellectual	Manual	GED	SVP	DATA	PEOPLE	THINGS	LEAD	SALES	HEAVY	INDEP	Int/Man[a]	Int/Man[b]	$\bar{R}$	F	$\bar{s}_e$
5,739	1,070 (11.08)	309 (3.18)												.600	66.53	1,489
5,668	945 (8.14)	180 (1.52)										991 (1.90)		.608	46.05	1,481
5,745	1,079 (9.09)	320 (2.59)											−66 (.13)	.600	44.17	1,492
7,322	877 (4.56)	208 (1.50)			−29 (.46)	−167 (2.90)	−77 (1.48)							.620	29.16	1,470
7,340	633 (2.42)	−89 (.43)			−95 (1.33)	−174 (2.89)	−84 (1.39)	−273 (.70)	674 (1.60)	373 (1.06)	803 (2.08)	1,737 (2.98)		.651	16.78	1,438
2,196			802 (5.53)	112 (1.46)										.578	59.09	1,520

[a]Dummy variable; equal to 1 if required level of intellectual and manual capability both surpass mean plus 1 standard deviation.
[b]Dummy variable; equal to 1 if required level of intellectual and manual capability both surpass mean plus .5 standard deviation.

again demonstrates the relevance of these two capabilities. As in the 1970 *Census* sample analyzed earlier, interaction between the intellectual and the manual should not be neglected, provided it is measured at a sufficiently high level (surpassing one standard deviation). Interaction will be studied in greater detail later in this chapter.

The data set can be used to search for other relevant capabilities. The intellectual factor is a cognitive capability; the manual factor is a mixture of a cognitive capability as represented through P and S and such clearly noncognitive variables as K, F, and M. The remaining variables in this data set can now be helpful in tracing other noncognitive capabilities. To this end, the fourth and the fifth regressions were run. Judging from *t*-ratios, these regressions bring out the relevance of the variables of PEOPLE and INDEP. The latter variable cannot be taken as a capability without qualifications. It was measured as a dummy distinguishing employees from the self-employed. The capability to operate independently, to make decisions, may be equally relevant for many salaried positions. For proper representation, the degree of independent operation should also be measured for that category. In fact, INDEP only identifies the jobs in which individuals also accept the financial consequences of their activities. Hence, INDEP may catch the return to accepting risk or the return to capital.

A better case can be made for the variable of PEOPLE. It represents the level of complexity in relationships with other people and therefore may be interpreted as a measure of a social capability. The relevance of social capability is also brought out by the results for the SALES variable, which borders on significance. SALES identifies job situations in which other people must be convinced. Jointly, the results on PEOPLE and SALES are taken as evidence that a social capability is also relevant for explaining earnings differentials.

Two other aspects of the fifth equation merit further discussion. First, LEAD comes out as an insignificant variable with the wrong sign. This result may be linked to the frequency distributions given in an earlier section. According to these distributions, 40 percent of the labor force would exert leadership, which can never be true of leadership in a restricted sense. It therefore cannot be considered a very adequate variable. Second, the results with respect to the variable of HEAVY are interesting. In some specifications (not reproduced here), this variable comes out with the wrong sign. However, if the factor analytic capabilities are included, the sign is rightly positive (although the coefficient is insignificant). This seems to indicate that the classical compensatory argument with respect to heavy work is valid on a ceteris paribus basis: it applies only when other factors are held constant. Omission of this stipulation naturally produces the wrong sign, since heavy work in the physical sense is associated with low-paying jobs.[20]

As already noted, other specifications were also run. In particular, these specifications employed factor scores based on the alternative factor analyses.

Relative prices of the three capabilities are maintained under these different specifications, as can be seen from Table 8.19. The table presents β-coefficients to make the results comparable among variables with different standard deviations.[21] Intellectual capability comes out as the one with the highest price; the next highest coefficient applies to interaction. The social capability (PEOPLE/SALES) comes next, while the manual capability appears to carry the lowest rewards.

To judge the performance of the multicapability theory as formulated in the foregoing chapters, the results may be compared with other specifications. Table 8.20 summarizes some results on the effect of a logarithmic transformation of income, implying a multiplicative model rather than an additive one. The multiplicative model is now inferior, judged by correlation coefficient and standard error. The results show that R diminishes. As explained in Section 8.2.2., there are grounds for replacing the judgment on the basis of the values of R with a comparison of standard error to standard error multiplied by geometric mean of the dependent.

All the values given at the bottom of Table 8.20 appear higher than the corresponding values for the linear model. Similar conclusions emerge from specifications using the alternative factor analyses. Clearly, in this comparison, there is no reason to reject the additive model.

Next, consider the prediction of human capital theory. According to this theory, the time dimension of education and training is essential because it re-

Table 8.19. β-Coefficients for Some Capabilities, 1959

	Factor Scores Derived from:		
Variable	GATB[b]	GATB, GED, SVP[c]	GATB, E, C, GED, SVP, DATA, PEOPLE THINGS[d]
Intellectual	.34	.41	.57
Interaction[a]	.24	.35	.29
Manual	.05	.06	.05
THINGS	.14	.13	
PEOPLE	.21	.18	
SALES	.09	.12	.10

[a]As in Table 8.18, Note a.

[b]Regression equation also contains DATA, LEAD, HEAVY, INDEP.

[c]Regression equation also contains DATA, LEAD, HEAVY, INDEP, and some insignificant other interaction dummies.

[d]Regression equation also contains LEAD, HEAVY, INDEP, and another insignificant interaction dummy.

Table 8.20. Effect of Log Transformation, 1959

	Intercept	Intellectual	Manual	DATA	PEOPLE	THINGS	LEAD	SALES	HEAVY	INDEP	Interaction[a]	$\bar{R}$	F	$\bar{s}_e$
Income	5,759	1,070 (11.08)	309 (3.18)									.600	66.53	1,489
ln Income	8.599	.186 (9.52)	.058 (2.97)									.545	49.84	.301[b]
Income	5,668	945 (8.14)	180 (1.52)	-95 (1.33)	-174 (2.89)	-84 (1.39)					991 (1.90)	.608	46.05	1,481
ln Income	8.598	.185 (7.83)	.058 (2.40)	-.033 (2.24)	-.018 (1.41)	-.014 (1.13)					.004 (.04)	.545	33.09	.302[c]
Income	7,340	633 (2.42)	-89 (.43)				-273 (.70)	674 (1.60)	373 (1.06)	803 (2.08)	1,737 (2.98)	.651	16.78	1,438
ln Income	8.847	.101 (1.88)	-.006 (.13)				-.028 (.34)	.067 (.77)	.091 (1.25)	.116 (1.46)	.187 (1.55)	.587	12.00	.296[d]

[a]As in Table 8.18, Note a.
[c] The product of $\bar{s}_e$ and geometric mean of the dependent equals:
[b]1,633;
[c]1,639;
[d]1,606.

lates to the most important component of the cost of training, foregone earnings. The theory requires a specification in which the logarithm of earnings depends linearly on training time. In the empirical work that has been published so far, formal education is measured by duration, but on-the-job training is not measured explicitly. The latter has only been inferred from the specification of the estimated earnings function. The DOT data contain a variable – SVP – that explicitly covers the required training time, be it in vocational schools, company schools, or informal on-the-job training. Admittedly, the measure is a crude one, but, as mentioned, it has the advantage of being measured independently of the earnings profile.

Table 8.21 collects evidence on the performance of the specification promoted by human capital theory. SVP has been transformed to a time-equivalent scale, as in Section 8.3.2, by using the approximate midpoint of an interval. The first thing to note about these results is that adding SVP (in the original measurement) does not add explanatory power to the equation and barely affects the estimated coefficients or their t-ratios (with one exception, intellectual in the equation containing all variables). Again, using the time dimension of SVP does not affect the explanatory power of the equations. In the specification that includes only two capabilities, SVP has a coefficient that differs significantly from zero, but this is not the case in the other specification. Comparing the equation without the training variable with the one containing the time-equivalent training scale, the effect on coefficients and explanatory power is negligible. However, important differences occur in the specification in which the logarithm of income is matched with the time-equivalent training variable. The explanatory power diminishes: $\bar{R}^2$ decreases from .36 to .31 in the first set of equations and from .42 to .35 in the second set, while the comparable standard error of estimate increases from about 1,450 to 1,600 in both sets. Clearly, there is no reason to give up the specification developed in the multicapability theory in favor of the one promoted by human capital theory.[22]

On a number of earlier occasions, an interaction term has entered the discussion. Because of its important place in the multicapability theory, a fuller evaluation of its empirical relevance is warranted. Recall that the multicapability model postulates an earnings function that is linear in the capabilities; this postulate is intimately tied to the assumption that capabilities are separable. The interaction term was devised to test this assumption. A number of species of potentially relevant interaction will now be studied. Interaction will be measured by a dummy variable, which assumes the value 1 if a number of variables simultaneously score beyond a certain, critical level, the value 0 otherwise. The dummy thus measures the contribution to income differences of simultaneously high requirements for a number of variables. Such interaction terms were specified for a number of combinations. Moreover, two continuously valued interac-

Table 8.21. The Effect of a Time-Equivalent SVP Scale: 1959 Income, Factor Analysis on GATB

	Intercept	Intellectual	Manual	SVP	SVP[a]	DATA	PEOPLE	THINGS	LEAD	SALES	HEAVY	INDEP	Interaction[b]	$\bar{R}$	F	$\bar{s}_e$
Income	5,739	1,070 (11.08)	309 (3.18)											.600	66.53	1,489
Income	5,080	900 (6.70)	244 (2.39)	121 (1.81)										.607	45.90	1,482
Income	5,380	866 (7.33)	222 (2.22)		.466 (2.92)									.618	48.62	1,466
ln Income	8.536	.150 (6.25)	.043 (2.13)		.00008 (2.53)									.562	36.16	.298[c]
Income	7,340	633 (2.42)	-89 (.43)			-95 (1.33)	-174 (2.89)	-84 (1.39)	-273 (.70)	674 (1.60)	373 (1.06)	803 (2.08)	1,737 (2.98)	.651	16.78	1,438
Income	5,642	347 (1.13)	-40 (.19)	199 (1.74)		-41 (.52)	-136 (2.13)	-31 (.45)	-237 (.61)	826 (1.93)	44 (.11)	862 (2.24)	1,910 (3.25)	.657	15.67	1,432
Income	6,652	566 (2.14)	-47 (.22)		.303 (1.50)	-71 (.97)	-135 (2.05)	-48 (.74)	-319 (.82)	660 (1.57)	259 (.72)	874 (2.26)	1,587 (2.69)	.656	15.54	1,434
ln Income	8.779	.094 (1.72)	-.001 (.03)		.00003 (.72)	-.031 (2.02)	-.014 (1.00)	-.010 (.78)	-.032 (.40)	.065 (.75)	.080 (1.07)	.123 (1.54)	.172 (1.41)	.588	10.93	.296[d]

[a] SVP time-equivalent scale as given in Section 8.2.2.
[b] As in Table 8.18, Note a.
The product of $\bar{s}_e$ and geometric mean of the dependent equals:
[c] 1,617;
[d] 1,606.

tion terms were defined. The first equals the product of the manual and the intellectual factor and thus allows for substitution. (Medium scores on both factors are valued equal to a high score on one factor and a low score on the other.) Substitution is prohibited in the other continuous interaction variable, the minimum of the two factor scores. In this case, interaction is very strong: the importance of the factors cannot surpass the value of the lowest requirement. In other words, a high requirement of one factor is only relevant (with respect to earnings) if the other factor is also required at a high level.[23]

Table 8.22 summarizes the evidence on the relevance of interaction: most species are insignificant and/or have the wrong sign (all were defined so as to require a nonnegative coefficient). The outcome on interaction defined as the minimum level of the two factors is remarkable: strongly and significantly negative (and thus not supportive of the hypothesis of interaction). The negative sign may be related to the strong correlation between the interaction term and "-manual" (.803).

Only one interaction term comes out significantly: the interaction between manual and intellectual, provided it is defined at a sufficiently high level. Such interaction is relevant for the following jobs (the dummy equals 1): architects, chiropractors, dentists, designers, seven types of engineers, foresters, chemists, optometrists, physicians/surgeons, and veterinarians. All these jobs belong to the professional occupations. It was noticed before (in Section 8.3.1) that the professions stand out among the high-level occupations for all capabilities. In other words, high levels of the manual capability occur in those occupations in which both incomes and intellectual requirements are high. The interaction term appears to be an effective way of picking out these occupations. The dummy selection is all the more effective in view of the fact that the variation in K, F, and M, which are important variables in the manual factor, is quite limited (see Section 8.3.1); the bulk concentrates at levels 3 and 4, with only a few observations in 2 (mainly the professions). This ties in with the result that interaction is only significant in the dummy specification and not in the continuous specifications that were tried.

The outcome may also be interpreted as evidence of some nonlinearity in the reward for the manual capability. The fact that the interaction dummy manages to select the occupations with high manual levels and high incomes supports this view. Support comes also from the results of the logarithmic transformation. In the semilog specification, interaction is insignificant (see Tables 8.20 and 8.21), which means that the logarithmic transformation of the income scale can make the earnings function linear in the capabilities, without further need to allow for extra reward at high levels of the manual capability. In this connection, it is worth repeating that separability could only be tested on the assumption that the DOT measurements have cardinal properties.

Table 8.22. Testing for Interaction, 1959

Factor Analysis Applied to	Int/Man[a]	Int/Man[b]	Int/Man[c]	Min Int/Man[d]	Int/Man LEAD[e]
GATB	991 (1.90)				
		−66 (.13)			
	1,915 (3.24)				
	1,967 (4.57)				
GATB, GED, SVP	1,220 (2.50)				
			10 (.10)		
				−1,194 (3.60)	
	1,730 (3.08)				
			83 (.72)		
				−1,196 (3.27)	
	2,488 (2.97)				
GATB, E, C, GED, SVP, DOT 3	1,905 (4.54)				
	1,923 (3.11)				−470 (.64)
	2,156 (3.34)				−262 (.30)

Note: All variables were measured so as to have nonnegative expected sign. DOT 3: DATA, PEOPLE, THINGS; int = intellectual, man = manual.

[a]Intellectual and manual each at least 1 standard deviation above the mean.
[b]Intellectual and manual each at least .5 standard deviation above the mean.
[c]Intellectual x manual.
[d]Minimum of intellectual and manual.
[e]Intellectual and manual as in (a), and leadership = 1.
[f]Intellectual as in (a), and leadership = 1.
[g]Intellectual as in (a), and data = 0 (highest level).
[h]Intellectual as in (a), and people = 0 (highest level).

$Int/LEAD^f$	$Int/DATA^g$	$Int/PEOPLE^h$	Other Variables Included in the Regression
			Int, man
			Int, man
			Int, man, GED, SVP, DOT 3, LEAD, SALES, HEAVY, INDEP
			Int, SVP, PEOPLE, SALES, INDEP
			Int, man
			Int, man
			Int, man
582 (1.57)			Int, man
			Int, man, DOT 3, LEAD, SALES, HEAVY, INDEP
			Int, man
			Int, man
621 (1.39)			Int, man
	−1,014 (1.21)	−417 (.55)	Int, man
			Int, SALES, HEAVY, INDEP
			Int, man
			Int, man, LEAD, SALES, HEAVY, INDEP

How damaging are these results to the assumption of separability of capabilities? Naturally, they increase the desire for an analytical framework that is not restricted by this assumption. But it may be pointed out that although this species of interaction has its coefficient significantly different from zero, it does not contribute to the explanatory power of the model. Hence, the claim that inseparability accounts for a negligible secondary effect on income differences is strongly reconfirmed. It may be seen from Table 8.18, for example, that adding the interaction term to an equation containing intellectual and manual capabilities only raises $\bar{R}$ from .600 to .608 (and thereby $\bar{R}^2$ from .36 to .37), while the standard error of estimate is reduced by only .5 percent. It may also be stated that the evidence collected here is by no means definitive. Further testing on different data is required. Finer scaling of the variables than that used for the GATB capabilities (given in intervals) may lead to additional observations in which the impact of nonlinearity or interaction will be reduced.

Since observations are available on income in two years, 1949 and 1959, the data may be used to find out whether capability prices have changed over time. At the outset, the warning about the differences in income concept should be recalled: the 1949 concept deviates more from the ideal than does the 1959 concept, since it contains transfer elements and more components of capital income. As was indicated before, one may be confident that the disturbances will not be systematic or large, with the possible exception of capital income (dividends, interest, etc.). Care should therefore be taken when relative prices between the two years are compared.

To get some initial idea of the changes in relative incomes that took place in ten years time, 1959 incomes were regressed on 1949 incomes, with the following result:

$$y\,(1959) = -93 + 1.65\,y\,(1949) \qquad \bar{R} = .969, F = 3614, \bar{s}_e = 461.$$

$$(60.11)$$

This suggests a fairly stable structure since a linear regression explains 94 percent of the variance.[24] But it leaves open the question of whether there is any system in the deviations from the straight line that would have changed relative capability prices. To answer this question, Table 8.23 was constructed. The table collects price changes estimated through a number of variants of the regression equation. In particular, the equations differ according to the estimation of the factor-analytic components and according to the selection of variables: factor-analytic capabilities only, factor-analytic capabilities plus interaction, and the list of variables selected through stepwise regression with termination at insignificant coefficients. The results all tend to tell the same tale. The price of the intellectual capability is lagging behind, the social capability (PEOPLE/SALES) has increased in relative price, and, in particular, the manual capability has become

Table 8.23. Changes in Relative Prices: 1959 Regression Coefficients Divided by 1949 Coefficients

Factor Analysis on	Intercept	Intellectual	Manual	SVP	PEOPLE	SALES	INDEP	Interaction[a]
1. *Regression on Factors Only*								
GATB	1.62	1.67	2.92					
GATB, GED, SVP	1.62	1.67	3.57					
DOT 3, GATB, GED, SVP, E, C	1.62	1.65	3.96					
2. *Regression on Factors and Interaction*[a]								
GATB	1.62	1.60	3.22					2.60
GATB, GED, SVP	1.62	1.61	14.43					2.33
DOT 3, GATB, GED, SVP, E, C	1.62	1.60	1.43					2.62
3. *Stepwise Regression; Termination at Insignificant Coefficients (2.5% Level)*								
GATB	1.57	1.16		1.90	1.83	1.82	1.62	2.39
GATB, GED, SVP	1.84	1.49			2.88		1.86	2.22
DOT 3, GATB, GED, SVP, E, C	1.60	1.62				1.88	1.58	2.38

Note: DOT 3: DATA, PEOPLE, THINGS.
[a]Interaction between manual and intellectual as defined in Table 8.18, Note a.

149

worth more. Note that the price increase of the manual capability is reflected in the price increase of the interaction variable. There is another way in which the price increase of the manual capability manifests itself: its t-value rose between 1949 and 1959 in such a way that in some specifications an insignificant coefficient became significant.

Plausible as these results may be, it is still important to recall the differences in income concept between the 1950 *Census of Population* and that of 1960 (i.e., that the 1950 *Census* includes transfer elements and capital income). Thus, if in 1949 these income components tend to be higher for incomes that depend to a larger extent on income from the intellectual capability (i.e., positive correlation between these transfers and the income share from the intellectual capability), the decrease in the price of intellectual capability is artificial. Although this situation cannot be ruled out, it is quite conceivable that the transfer elements and the capital income components tend to cancel each other with respect to their relation to the level of earnings. In that case, the estimates of capability prices will not be biased.

8.3.5 Conclusions

The following important findings emerge from the empirical analysis:

1. As in earlier sections, the multicapability theory shows its relevance. The implication of the empirical analysis is that the labor market may be structured in terms of a number of continuous variables rather than in terms of disjunct groups. Such a distinction as the one made between blue-collar and white-collar workers is too rigid; there is a continuum of capability requirements that crosses such boundaries. Professional occupations (like dentistry or chemistry) may have high requirements of such blue-collar-like capabilities as motor coordination and manual and finger dexterity.

2. Considering the capability structure of the labor market, it appears that blue-collar work is not shaped distinctly in terms of motor coordination or manual and finger dexterity; rather, it is shaped in terms of spatial orientation and form perception.

3. Considering the frequency distribution of required capability levels, one can conclude that there is a very low frequency of workers in jobs requiring capability levels not surpassing the level possessed by the lowest 10 percent of the population. The professional occupations stand out as requiring high levels on all capabilities, or, stated in reverse, the high-level occupations on all capabilities are primarily professional occupations.

4. The income distribution by capability level shows a clear positive association between income and capability requirement for a number of capability variables. For some other capability variables, the relation with income also shows a tendency to positive association, although a less straightforward one; in particular, the range does not respond monotonically to the capability level.

5. Factor analysis reveals a capability structure identical to the one discovered earlier. There are two clearly distinct factors—intellectual and manual. The new variables of the data set analyzed here smoothly merge with this factor structure: the relation to data submerges in the intellectual factor, the relation to things in the manual factor. The relation to people, however, does not fit in so well and does not emerge as a separate factor.

6. Up to 40 percent of the income variance can be attributed to the capability variables used here. Three types of variables stand out: intellectual, social, and manual capabilities, with relative prices in this order. All these coefficients have their theoretically expected signs.

7. There is evidence of changes in relative prices over time. Comparing 1959 to 1949, the intellectual capability has become cheaper, the price of the social capability has increased somewhat, and, in particular, the price of the manual capability has risen. Comparing the 1959 prices to those of 1969, one is tempted to conclude that there was a fall in the manual capability price, but because of differences in the data set, this comparison has limited value.

8. The tests for interaction between variables, which imply a test on the assumption of separability of capabilities, point to the insignificance of most species of interaction. One type of interaction comes out strongly and significantly and with the proper sign: interaction defined as having a simultaneously high requirement on the intellectual and the manual capabilities, as measured with a zero-one dummy. The relevance of this type of interaction for the explanatory power of the model is almost zero, thus supporting the view that inseparability has a negligible secondary effect on income differences.

9. The human capital prediction that length of (specific vocational) training should be related to the logarithm of income does not lead to an improvement over the additive models predicted by the multicapability theory.

9 EVALUATION AND EXPANSION

O rijkdom van het onvoltooide.[1]

—J.H. Leopold, 1977

The theory developed so far consists of explicit specifications of a number of basic concepts. Among these basic concepts are the notions of a multitude of capabilities structuring labor force and labor pay, of the distinction between capability stocks and effective capability supply, and, concomitantly, of effort as the discrepancy between capability stock and capability supply.

In the specifications used in the foregoing chapters, these concepts appeared to be valuable tools in understanding the job wage structure and the shape of the income distribution, as well as in applying comparative static analysis of exogenous shifts in parameters. Moreover, Chapters 7 and 8 indicated that the available empirical evidence does not conflict with the theory.

152

Obviously, the present theory is not without its shortcomings. Assumptions were made to study income distribution within the smooth and ideal world of pure competition, involving individually negligible market participants, costless and complete information, and no uncertainty. In income distribution theory, it is particularly relevant not to stop the analysis at this point, but to go on to study the impact of such things as monopoly elements and imperfect information.

As to the problem of information, it has been assumed that every actor has immediate and costless access to all relevant information. However, neither individual employees nor employers will always know what individual capability stocks are, nor will they know what the exact situation in the labor market is in terms of jobs available and prices paid. Such information will have to be produced, at a cost, by searching, by trying a job, or by trying an employee. Lack of knowledge on capabilities naturally poses a question about indicators of capabilities: How can capabilities be known; how can individual productivity and performance be predicted? In the actual labor market, a number of methods are in use. The simplest method by which employers try to generate predictions on individual performance is the personal interview. Another method is the psychological testing of candidates. A third method employs immediately observable indicators of potential performance, such as age, experience, education, and parental status. Situations in which the required information is not immediate and not costless may be analyzed with a view to such matters as the selection of performance indicators, the convergence between the informational value ascribed to an indicator and the actual predictive value, and the problem of optimal allocation of individuals to tasks if each individual's performance on the different tasks is not known a priori. Analysis of the problem in the context of a multicapability world no doubt can take advantage of the work on screening and signaling as carried out by Spence (1974) and Arrow (1973).

Work in progress (Hartog, 1978b) demonstrates that the gradual emergence of capability information, through monitoring individuals at work, can lead to observed patterns of allocation and age-income profiles. Upon entering the labor force, individuals are allocated on the basis of the information that is then available. If this information is imperfect, the resulting allocation will also be imperfect. Observing individuals in their work reveals their qualities and allows a better match of workers and jobs. Later in working life, individuals can then be paid their "true worth," whereas initially their salary is based on expected marginal productivity in the group to which they belong, and this group will usually contain less productive individuals. Such a model can be enriched by developing a life-cycle model in which the stock of a capability changes with experience in response to the extent to which an individual uses this capability in his work. In other words, experience accumulation of a capability only occurs if the individual employs this capability. The optimal career plan would then follow from evaluating the consequences of capability supply at any point in life with respect to immediate job satisfaction and job earnings, as well as with respect to future satisfaction and earnings.

Further work should also investigate the relation between schooling and capabilities in producing earnings. Schooling has been studied extensively, in large part because of the role it can play in egalitarian policies. Obviously, then, it is important to know the contribution of schooling, independent of other variables. Some studies claim that this contribution is a strong and large one (Griliches and Mason, 1972), while others have found that the ability bias in the schooling coefficient may be very high, up to 50 percent (Olneck, 1976; Welland, 1976). In view of this debate and the magnitude of this bias, it seems that starting from capabilities rather than schooling is justified. However, further work should assess the contribution of each component. No doubt, schooling conveys information on capabilities and to some extent operates as a signal in the sense of Spence (1974). But it also plays a role in augmenting individual productivities, providing training that in earlier days was given as on-the-job training. The relative importance of these two interpretations of schooling may be expected to differ by type of school and can only be established by detailed analysis by type of education (contrasting, e.g., vocational education and general education).

Finally, an important route for empirical research can be derived from the distinction between individuals' capability levels and the levels required in their jobs. It seems clear that individual capabilities have different relevance in different jobs (as demonstrated in Taubman, 1975, where ability rewards were found to differ by occupation). This can only be investigated properly in a data set that combines observations on individuals' capabilities with detailed information on the jobs they hold. Such data can separately identify allocation (the job-worker match) and the pay structure. First steps toward such research have been made, and it is hoped that the results can be presented in the near future.

APPENDIX 1
THE TIME DERIVATIVES OF Π_t

As Equation (2.39) indicates,

$$\Pi_t = \alpha_c \left(\frac{p}{P_{Ut}}\right)^{1-s_0}. \tag{a1.1}$$

Variables without the subscript t, such as α_c and p, are assumed constant over time. Straightforward differentiation then yields

$$\frac{d\Pi_t}{dt} = \alpha_c \, p^{1-s_0} \, (s_0 - 1) \, P_U^{s_0-2} \, \frac{dP_U}{dt} = \Pi_t \, (s_0 - 1) \, \frac{dP_U}{dt} \, \frac{1}{P_U}. \tag{a1.2}$$

To find dP_U/dt, write

$$\frac{dP_U}{dt} = \frac{\partial P_U}{\partial P_L} \frac{dP_L}{dt} = \alpha_L \left(\frac{P_U}{P_L}\right)^{s_0} \frac{dP_L}{dt}$$

$$= \alpha_L \left(\frac{P_U}{P_L}\right)^{s_0} \sum_m \alpha_{Lm} \left(\frac{P_L}{P_{Lm}}\right)^{s_1} \frac{dP_{Lm}}{dt} \geqslant 0. \tag{a1.3}$$

The last step follows from Equation (2.7) and the behavior of (2.46). Thus, $d\Pi_t/dt$ critically depends on s_0.

To find the second derivative, differentiate (a1.2):

$$\frac{d^2\Pi_t}{dt^2} = (s_0 - 1)\frac{dP_U}{dt}\frac{1}{P_U}\frac{d\Pi_t}{dt}$$

$$+ (s_0 - 1)\,\Pi_t\left\{\frac{d^2P_U}{dt^2}\frac{1}{P_U} - \left(\frac{dP_U}{dt}\right)^2\frac{1}{P_U{}^2}\right\}. \qquad (a1.4)$$

Substituting (a1.2) and combining terms yields

$$\frac{d^2\Pi_t}{dt^2} = (s_0 - 1)\,\Pi_t\left\{(s_0 - 2)\left(\frac{dP_U}{dt}\right)^2\frac{1}{P_U{}^2} + \frac{d^2P_U}{dt^2}\frac{1}{P_U}\right\}; \qquad (a1.5)$$

d^2P_U/dt^2 is negative. This follows from the differentiation of the terms after the first equality sign in (a1.3), realizing that P_U and P_L are composite terms, to be differentiated with the chain rule and utilizing

$$\frac{\partial^2 P_U}{\partial P_L{}^2} = -\alpha_L\,s_0\left(\frac{P_U}{P_L}\right)^{s_0}\frac{1}{P_L}\frac{\tilde{y}}{R} < 0; \qquad (\text{a1.6})$$

$$\frac{\partial^2 P_L}{\partial P_{Lm}{}^2} = -\alpha_{Lm}\,s_1\left(\frac{P_L}{P_{Lm}}\right)^{s_1}\frac{1}{P_{Lm}}\left(1 - \frac{f_m P_{Lm}}{L P_L}\right) < 0. \qquad (a1.7)$$

Equations (a1.2) and (a1.5) then lead to the following result:

$$\text{if } 0 \leqslant s_0 < 1, \frac{d\Pi_t}{dt} < 0 \quad \text{and } \frac{d^2\Pi_t}{dt^2} > 0;$$

$$\text{if } \quad s_0 = 1, \frac{d\Pi_t}{dt} = 0 \quad \text{and } \frac{d^2\Pi_t}{dt^2} = 0;$$

$$\text{if } 1 < s_0 \leqslant 2, \frac{d\Pi_t}{dt} > 0 \quad \text{and } \frac{d^2\Pi_t}{dt^2} < 0.$$

In case $s_0 > 2$, $d\Pi_t/dt$ is still positive, but the second derivative may switch sign.

APPENDIX 2
THE LABOR DEMAND MODEL

To derive the minimum cost combination of inputs producing a fixed output quantity Q, form the Lagrangean:

$$L = O + \lambda \left\{ Q - \left(\sum_j \beta_{jm}^{1-\rho_q} E_j^{\rho_q} \right)^{1/\rho_q} \right\}$$

where

$$O = \sum_m \sum_j w_m \ell_{jm} + \sum_j r_j K_j + \sum_j p_j N_j$$

and E_j is given in the full specification of the production function (Equations [3.6] and [3.1]).

One of the first-order conditions for a minimum of L is

$$\frac{\partial L}{\partial \ell_{jm}} = 0$$

or

$$w_m = \beta_{jm}^{1-\rho_{aj}} \beta_{aj}^{1-\rho_{ej}} \beta_j^{1-\rho_q} A_j^{\rho_{ej}-\rho_{aj}} E_j^{\rho_q-\rho_{ej}} Q^{1-\rho_q} \ell_{jm}^{\rho_{aj}-1}. \quad \text{(a2.1)}$$

A similar equation can be found for w_n, which may be used to derive, from dividing and rearranging:

$$\ell_{jn} = \frac{\beta_{jn}}{\beta_{jm}} \left(\frac{w_n}{w_m}\right)^{-s_{aj}} \ell_{jm} \,. \tag{a2.2}$$

Substitution of (a2.2) for $n = 1, 2, \ldots, M$ in the production function A_j (3.1) yields

$$A_j = P_{aj}^{(1-s_{aj})/\rho_{aj}} \, w_m^{s_{aj}} \, \beta_{jm}^{-1} \, \ell_{jm} \,. \tag{a2.3}$$

Using the marginal equalities

$$\frac{\partial O}{\partial K_j} = \lambda \frac{\partial Q}{\partial K_j} \tag{a2.4}$$

and

$$\frac{\partial O}{\partial N_j} = \lambda \frac{\partial Q}{\partial N_j}, \tag{a2.5}$$

equations for K_j and N_j can be derived, expressed in prices, β's, and A_j similar to (a2.1). Substituting these equations and (a2.2) in the production function E_j (3.6) yields

$$E_j = P_{ej}^{-s_{ej}} \, P_{aj}^{s_{ej} - s_{aj}} \, \beta_{aj}^{-1} \, \beta_{jm}^{-1} \, w_m^{s_{aj}} \, \ell_{jm} \,. \tag{a2.6}$$

Substituting (a2.3) and (a2.6) into (a2.1) yields

$$\ell_{jm} = \beta_{jm} \, \beta_{aj} \, \beta_j \, P_{aj}^{s_{aj} - s_{ej}} \, P_{ej}^{s_{ej} - s_q} \, w_m^{-s_{aj}} \, Q. \tag{a2.7}$$

Optimum values for the other variables then follow: A_j from (a2.3), E_j from (a2.6), K_j and N_j from the equations derived from (a2.4) and (a2.5).

The solutions can be rewritten. Substituting the optimum values of ℓ_{jm}, K_j, and N_j in the cost function (3.18) allows the writing of

$$O = \sum_j E_j P_{ej} = \sum_j \beta_j P_{ej}^{1-s_q} Q = P_Q^{1-s_q} Q \tag{a2.8}$$

where P_Q is defined implicitly. Substituting (a.2.8) in the optimum solutions yields the equations given in the text.

APPENDIX 3
PROPERTIES
OF TRANSFORMATIONS

This appendix will focus on properties of distributions of random variables when the random variables are subject to transformation. A distinction will be made between unidimensional transformations (from one random variable to another) and multidimensional transformations (from a number of random variables to one random variable, as in summation or multiplication). Some results will be derived here; others are borrowed from the literature. In a sense, the results presented here are like a catalog of properties relevant to income distribution theory. They will not all be used in the main text, but the listing given here also indicates how the literature on income distribution might be classified according to the transformation that is involved.

PROPERTIES OF UNIDIMENSIONAL TRANSFORMATIONS

Let the stochastic variable y (income) be related to the stochastic variable x through the invertible one-to-one relation:

$$y = h(x) \qquad\qquad (a3.1)$$

with

$$x = g(y). \qquad\qquad (a.3.2)$$

159

Hence, $g\{h(x)\} = x$. Let the unimodal probability density function of x be given by $f(x)$. The following statements can then be made:

U.1.

$$\Phi(y) = f\{g(y)\}\ J \qquad (a3.3)$$

where J is the Jacobian of the transformation:

$$J = \left|\frac{\partial g}{\partial y}\right|.$$

The *density function* of y follows from the density function of x by inserting the inverse relation $x = g(y)$ and postmultiplying by the Jacobian (see Hogg and Craig, 1970, p. 125).

U.2. The *slope* of the income-generating function conveys information on the way inequality across individuals in x endowment is transformed into income inequality. If this slope is positive, the ranking of individuals by the size of x is conserved in the ranking by incomes (for getting an income, x is a "good"); a negative slope reverses this ranking (x is a "bad"). The absolute magnitude of this slope indicates how much difference in income is associated with a given difference in x. In a world in which only one variable determines an individual's income, this slope $|\partial y/\partial x|$ is a truly meaningful measure of income inequality. It conveys all the relevant information and may range from zero to infinity.

U.3. Moments of $\Phi(y)$ are related to moments of $f(x)$; the following results may be mentioned. As a crude approximation to the mean, consider

$$\bar{y} = \int y\ \Phi(y)\ dy = \int h(x)\ f(x)\ dx \approx h(\bar{x}) + \frac{1}{2}\frac{\partial^2 \bar{h}}{\partial x^2}\sigma_x^2. \qquad (a3.4)$$

This latter part follows from approximating $g(x)$ by a Taylor's series expansion about the mean $\bar{x}$, and breaking off after the second derivative. The position of the mode under a transformation may be studied as follows: Starting from

$$\Phi(y) = f\{g(y)\}\left|\frac{\partial g}{\partial y}\right| = f\{x|x = g(y)\}\left|\frac{\partial g}{\partial y}\right|,$$

the slope may be expressed as

$$\frac{\partial \Phi}{\partial y} = \left\{\frac{\partial f}{\partial x}\frac{\partial x}{\partial y}\,|\,x = g(y)\right\}\left|\frac{\partial g}{\partial y}\right| + f\{x|x = g(y)\}\frac{\partial}{\partial y}\left|\frac{\partial g}{\partial y}\right|.$$

Consider the transformation of the mode $\tilde{x}$ (i.e., the point at which $\partial f/\partial x$ = 0). The first component of the equation then vanishes and

$$\left(\frac{\partial \Phi}{\partial y} \mid y = h(\tilde{x})\right) = f(\tilde{x}) \frac{\partial \mid \partial g/\partial y \mid}{\partial y} \mid y = h(\tilde{x}).$$

This implies that

$$\left(\frac{\partial \Phi}{\partial y} \mid y = h(\tilde{x})\right) > 0 \text{ if } \frac{\partial}{\partial y}\left|\frac{\partial g}{\partial y}\right| > 0 \to \tilde{y} > h(\tilde{x})$$

$$= 0 \qquad\qquad\quad = 0 \to \tilde{y} = h(\tilde{x})$$

$$< 0 \qquad\qquad\quad < 0 \to \tilde{y} < h(\tilde{x}). \qquad \text{(a3.5)}$$

The implication on the position of $\tilde{y}$ relative to the transformed mode $h(\tilde{x})$ follows from the fact that in a unimodal distribution, the point with slope zero is enclosed between points with positive slope and points with negative slope. Assuming the distribution of y to be unimodal puts restrictions on the transformation $h(x)$, but this is not unrealistic if y is identified as income.

U.4. *Asymmetry* can be considered most fruitfully in the following direct approach. (The approach was suggested by Dr. L.F.M. de Haan, associated with the Econometric Institute of Erasmus University.)

Define the point $x = \hat{x}$ as the axis of symmetry in the density function of x. Select two points, $x_1 < \hat{x}$ and $x_2 > \hat{x}$, so that $f(x_1) = f(x_2)$ (i.e., points of equal density). Clearly, a distribution is symmetrical if, for any $f(x)$ so chosen, $|x_1 - \hat{x}|$ = $|x_2 - \hat{x}|$. Generally, asymmetry about a point $x = \hat{x}$ can be measured by

$$A(\hat{x}) = \frac{|\hat{x}+\delta_2-\hat{x}| - |\hat{x}-\delta_1-\hat{x}|}{\hat{x}} \mid f(\hat{x}+\delta_2) = f(\hat{x}-\delta_1), \delta_1, \delta_2 > 0. \qquad \text{(a3.6)}$$

Define positive asymmetry by $A > 0$, negative asymmetry by $A < 0$, symmetry by $A = 0$. $A(\hat{x})$ applies to particular points, which are identified by the choice of f (.): A $(\hat{x})$ is short for $A(\hat{x}, f)$. Defining $A(\hat{y})$ similarly, and realizing that $y = h(x)$, write

$$A(\hat{y}) = \left\{ \frac{|h(\hat{x}+\delta_2) - h(\hat{x})| - |h(\hat{x}-\delta_1) - h(\hat{x})|}{h(\hat{x})} \mid f(\hat{x} + \delta_2) = f(\hat{x} - \delta_1) \right\}. \qquad \text{(a3.7)}$$

Equation (a3.7) uses the fact that a given density $f(\tilde{x})$ corresponding to a point $x = \tilde{x}$ will now correspond to a point $y = h(\tilde{x})$. The asymmetry in the distribution of y can be evaluated conveniently with a Taylor's series expansion:

$$h(\hat{x} + \delta) = h(\hat{x}) + \delta h'(\hat{x}) + \tfrac{1}{2} h''(\hat{x}) \delta^2 \qquad \text{(a3.8)}$$

where $h'(x)$ represents $\partial h/\partial x$ and $h''(x) = \partial^2 h/\partial x^2$ and the higher order derivatives are assumed negligible. Substituting such expansions in (a3.7) yields

$$A(\hat{y}) = \left\{ \frac{|\delta_2 h'(\hat{x}) + \frac{1}{2} h''(\hat{x}) \delta_2^2| - |-\delta_1 h'(\hat{x}) + \frac{1}{2} h''(\hat{x}) \delta_1^2|}{\hat{y}} \right.$$
$$\left. |f(\hat{x} + \delta_2) = f(\hat{x} - \delta_1)| \right\}. \tag{a3.9}$$

Equation (a3.9) can be used to evaluate $A(\hat{y})$. The simplest case arises when $f(x)$ is symmetrical about $\hat{x}$—that is, $\delta_1 = \delta_2$, all $f(.)$. Denoting the first component in the numerator of (a3.9) by d_2 and the second by d_1, then $A(\hat{y}) \gtreqless 0$ according to $d_2 \gtreqless d_1$. A little reflection reveals the following implications:

If $h'(\hat{x}) > 0, h''(\hat{x}) > 0 \rightarrow A(\hat{y}) > 0$.
If $h'(\hat{x}) < 0, h''(\hat{x}) < 0 \rightarrow A(\hat{y}) > 0$.
If $h'(\hat{x}) > 0, h''(\hat{x}) < 0 \rightarrow A(\hat{y}) < 0$.
If $h'(\hat{x}) < 0, h''(\hat{x}) > 0 \rightarrow A(\hat{y}) < 0$.
If $\qquad\qquad h''(\hat{x}) = 0 \rightarrow A(\hat{y}) = 0$.

If $\delta_1 \neq \delta_2$, and hence $A(\hat{x}) \neq 0$, these conclusions may be generalized by stating that equal signs of $h'(\hat{x})$ and $h''(\hat{x})$ produce a tendency toward positive asymmetry in y, opposite signs produce a tendency toward negative asymmetry, while $h''(\hat{x}) = 0$ leaves the sign of asymmetry unaffected.

Note that if $h'(\hat{x}) > 0$, it also follows that $h(x_2) > h(x_1)$ (from $x_2 > x_1$), and there is no need to use the absolute values in (a3.6). In this case, the formula simplifies to

$$A(\hat{y}) = \hat{y}^{-1} \{h'(\hat{x}) (\delta_2 - \delta_1) + \frac{1}{2} h''(\hat{x}) (\delta_1^2 + \delta_2^2) \,|\, f(\hat{x} + \delta_2) = f(\hat{x} - \delta_1)\}.$$

This result is used in Section 5.2.3, with a slight change in notation.

PROPERTIES OF MULTIDIMENSIONAL TRANSFORMATIONS

The above results on unidimensional transformations were derived from first principles. Although the same general methods apply here, analytical results are much harder to derive. Moreover, the literature contains a number of valuable results. This section will therefore primarily summarize existing knowledge.

M.1. *Moments* of y, where y is a function of a number of variables $x_1, x_2, \ldots, x_m$, can be derived from moments of x_i, $i = 1, 2, \ldots, m$. In particular, the following cases are relevant:

1. *The sum of random variables.* Let $y = k'x$ and let the vector x have a vector of means μ and a disperson matrix V. Then,

$$\mu_y = k'\mu,$$
$$\sigma_y^2 = k'Vk.$$

2. *The sum of independent random variables.* In case of mutual stochastic independence, mean μ, variance σ^2, and skew sk (third moment about the mean), moments follow as the linear combination of the moments of the x_i, (cf. Cramér, 1946, p. 191). Thus, if $y = \Sigma_i k_i x_i$, this implies

$$\mu_y = \sum_i k_i \mu_i;$$

$$\sigma_y^2 = \sum_i k_1^2 \sigma_i^2;$$

$$sk_y = \sum_i k_i^3 sk_i.$$

3. *The product of random variables.* Products can be reduced to sums by invoking a logarithmic transformation. Thus, if $y = \Pi_i x_i^{k_i}$, then $\log y = k'x^*$, where $x_i^* = \log x_i$, and the results stated above can be used.

Another result was produced by Goodman (1960). In the case of two random variables x_1 and x_2, with variance σ_1^2 and σ_2^2 and means μ_1 and μ_2, the variance of the product $y = x_1 x_2$ equals

$$\sigma_y^2 = \mu_1^2 \sigma_2^2 + \mu_2^2 \sigma_1^2 + 2\mu_1\mu_2 E\{(x_1-\mu_1)(x_2-\mu_2)\} + 2\mu_1 E\{(x_1-\mu_1)(x_2-\mu_2)^2\} +$$
$$+ 2\mu_2 E\{(x_1-\mu_1)^2 (x_2-\mu_2)\} + E\{(x_1-\mu_1)^2 (x_2-\mu_2)^2\} +$$
$$- [E(x_1-\mu_1)(x_2-\mu_2)\}]^2.$$

M.2. This section will explore the sums of random variables.

1. *The sum of correlated normal variables.* The sum of correlated normal variables is normally distributed (see Hogg and Craig, 1970, p. 383). In particular, let $y = \Sigma_i k_i x_i = k'x$ and let $x = (x_1, x_2, \ldots, x_n)'$ have a multivariate normal distribution with vector of means μ and positive definite

covariance matrix $\mathbf{V}$. The random variable y then has normal distribution $N(\mathbf{k}'\mu, \mathbf{k}'\mathbf{V}\mathbf{k})$. An application of this property has not been discovered in the income distribution literature, presumably because of the preoccupation of theorists with nonsymmetrical distributions, such as the lognormal and Pareto. However, as was pointed out by Staehle (1943) and Miller (1955), if more homogeneous groups are considered, their income distribution becomes less skewed, and in such cases, the normal distribution may be a good approximation.

2. *The sum of gamma variables.* The sum of mutually stochastically independent variables, each distributed as a gamma distribution, is another gamma distribution (Raiffa and Schlaifer, 1968, p. 224). In particular, let $y = \Sigma_i x_i$ where $x_i \sim \Gamma(r_i, Z)$; then $y \sim \Gamma(\Sigma_i r_i, Z)$. Note that the scale parameter Z is assumed equal for each element. This so-called two-parameter gamma function has been used in empirical applications by Salem and Mount (1974) and Bartels and van Metelen (1975). The latter found this distribution a clear improvement over the lognormal when applied to Dutch data. Kloek and van Dijk (1978), using a much smaller sample, were less enthusiastic about it.

3. *The sum of Poisson variables.* The sum of mutually stochastically independent variables, each Poisson-distributed, is another Poisson distribution (Hogg and Craig, 1970, p. 161). In particular, let $y = \Sigma_i x_i$ where $x_i \sim$ Poisson (μ_i); then $y \sim$ Poisson $(\Sigma_i \mu_i)$. No applications of this distribution have been spotted.

4. *Pareto-Lévy stable laws.* Let x_1 and x_2 be two stochastically independent random variables that are distributed according to the same "law." If the sum is also distributed according to this law (with appropriate adjustment of scale and origin), the law is called Pareto-Lévy stable (Mandelbrot, 1960). The family of Pareto-Lévy stable laws includes the normal distribution and the asymptotic Pareto distribution (provided $0 < \alpha < 2$). Mandelbrot has applied these properties in his theory on the distribution of incomes in the upper tail (Mandelbrot, 1960, 1962).

5. *Central limit theorems.* Under suitable conditions, the sum of a large number of independent random variables converges to a normal distribution (see, e.g., Dhrymes, 1970). (Applications of the central limit theorem all involve products of components; after logarithmic transformation this leads to sums of variables.) According to Mandelbrot (1960), the Pareto-Lévy stable laws are the only possible limit laws of weighted sums of identically and mutually independently distributed random variables. In other words, the (asymptotic) Pareto distribution (with $\alpha < 2$) may result from the addition of a large number of components.

M.3. The focus of this section will be the products of random variables.

1. *The lognormal transformation.* A multiplicative structure can be reduced
    to an additive one through logarithmic transformation; the properties of
    additive structures may then be applied to the transformed variables. In
    particular (Aitchison and Brown, 1957, p. 12), if x is multivariate lognor-
    mal, where the logarithms of the variables have vector of means μ and dis-
    persion matrix V and k is a column vector of constants, then the product
    $y = c \, \Sigma_i \, x_i^{k_i}$ is $\Lambda(a + \mathbf{k}'\mu, \mathbf{k}'\mathbf{V}\mathbf{k})$, where $c = e^a$ is a positive constant.
2. *The central limit theorem.* The central limit theorem on sums of mutually
    independent random variables has its counterpart in products of indepen-
    dent random variables. Under suitable conditions (Aitchison and Brown,
    1957, p. 14), the product

$$y = \prod_{i=1}^{n} x_i,$$

where the x_i are independent positive variables and $\log x_i$ has mean μ_i and
variance σ_i^2, is asymptotically distributed as $\Lambda(\Sigma\mu_i, \Sigma_i \, \sigma_i^2)$. One application of this theorem was made by Roy (1950), who argued that output
depends on a compound ability that results from multiplicative interaction of a number of elementary abilities. Another application is the so-
called law of proportionate effect, in which the change in income is a
random proportion of income itself. This law is the basis of the so-called
stochastic approach to income distribution, as applied by Gibrat, Champernowne, and others (see Mincer, 1970).

3. *Product of normal variables.* Haldane (1942) presented a number of
    results with respect to products of normal variables, specifying moments
    of the product in terms of moments of the components. One conclusion
    from his results, used by Roy (1950), states that the product of a number
    of correlated normal variables does not differ markedly in distribution
    from the product of independent normal variables if the coefficients of
    variation are approximately equal.

    Another interesting result is worth reproducing here. Let $y = x_1 x_2$ and
    let the x_i have mean μ_i and coefficient of variation v_i. Let μ_y, σ_y^2, and sk_y
    indicate the mean of y, the variance of y, and the skewness of y as mea-
    sured by the third moment about the mean. Let ρ indicate the coefficient
    of correlation between x_1 and x_2. Then

$$\mu_y = \mu_1 \, \mu_2 \, (1 + \rho \, \nu_1 \, \nu_2); \tag{a3.10}$$

$$\sigma_y^2 = \mu_1^2 \, \mu_2^2 \, \{\nu_1^2 + 2 \, \rho \, \nu_1 \, \nu_2 + \nu_2^2 + (1 + \rho^2) \, \nu_1^2 \, \nu_2^2\}; \tag{a3.11}$$

$$sk_y = 2 \, \mu_1^3 \, \mu_2^3 \, \nu_1 \, \nu_2 \, [3 \, \{\rho\nu_1^2 + (1 + \rho^2)\nu_1 \, \nu_2 + \rho\nu_2^2\}$$
$$+ \rho \, (3 + \rho^2) \, \nu_1^2 \, \nu_2^2]. \tag{a3.12}$$

Many interesting conclusions can be drawn from these equations. Consider only some results about skewness. Equation (a3.12) implies that $sk_y > 0$ if $\rho \geqslant 0$ (thus, the product of independent normal variables yields a positively skewed distribution) and that $sk_y < 0$ if $\rho = -1$; $sk_y = 0$ requires $-1 < \rho < 0$.

4. *The product of independent binomial variables.* The product of a number of mutually independent binomially distributed variables has a skewed distribution. Boissevain (1939) calculated examples to this effect, which show that in case of two variates, the resulting distribution is already very similar to the observed income distribution (i.e., positively skewed). Increasing the number of variables (up to four) leads to a distribution that approaches the Pareto. Boissevain identified the variables as abilities relevant to the generation of income.

M.4. The preceding section focused on results concerning the addition of random income components. However, in aggregation of distributions, which will be the subject of this section, frequencies, rather than income components, are added. Clearly, if disjoint distributions are added, the aggregate distribution may have any shape. The argument has been invoked on a number of occasions. Pigou (1924) used it to save the argument of normally distributed abilities; the skew of the aggregate result should stem from the existence of noncompetitive groups. Staehle (1943) has demonstrated that this effect can be actually observed.

The most general statement on aggregation would seem to be that, depending on the component distributions, any distribution may result. However, a few more specific cases may be distinguished:

1. *Dominance of sizes and averages.* According to Bowley (1915, p. 114), combination of a number of frequency curves leads to a result that is dominated by sizes and averages, rather than by shapes, of the separate curves.

2. *Moments.* Consider M disjoint income categories, with means μ_i, variance σ_i^2, skew (third moment about the mean) sk_i, and let the sizes be given by n_i, $\Sigma_i \, n_i = 1$. Define $d_i = \mu_i - \mu$. Then, moments of the aggregated distribution are given by

$$\mu = \sum_i n_i \, \mu_i;$$

$$\sigma^2 = \sum_i n_i \, \sigma_i^2 + \sum_i n_i \, d_i^2;$$

$$sk = \frac{1}{\sigma^3} \left\{ \sum_i n_i \, \sigma_i^3 \, sk_i + \sum_i n_i \, d_i \, (3\sigma_i^2 + d_i^2) \right\}.$$

The first two results are standard; the third can be found in Mincer (1974), who used work by Bates published in 1935.

3. *Lognormal distributions.* Suppose, in separate income-earning categories, the distribution is lognormal. The aggregate income distribution is then also lognormal, provided the variance of log income in all categories is equal and the distribution of mean income (of the categories) is lognormal (Aitchison and Brown, 1957, p. 110).

APPENDIX 4
EFFECTS OF TAX RATE CHANGES

Notation: σ_z^2 represents the variance in z, and sk_z the skew (third moment about the mean).

1. Only tastes α_c differ.

$$\tilde{y} = \alpha_c \sum_m \tilde{w}_m x_m - \alpha_c \Theta_0$$

$$y = \alpha_c \sum_m w_m x_m + (1 - \alpha_c) \frac{\Theta_0}{1 - \Theta_0}$$

$$\tilde{y} = \alpha_c \left\{ \sum_m \tilde{w}_m x_m - \Theta_0 \right\} = \alpha_c R$$

$$y = \alpha_c \left\{ \sum_m w_m x_m - \frac{\Theta_0}{1 - \Theta_0} \right\} + \frac{\Theta_0}{1 - \Theta_0}$$

$$\sigma_{\widetilde{y}}^2 = \sigma_\alpha^2 \left\{ \sum_m \widetilde{w}_m x_m - \Theta_0 \right\}^2$$

$$\sigma_y^2 = \sigma_\alpha^2 \left\{ \sum_m w_m x_m - \frac{\Theta_0}{1 - \Theta_1} \right\}^2$$

$$sk_{\widetilde{y}} = sk_\alpha \left\{ \sum_m \widetilde{w}_m x_m - \Theta_0 \right\}^3$$

$$sk_y = sk_\alpha \left\{ \sum_m w_m x_m - \frac{\Theta_0}{1 - \Theta_1} \right\}^3$$

$$\frac{d\sigma_{\widetilde{y}}^2}{d\Theta_1} = \sigma_\alpha^2 \, 2 \, R \sum_m x_m \frac{d\widetilde{w}_m}{d\Theta_1} \leqslant 0$$

$$\frac{d\sigma_y^2}{d\Theta_1} = \sigma_\alpha^2 \, 2 \, \frac{R}{1 - \Theta_1} \left\{ \sum_m x_m \frac{dw_m}{d\Theta_1} - \frac{\Theta_0}{(1 - \Theta_1)^2} \right\} \geqslant 0$$

$$\frac{d\sigma_{\widetilde{y}}^2}{d\Theta_0} = \sigma_\alpha^2 \, 2 \, R \left\{ \sum_m x_m \frac{d\widetilde{w}_m}{d\Theta_0} - 1 \right\} \leqslant 0$$

$$\frac{d\sigma_y^2}{d\Theta_0} = \sigma_\alpha^2 \, \frac{R}{1 - \Theta_1} \left\{ \sum_m x_m \frac{dw_m}{d\Theta_0} - \frac{1}{1 - \Theta_1} \right\} \leqslant 0$$

$$\frac{dsk_{\widetilde{y}}}{d\Theta_1} = sk_\alpha \, 3 \, R^2 \left\{ \sum_m x_m \frac{d\widetilde{w}_m}{d\Theta_1} \right\} \leqslant 0$$

$$\frac{dsk_y}{d\Theta_1} = sk_\alpha \, 3 \left(\frac{R}{1 - \Theta_1} \right)^2 \left\{ \sum_m x_m \frac{dw_m}{d\Theta_1} - \frac{\Theta_0}{(1 - \Theta_1)^2} \right\} \geqslant 0$$

$$\frac{dsk_{\widetilde{y}}}{d\Theta_0} = sk_\alpha \, 3 \, R^2 \left\{ \sum_m x_m \frac{d\widetilde{w}_m}{d\Theta_0} - 1 \right\} \leqslant 0$$

$$\frac{dsk_y}{d\Theta_0} = sk_\alpha 3 \left(\frac{R}{1-\Theta_1}\right)^2 \left\{\sum_m x_m \frac{dw_m}{d\Theta_0} - \frac{1}{1-\Theta_1}\right\} \leqslant 0$$

The inequality transformations follow Section M.1, Appendix 3; the signs of the derivatives are based on the inequalities (5.20).

2. Only capabilities x_m differ, distributions mutually stochastically independent.

$$\tilde{y} = \alpha_c \sum_m \tilde{w}_m x_m - \alpha_c \Theta_0 \qquad\qquad y = \alpha_c \sum_m w_m x_m + (1-\alpha_c)\frac{\Theta_0}{1-\Theta_1}$$

$$\sigma_{\tilde{y}}^2 = \alpha_c^2 \sum_m \tilde{w}_m^2 \sigma_m^2 \qquad\qquad \sigma_y^2 = \alpha_c^2 \sum_m w_m^2 \sigma_m^2$$

$$sk_{\tilde{y}} = \alpha_c^3 \sum_m \tilde{w}_m^3 sk_m \qquad\qquad sk_y = \alpha_c^3 \sum_m w_m^3 sk_m$$

$$\frac{d\sigma_{\tilde{y}}^2}{d\Theta_1} = \alpha_c^2 \sum_m \sigma_m^2 2\tilde{w}_m \frac{d\tilde{w}_m}{d\Theta_1} \leqslant 0 \quad \frac{d\sigma_y^2}{d\Theta_1} = \alpha_c^2 \sum_m \sigma_m^2 2w_m \frac{dw_m}{d\Theta_1} \geqslant 0$$

$$\frac{d\sigma_{\tilde{y}}^2}{d\Theta_0} = \alpha_c^2 \sum_m \sigma_m^2 2\tilde{w}_m \frac{d\tilde{w}_m}{d\Theta_0} \leqslant 0 \quad \frac{d\sigma_y^2}{d\Theta_0} = \alpha_c^2 \sum_m \sigma_m^2 2w_m \frac{dw_m}{d\Theta_0} \leqslant 0$$

$$\frac{dsk_{\tilde{y}}}{d\Theta_1} = \alpha_c^3 \sum_m sk_m 3\tilde{w}_m^2 \frac{d\tilde{w}_m}{d\Theta_1} \leqslant 0 \quad \frac{dsk_y}{d\Theta_1} = \alpha_c^3 \sum_m sk_m 3w_m^2 \frac{dw_m}{d\Theta_1} \geqslant 0$$

$$\frac{dsk_y}{d\Theta_0} = \alpha_c^3 \sum_m sk_m 3\tilde{w}_m^2 \frac{d\tilde{w}_m}{d\Theta_0} \leqslant 0 \quad \frac{dsk_y}{d\Theta_0} = \alpha_c^3 \sum_m sk_m 3w_m^2 \frac{dw_m}{d\Theta_0} \leqslant 0$$

The inequality transformations are based on Section M.1, Appendix 3, the signs of the derivatives on (5.20). It has been assumed that sk_m (short for sk_{xm}, just as σ_m is short for σ_{xm}) is always nonnegative and positive for at least some m.

3. Taste and talent differ.

$$\tilde{y} = \alpha_c R \qquad\qquad y = \alpha_c \frac{R}{1 - \Theta_1} = \alpha_c \frac{\sum\limits_m \tilde{w}_m x_m - \Theta_0}{1 - \Theta_1}$$

It is now assumed that both α_c and R are distributed normally across the population, with zero correlation. A result of Haldane (1942) can then be applied (Section M.3, Appendix 3). Start from two normally distributed variables with moments (μ_1, σ_1^2), (μ_2, σ_2^2). The product of these two variables has moments μ, σ^2, and sk (third moment), which relate as follows to the underlying moments:

$$\mu = \mu_1 \mu_2; \tag{a4.1}$$

$$\sigma^2 = \mu_2^2\, \sigma_1^2 + \mu_1^2\, \sigma_2^2 + \sigma_1^2\, \sigma_2^2; \tag{a4.2}$$

$$sk = 6\mu_1\, \mu_2\, \sigma_1^2\, \sigma_2^2. \tag{a4.3}$$

Now associate the first variable with α_c, the second with R, resp., $R/(1 - \Theta_1)$. This latter distribution then has the following moments and sensitivities (the x_m are distributed independently normal):

$$\mu_2 = \mu_R = \sum_m \tilde{w}_m \mu_{x_m} - \Theta_0 \qquad \mu_2 = \frac{R}{1 - \Theta_1} = \sum_m w_m x_m - \frac{\Theta_0}{1 - \Theta_1}$$

$$\sigma_2^2 = \sigma_R^2 = \sum_m \tilde{w}_m^2\, \sigma_{x_m}^2 \qquad\qquad \sigma_2^2 = \quad = \sum_m w_m^2\, \sigma_{x_m}^2$$

$$\frac{d\mu_2}{d\Theta_1} = \sum_m \mu_{x_m} \frac{d\tilde{w}_m}{d\Theta_1} \leqslant 0 \qquad \frac{d\mu_2}{d\Theta_1} = \sum_m \mu_{x_m} \frac{dw_m}{d\Theta_1} - \frac{\Theta_0}{(1 - \Theta_1)^2} \geqslant 0$$

$$\frac{d\mu_2^2}{d\Theta_1} = 2\mu_2 \frac{d\mu_2}{d\Theta_1} \leqslant 0 \qquad\qquad \frac{d\mu_2^2}{d\Theta_1} = 2\mu_2 \frac{d\mu_2}{d\Theta_1} \geqslant 0$$

$$\frac{d\sigma_2^2}{d\Theta_1} = 2 \sum_m \sigma_{x_m}^2 \frac{d\tilde{w}_m}{d\Theta_1} \leqslant 0 \qquad \frac{d\sigma_2^2}{d\Theta_1} = 2 \sum_m \sigma_{x_m}^2 \frac{dw_m}{d\Theta_1} \geqslant 0$$

$$\frac{d\mu_2}{d\Theta_0} = \sum_m \mu_{x_m} \frac{d\tilde{w}_m}{d\Theta_0} - 1 \leqslant 0 \qquad \frac{d\mu_2}{d\Theta_0} = \sum_m \mu_{x_m} \frac{dw_m}{d\Theta_0} - \frac{1}{1 - \Theta_1} < 0$$

$$\frac{d\mu_2^2}{d\Theta_0} = 2\,\mu_2\frac{d\mu_2}{d\Theta_0} \leqslant 0 \qquad\qquad \frac{d\mu_2^2}{d\Theta_0} = 2\,\mu_2\frac{d\mu_2}{d\Theta_0} < 0$$

$$\frac{d\sigma_2^2}{d\Theta_0} = 2\sum_m \sigma_{x_m}^2\frac{d\widetilde{w}_m}{d\Theta_0} \leqslant 0 \qquad\qquad \frac{d\sigma_2^2}{d\Theta_0} = 2\sum_m \sigma_{x_m}^2\frac{dw_m}{d\Theta_0} < 0$$

Tax rate sensitivities of the income distribution now have to be deduced from differentiating (a4.1), (a4.2), and (a4.3), realizing that the moments of the first distribution (α_c) are not affected.

$$\frac{d\mu}{d\Theta_i} = \mu_1\frac{d\mu_2}{d\Theta_i} \qquad\qquad (a4.4)$$

$$\frac{d\sigma^2}{d\Theta_i} = \sigma_1^2\frac{d\mu_2^2}{d\Theta_1} + (\mu_1^2 + \sigma_1^2)\frac{d\sigma_2^2}{d\Theta_i} \qquad\qquad (a4.5)$$

$$\frac{dsk}{d\Theta_i} = \frac{sk}{\mu_2}\frac{d\mu_2}{d\Theta_i} + \frac{sk}{\sigma_2^2}\frac{d\sigma_2^2}{d\Theta_i} \qquad\qquad (a4.6)$$

This leads to

$$\frac{d\sigma^2}{d\Theta_1} \leqslant 0 \text{ for } \widetilde{y}, \text{ and} \qquad\qquad \frac{d\sigma^2}{d\Theta_1} \geqslant 0 \text{ for } y$$

$$\frac{d\sigma^2}{d\Theta_0} \leqslant 0 \qquad\qquad\qquad\qquad \frac{d\sigma^2}{d\Theta_0} \leqslant 0$$

$$\frac{dsk}{d\Theta_1} \leqslant 0 \text{ (if } sk \geqslant 0) \qquad\qquad \frac{dsk}{d\Theta_1} \geqslant 0$$

$$\frac{dsk}{d\Theta_0} \leqslant 0 \qquad\qquad\qquad\qquad \frac{dsk}{d\Theta_0} \leqslant 0$$

APPENDIX 5
EXPLANATION OF DOT
VARIABLES

Explanation of Relationships Within Data, People, Things Hierarchies

Much of the information in this edition of the Dictionary is based on the premise that every job requires a worker to function in relation to Data, People, and Things, in varying degrees. These relationships are identified and explained below. They appear in the form of three hierarchies arranged in each instance from the relatively simple to the complex in such a manner that each successive relationship includes those that are simpler and excludes the more complex.[1] The identifications attached to these relationships are referred to as worker functions, and provide standard terminology for use in summarizing exactly what a worker does on the job by means of one or more meaningful verbs.

A job's relationship to Data, People, and Things can be expressed in terms of the highest appropriate function in each hierarchy to which the worker has an occupationally significant relationship, and these functions taken together indicate the total level of complexity at which he must perform. The last three digits of the occupational code numbers in the Dictionary reflect significant relationships to Data, People, and Things, respectively.[2] These last three digits express a job's relationship to Data, People, and Things by identifying the highest appropriate function in each hierarchy to which the job requires the worker to have a significant relationship, as reflected by the following table:

DATA (4th digit)	PEOPLE (5th digit)	THINGS (6th digit)
0 Synthesizing	0 Mentoring	0 Setting-Up
1 Coordinating	1 Negotiating	1 Precision Working
2 Analyzing	2 Instructing	2 Operating-Controlling
3 Compiling	3 Supervising	3 Driving-Operating
4 Computing	4 Diverting	4 Manipulating
5 Copying	5 Persuading	5 Tending
6 Comparing	6 Speaking-Signaling	6 Feeding-Offbearing
7⎫ No significant relationship	7 Serving	7 Handling
8⎭	8 No significant relationship	8 No significant relationship

DATA: Information, knowledge, and conceptions, related to data, people, or things, obtained by observation, investigation, interpretation, visualization, mental creation; incapable of being touched; written data take the form of numbers, words, symbols; other data are ideas, concepts, oral verbalization.

[1] As each of the relationships to People represents a wide range of complexity, resulting in considerable overlap among occupations, their arrangement is somewhat arbitrary and can be considered a hierarchy only in the most general sense.

[2] Only those relationships which are occupationally significant in terms of the requirements of the job are reflected in the code numbers. The incidental relationships which every worker has to Data, People, and Things, but which do not seriously affect successful performance of the essential duties of the job, are not reflected.

0 Synthesizing: Integrating analyses of data to discover facts and/or develop knowledge concepts or interpretations.

1 Coordinating: Determining time, place, and sequence of operations or action to be taken on the basis of analysis of data; executing determinations and/or reporting on events.

2 Analyzing: Examining and evaluating data. Presenting alternative actions in relation to the evaluation is frequently involved.

3 Compiling: Gathering, collating, or classifying information about data, people, or things. Reporting and/or carrying out a prescribed action in relation to the information is frequently involved.

4 Computing: Performing arithmetic operations and reporting on and/or carrying out a prescribed action in relation to them. Does not include counting.

5 Copying: Transcribing, entering, or posting data.

6 Comparing: Judging the readily observable functional, structural, or compositional characteristics (whether similar to or divergent from obvious standards) of data, people, or things.

PEOPLE: Human beings; also animals dealt with on an individual basis as if they were human.

0 Mentoring: Dealing with individuals in terms of their total personality in order to advise, counsel, and/or guide them with regard to problems that may be resolved by legal, scientific, clinical, spiritual, and/or other professional principles.

1 Negotiating: Exchanging ideas, information, and opinions with others to formulate policies and programs and/or arrive jointly at decisions, conclusions, or solutions.

2 Instructing: Teaching subject matter to others, or training others (including animals) through explanation, demonstration, and supervised practice; or making recommendations on the basis of technical disciplines.

3 Supervising: Determining or interpreting work procedures for a group of workers, assigning specific duties to them, maintaining harmonious relations among them, and promoting efficiency.

4 Diverting: Amusing others.

5 Persuading: Influencing others in favor of a product, service, or point of view.

6 Speaking-Signaling: Talking with and/or signaling people to convey or exchange information. Includes giving assignments and/or directions to helpers or assistants.

7 Serving: Attending to the needs or requests of people or animals or the expressed or implicit wishes of people. Immediate response is involved.

THINGS: Inanimate objects as distinguished from human beings; substances or materials; machines, tools, equipment; products. A thing is tangible and has shape, form, and other physical characteristics.

0 Setting Up: Adjusting machines or equipment by replacing or altering tools, jigs, fixtures, and attachments to prepare them to perform their functions, change their performance, or restore their proper functioning if they break down. Workers who set up one or a number of machines for other workers or who set up and personally operate a variety of machines are included here.

1 Precision Working: Using body members and/or tools or work aids to work, move, guide, or place objects or materials in situations where ultimate responsibility for the attainment of standards occurs and selection of appropriate tools, objects, or materials, and the adjustment of the tool to the task require exercise of considerable judgment.

2 Operating-Controlling: Starting, stopping, controlling, and adjusting the progress of machines or equipment designed to fabricate and/or process objects or materials. Operating machines involves setting up the machine and adjusting the machine or material as the work progresses. Controlling equipment involves observing gages, dials, etc., and turning valves and other devices to control such factors as temperature, pressure, flow of liquids, speed of pumps, and reactions of materials. Setup involves several variables and adjustment is more frequent than in tending.

3 Driving-Operating: Starting, stopping, and controlling the actions of machines or equipment for which a course must be steered, or which must be guided, in order to fabricate, process, and/or move things or people. Involves such activities as observing gages and dials; estimating distances and determining speed and direction of other objects; turning cranks and wheels; pushing clutches or brakes; and pushing or pulling gear lifts or levers. Includes such machines as cranes, conveyor systems, tractors, furnace charging machines, paving machines and hoisting machines. Excludes manually powered machines, such as handtrucks and dollies, and power assisted machines, such as electric wheelbarrows and handtrucks.

4 Manipulating: Using body members, tools, or special devices to work, move, guide, or place objects or materials. Involves some latitude for judgment with regard to precision attained and selecting appropriate tool, object, or material, although this is readily manifest.

5 Tending: Starting, stopping, and observing the functioning of machines and equipment. Involves adjusting materials or controls of the machine, such as changing guides, adjusting timers and temperature gages, turning valves to allow flow of materials, and flipping switches in response to lights. Little judgment is involved in making these adjustments.

6 Feeding-Offbearing: Inserting, throwing, dumping, or placing materials in or removing them from machines or equipment which are automatic or tended or operated by other workers.

7 Handling: Using body members, handtools, and/or special devices to work, move, or carry objects or materials. Involves little or no latitude for judgment with regard to attainment of standards or in selecting appropriate tool, object, or material.

NOTE: Included in the concept of Feeding-Offbearing, Tending, Operating-Controlling, and Setting Up, is the situation in which the worker is actually part of the setup of the machine, either as the holder and guider of the material or holder and guider of the tool.

Explanation of Worker Trait Components

Those abilities, personal traits, and individual characteristics required of a worker in order to achieve average successful job performance are referred to as worker traits. Occupational information presented in volumes I and II is based in part on analysis of required worker traits in terms of the six distinct worker trait components described in this appendix. These six components have been selected for this purpose because they provide the broadest and yet most comprehensive framework for the effective presentation of worker trait information. Within this framework the user will find data concerning the requirements of jobs for: (1) The amount of general educational development and specific vocational preparation a worker must have, (2) the specific capacities and abilities required of him in order to learn or perform certain tasks or duties, (3) preferences for certain types of work activities or experiences considered necessary for job success, (4) types of occupational situations to which an individual must adjust, (5) physical activities required in work situations, and (6) physical surroundings prevalent in jobs.

Information reflecting significant worker trait requirements is contained, explicitly or by implication, in the job definitions in volume I. In the Worker Traits Arrangement in volume II, the qualifications profile for each worker trait group shows the range of required traits and/or levels of traits for the first five of these components. Numbers or letters are used to identify each specific trait and level. In this appendix, these identifying numbers and letters appear in italics.

The worker trait components are:
I. Training time (general educational development, specific vocational preparation)
II. Aptitudes
III. Interests
IV. Temperaments
V. Physical demands
VI. Working conditions [1]

I. Training Time

The amount of general educational development and specific vocational preparation required for a worker to acquire the knowledge and abilities necessary for average performance in a particular job.

General Educational Development: This embraces those aspects of education (formal and informal) which contribute to the worker's (a) reasoning development and ability to follow instructions, and (b) acquisition of "tool" knowledges, such as language and mathematical skills. It is education of a general nature which does not have a recognized, fairly specific, occupational objective. Ordinarily such education is obtained in elementary school, high school, or college. It also derives from experience and individual study.

The following is a table explaining the various levels of general educational development.

---

[1] Working conditions were recorded as part of each job analysis, and are reflected, when appropriate, in job definitions in volume I. However, because they did not contribute to the homogeneity of worker trait groups, they do not appear as a component in the Worker Traits Arrangement.

GENERAL EDUCATIONAL DEVELOPMENT

Level	Reasoning Development	Mathematical Development	Language Development
6	Apply principles of logical or scientific thinking to a wide range of intellectual and practical problems. Deal with non-verbal symbolism (formulas, scientific equations, graphs, musical notes, etc.) in its most difficult phases. Deal with a variety of abstract and concrete variables. Apprehend the most abstruse classes of concepts.	Apply knowledge of advanced mathematical and statistical techniques such as differential and integral calculus, factor analysis, and probability determination, or work with a wide variety of theoretical mathematical concepts and make original applications of mathematical procedures, as in empirical and differential equations.	Comprehension and expression of a level to —Report, write, or edit articles for such publications as newspapers, magazines, and technical or scientific journals. Prepare and draw up deeds, leases, wills, mortgages, and contracts. —Prepare and deliver lectures on politics, economics, education, or science. —Interview, counsel, or advise such people as students, clients, or patients, in such matters as welfare eligibility, vocational rehabilitation, mental hygeine, or marital relations. —Evaluate engineering technical data to design buildings and bridges.
5	Apply principles of logical or scientific thinking to define problems, collect data, establish facts, and draw valid conclusions. Interpret an extensive variety of technical instructions, in books, manuals, and mathematical or diagrammatic form. Deal with several abstract and concrete variables.		
4	Apply principles of rational systems [1] to solve practical problems and deal with a variety of concrete variables in situations where only limited standardization exists. Interpret a variety of instructions furnished in written, oral, diagrammatic, or schedule form.	Perform ordinary arithmetic, algebraic, and geometric procedures in standard, practical applications.	Comprehension and expression of a level to —Transcribe dictation, make appointments for executive and handle his personal mail, interview and screen people wishing to speak to him, and write routine correspondence on own initiative. —Interview job applicants to determine work best suited for their abilities and experience, and contact employers to interest them in services of agency. —Interpret technical manuals as well as drawings and specifications, such as layouts, blueprints, and schematics.
3	Apply common sense understanding to carry out instructions furnished in written, oral, or diagrammatic form. Deal with problems involving several concrete variables in or from standardized situations.	Make arithmetic calculations involving fractions, decimals and percentages.	Comprehension and expression of a level to —File, post, and mail such material as forms, checks, receipts, and bills. —Copy data from one record to another, fill in report forms, and type all work from rough draft or corrected copy. —Interview members of household to obtain such information as age, occupation, and number of children, to be used as data for surveys, or economic studies. —Guide people on tours through historical or public buildings, describing such features as size, value, and points of interest.
2	Apply common sense understanding to carry out detailed but uninvolved written or oral instructions. Deal with problems involving a few concrete variables in or from standardized situations.	Use arithmetic to add, subtract, multiply, and divide whole numbers.	
1	Apply common sense understanding to carry out simple one- or two-step instructions. Deal with standardized situations with occasional or no variables in or from these situations encountered on the job.	Perform simple addition and subtraction, reading and copying of figures, or counting and recording.	Comprehension and expression of a level to —Learn job duties from oral instructions or demonstration. —Write identifying information, such as name and address of customer, weight, number, or type of product, on tags, or slips. —Request orally, or in writing, such supplies as linen, soap, or work materials.

[1] Examples of "principles of rational systems" are: Bookkeeping, internal combustion engines, electric wiring systems, house building, nursing, farm management, ship sailing.

Specific Vocational Preparation: The amount of time required to learn the techniques, acquire information, and develop the facility needed for average performance in a specific job-worker situation. This training may be acquired in a school, work, military, instutitional, or avocational environment. It does not include orientation training required of even every fully qualified worker to become accustomed to the special conditions of any new job. Specific vocational training includes training given in any of the following circumstances:

a. Vocational education (such as high school commercial or shop training, technical school, art school, and that part of college training which is organized around a specific vocational objective);

b. Apprentice training (for apprenticeable jobs only);

c. In-plant training (given by an employer in the form of organized classroom study);

d. On-the-job training (serving as learner or trainee on the job under the instruction of a qualified worker);

e. Essential experience in other jobs (serving in less responsible jobs which lead to the higher grade job or serving in other jobs which qualify).

The following is an explanation of the various levels of specific vocational preparation.

Level	Time	Level	Time
1	Short demonstration only.	5	Over 6 months up to and including 1 year.
2	Anything beyond short demonstration up and including 30 days.	6	Over 1 year up to and including 2 years.
		7	Over 2 years up to and including 4 years.
3	Over 30 days up to and including 3 months.	8	Over 4 years up to and including 10 years.
4	Over 3 months up to and including 6 months.	9	Over 10 years.

II. APTITUDES

Specific capacities and abilities required of an individual in order to learn or perform adequately a task or job duty.

G   INTELLIGENCE: General learning ability.   The ability to "catch on" or understand instructions and underlying principles.   Ability to reason and make judgments.   Closely related to doing well in school.

V   VERBAL: Ability to understand meanings of words and ideas associated with them, and to use them effectively.   To comprehend language, to understand relationships between words, and to understand meanings of whole sentences and paragraphs.   To present information or ideas clearly.

N   NUMERICAL: Ability to perform arithmetic operations quickly and accurately.

S   SPATIAL: Ability to comprehend forms in space and understand relationships of plane and solid objects.   May be used in such tasks as blueprint reading and in solving geometry problems.   Frequently described as the ability to "visualize" objects of two or three dimensions, or to think visually of geometric forms.

P   FORM PERCEPTION: Ability to perceive pertinent detail in objects or in pictorial or graphic material; To make visual comparisons and discriminations and see slight differences in shapes and shadings of figures and widths and lengths of lines.

Q   CLERICAL PERCEPTION: Ability to perceive pertinent detail in verbal or tabular material.   To observe differences in copy, to proofread words and numbers, and to avoid perceptual errors in arithmetic computation.

K   MOTOR COORDINATION: Ability to coordinate eyes and hands or fingers rapidly and accurately in making precise movements with speed.   Ability to make a movement response accurately and quickly.

F   FINGER DEXTERITY: Ability to move the fingers and manipulate small objects with the fingers rapidly or accurately.

M   MANAUL DEXTERITY: Ability to move the hands easily and skillfully.   To work with the hands in placing and turning motions.

E   EYE-HAND-FOOT COORDINATION: Ability to move the hand and foot coordinately with each other in accordance with visual stimuli.

C   COLOR DISCRIMINATION: Ability to perceive or recognize similarities or differences in colors, or in shades or other values of the same color; to identify a particular color, or to recognize harmonious or contrasting color combinations, or to match colors accurately.

Explanation of Levels

The digits indicate how much of each aptitude the job requires for satisfactory (average) performance.   The average requirements, rather than maximum or minimum, are cited.   The amount required is expressed in terms of equivalent amounts possessed by segments of the general working population.

The following scale is used:

1   The top 10 percent of the population.   This segment of the population possesses an extremely high degree of the aptitude.

2   The highest third exclusive of the top 10 percent of the population.   This segment of the population possesses an above average or high degree of the aptitude.

3   The middle third of the population.   This segment of the population possesses a medium degree of the aptitude, ranging from slightly below to slightly above average.

4   The lowest third exclusive of the bottom 10 percent of the population.   This segment of the population possesses a below average or low degree of the aptitude.

5   The lowest 10 percent of the population.   This segment of the population possesses a negligible degree of the aptitude.

Significant Aptitudes

Certain aptitudes appear in boldface type on the qualifications profiles for the worker trait groups.   These aptitudes are considered to be occupationally significant for the specific group; i.e., essential for average successful job performance.   All boldface aptitudes are not necessarily required of a worker for each individual job within a worker trait group, but some combination of them is essential in every case.

III. INTERESTS

Preferences for certain types of work activities or experiences, with accompanying rejection of contrary types of activities or experiences. Five pairs of interest factors are provided so that a positive preference for one factor of a pair also implies rejection of the other factor of that pair.

1 Situations involving a preference for activities dealing with things and objects.	vs.	*6* Situations involving a preference for activities concerned with people and the communication of ideas.
2 Situations involving a preference for activities involving business contact with people.	vs.	*7* Situations involving a preference for activities of a scientific and technical nature.
3 Situations involving a preference for activities of a routine, concrete, organized nature.	vs.	*8* Situations involving a preference for activities of an abstract and creative nature.
4 Situations involving a preference for working for people for their presumed good, as in the social welfare sense, or for dealing with people and language in social situations.	vs.	*9* Situations involving a preference for activities that are nonsocial in nature, and are carried on in relation to processes, machines, and techniques.
5 Situations involving a preference for activities resulting in prestige or the esteem of others.	vs.	*0* Situations involving a preference for activities resulting in tangible, productive satisfaction.

IV. TEMPERAMENTS

Different types of occupational situations to which workers must adjust.

1 Situations involving a variety of duties often characterized by frequent change.

2 Situations involving repetitive or short cycle operations carried out according to set procedures or sequences.

3 Situations involving doing things only under specific instruction, allowing little or no room for independent action or judgment in working out job problems.

4 Situations involving the direction, control, and planning of an entire activity or the activities of others.

5 Situations involving the necessity of dealing with people in actual job duties beyond giving and receiving instructions.

6 Situations involving working alone and apart in physical isolation from others, although the activity may be integrated with that of others.

7 Situations involving influencing people in their opinions, attitudes, or judgments about ideas or things.

8 Situations involving performing adequately under stress when confronted with the critical or unexpected or when taking risks.

9 Situations involving the evaluation (arriving at generalizations, judgments, or decisions) of information against sensory or judgmental criteria.

0 Situations involving the evaluation (arriving at generalizations, judgments, or decisions) of information against measurable or verifiable criteria.

X Situations involving the interpretation of feelings, ideas, or facts in terms of personal viewpoint.

Y Situations involving the precise attainment of set limits, tolerances, or standards.

V. PHYSICAL DEMANDS

Physical demands are those physical activities required of a worker in a job.

The physical demands referred to in this Dictionary serve as a means of expressing both the physical requirements of the job and the physical capacities (specific physical traits) a worker must have to meet the requirements. For example, "seeing" is the name of a physical demand required by many jobs (perceiving by the sense of vision), and also the name of a specific capacity possessed by many people (having the power of sight). The worker must possess physical capacities at least in an amount equal to the physical demands made by the job.

The Factors

1 **Lifting, Carrying, Pushing, and/or Pulling (Strength).** These are the primary "strength" physical requirements, and generally speaking, a person who engages in one of these activities can engage in all.

Specifically, each of these activities can be described as:

(1) Lifting: Raising or lowering an object from one level to another (includes upward pulling).

(2) Carrying: Transporting an object, usually holding it in the hands or arms or on the shoulder.

(3) Pushing: Exerting force upon an object so that the object moves away from the force (includes slapping, striking, kicking, and treadle actions).

(4) Pulling: Exerting force upon an object so that the object moves toward the force (includes jerking).

The five degrees of Physical Demands Factor No. 1 (Lifting, Carrying, Pushing, and/or Pulling), are as follows:

S Sedentary Work

Lifting 10 lbs. maximum and occasionally lifting and/or carrying such articles as dockets, ledgers, and small tools. Although a sedentary job is defined as one which involves sitting, a certain amount of walking and standing is often necessary in carrying out job duties. Jobs are sedentary if walking and standing are required only occasionally and other sedentary criteria are met.

L Light Work

Lifting 20 lbs. maximum with frequent lifting and/or carrying of objects weighing up to 10 lbs. Even though the weight lifted may be only a negligible amount, a job is in this category when it requires walking or standing to a significant degree, or when it involves sitting most of the time with a degree of pushing and pulling of arm and/or leg controls.

M Medium Work

Lifting 50 lbs. maximum with frequent lifting and/or carrying of objects weighing up to 25 lbs.

H Heavy Work

Lifting 100 lbs. maximum with frequent lifting and/or carrying of objects weighing up to 50 lbs.

V Very Heavy Work

Lifting objects in excess of 100 lbs. with frequent lifting and/or carrying of objects weighing 50 lbs. or more.

2 Climbing and/or Balancing:

(1) Climbing: Ascending or descending ladders, stairs, scaffolding, ramps, poles, ropes, and the like, using the feet and legs and/or hands and arms.

(2) Balancing: Maintaining body equilibrium to prevent falling when walking, standing, crouching, or running on narrow, slippery, or erratically moving surfaces; or maintaining body equilibrium when performing gymnastic feats.

3 Stooping, Kneeling, Crouching, and/or Crawling:

(1) Stooping: Bending the body downward and forward by bending the spine at the waist.

(2) Kneeling: Bending the legs at the knees to come to rest on the knee or knees.

(3) Crouching: Bending the body downward and forward by bending the legs and spine.

(4) Crawling: Moving about on the hands and knees or hands and feet.

4 Reaching, Handling, Fingering, and/or Feeling:

(1) Reaching: Extending the hands and arms in any direction.

(2) Handling: Seizing, holding, grasping, turning, or otherwise working with the hand or hands (fingering not involved).

(3) Fingering: Picking, pinching, or otherwise working with the fingers primarily (rather than with the whole hand or arm as in handling).

(4) Feeling: Perceiving such attributes of objects and materials as size, shape, temperature, or texture, by means of receptors in the skin, particularly those of the finger tips.

5 Talking and/or Hearing:

(1) Talking: Expressing or exchanging ideas by means of the spoken word.

(2) Hearing: Perceiving the nature of sounds by the ear.

6 Seeing:

Obtaining impressions through the eyes of the shape, size, distance, motion, color, or other characteristics of objects. The major visual functions are: (1) acuity, far and near, (2) depth perception, (3) field of vision, (4) accommodation, (5) color vision. The functions are defined as follows:

(1) Acuity, far—clarity of vision at 20 feet or more.

Acuity, near—clarity of vision at 20 inches or less.

(2) Depth perception—three dimensional vision. The ability to judge distance and space relationships so as to see objects where and as they actually are.

(3) Field of vision—the area that can be seen up and down or to the right or left while the eyes are fixed on a given point.

(4) Accommodation—adjustment of the lens of the eye to bring an object into sharp focus. This item is especially important when doing near-point work at varying distances from the eye.

(5) Color vision—the ability to identify and distinguish colors.

VI. WORKING CONDITIONS

Working conditions are the physical surroundings of a worker in a specific job.

1   Inside, Outside, or Both:

I   Inside: Protection from weather conditions but not necessarily from temperature changes.

O   Outside: No effective protection from weather.

B   Both: Inside and outside.

A job is considered "inside" if the worker spends approximately 75 per cent or more of his time inside, and "outside" if he spends approximately 75 per cent or more of his time outside. A job is considered "both" if the activities occur inside or outside in approximately equal amounts.

2   Extremes of Cold Plus Temperature Changes:

(1) Extremes of Cold: Temperature sufficiently low to cause marked bodily discomfort unless the worker is provided with exceptional protection.

(2) Temperature Changes: Variations in temperature which are sufficiently marked and abrupt to cause noticeable bodily reactions.

3   Extremes of Heat Plus Temperature Changes:

(1) Extremes of Heat: Temperature sufficiently high to cause marked bodily discomfort unless the worker is provided with exceptional protection.

(2) Temperature Changes: Same as 2 (2).

4   Wet and Humid:

(1) Wet: Contact with water or other liquids.

(2) Humid: Atmospheric condition with moisture content sufficiently high to cause marked bodily discomfort.

5   Noise and Vibration:

Sufficient noise, either constant or intermittent, to cause marked distraction or possible injury to the sense of hearing and/or sufficient vibration (production of an oscillating movement or strain on the body or its extremities from repeated motion or shock) to cause bodily harm if endured day after day.

6   Hazards:

Situations in which the individual is exposed to the definite risk of bodily injury.

7   Fumes, Odors, Toxic Conditions, Dust, and Poor Ventilation:

(1) Fumes: Smoky or vaporous exhalations, usually odorous, thrown off as the result of combustion or chemical reaction.

(2) Odors: Noxious smells, either toxic or nontoxic.

(3) Toxic Conditions: Exposure to toxic dust, fumes, gases, vapors, mists, or liquids which cause general or localized disabling conditions as a result of inhalation or action on the skin.

(4) Dust: Air filled with small particles of any kind, such as textile dust, flour, wood, leather, feathers, etc., and inorganic dust, including silica and asbestos, which make the workplace unpleasant or are the source of occupational diseases.

(5) Poor Ventilation: Insufficient movement of air causing a feeling of suffocation; or exposure to drafts.

The material in this appendix was reproduced from *Dictionary of Occupational Titles,* Vol. 2 (U.S. Department of Labor, 1965).

APPENDIX 6
THE 1970 CENSUS DATA SET

Table A6.1. Means and Variances

Variable	Mean	Variance
GED	4.261	1.044
SVP	6.090	1.909
G	2.079	.937
V	2.238	1.082
N	2.613	1.044
S	2.750	1.116
P	2.965	.850
Q	3.318	1.034
K	3.159	.676
F	3.193	.692
M	3.170	.629
Median income, 25–64	$10,847	3,596
Mean income, 25–64	$11,508	4,154
Median income, 25–34	$ 9,621	2,312
Mean income, 25–34	$ 9,885	2,478

Table A6.2. Frequency Distribution Explanatory Variables

Score	GED	SVP	G	V	N	S	P	Q	K	F	M
1	1	–	33	31	18	17	6	6	0	0	0
2	3	7	17	17	16	17	14	14	14	14	11
3	14	9	36	28	37	25	43	19	46	43	51
4	34	3	2	12	16	29	24	44	28	31	26
5	26	5	0	0	1	0	0	5	0	0	0
6	10	7									
7	0	40									
8	0	17									

Note: This table gives the frequencies based on jobs in the sample, not on workers in each occupation.

APPENDIX 7
DISTRIBUTION OF JOBS BY
CAPABILITY LEVEL

Table A7.1. Number of Jobs with Specified Level of Capability Requirements, by Occupational Group

Occupation	G					V					N					S					P				
	1	2	3	4	5	1	2	3	4	5	1	2	3	4	5	1	2	3	4	5	1	2	3	4	5
Professionals	27	12	1			25	12	3			13	8	18	1		16	5	6	13		2	19	6	13	
Managers	7	40	2			7	38	4				9	40				2		47				4	45	
Sales workers			9					9					2	7				7	2				9		
Clerical workers		4	8	4			4	10	2			2	7	6	1			1	15			1	6	9	
Craftsmen		3	56	2			3	39	19			2	40	18	1		32	24	5			5	53	3	
Operatives			23	9				6	26				5	19	8		2	13	17				19	13	
Laborers			4	2					6					4	2			1	5				3	3	
Farmers		1	1				1	1	1				2					1	1				1	1	
Farm laborers			1	1				1	1				1	1				1	1				1	1	
Service workers		2	17	3			2	9	11				4	17	1			3	19			1	5	16	
Total	34	62	122	21		32	60	82	65		13	21	119	72	14	16	41	57	125		2	26	107	104	

Table A7.1—Continued

Occupation	Q					K					F					M					Number of Observations
	1	2	3	4	5	1	2	3	4	5	1	2	3	4	5	1	2	3	4	5	
Professionals	3	8	10	19			10	17	13			11	16	13			10	18	12		40
Managers		36	2	11				2	47				2	47				2	47		49
Sales workers				9				7	2				7	2				9			9
Clerical workers		5	7	3	1		3	6	7			2	6	8				9	7		16
Craftsmen			1	55	5		2	54	5			1	55	5			6	53	2		61
Operatives			3	11	18			27	5				19	13				26	6		32
Laborers					6			6					3	3				4	2		6
Farmers		1						1	1				1	1				1	1		2
Farm Laborers				1	1			2					1	1				1	1		2
Service workers			1	18	3			1	5	16		1	5	16				13	9		22
Total	3	50	24	128	34		16	127	96	16		15	115	109			16	136	87		239

187

APPENDIX 8
SELECTION OF REGRESSION
RESULTS:
1950–1960 Census Data

Table A8.1. 1949 Income: Factor Analysis on GATB

Intercept	Intellectual	Manual	GED	SVP	DATA	PEOPLE	THINGS	LEAD	SALES	HEAVY	INDEP	Int/Man[a]	Int/Man[b]	$\bar{R}$	F	$\bar{s}_e$
3,533	642 (11.32)	106 (1.86)												.599	65.89	876
3,506	594 (8.67)	56 (.81)										382 (1.24)		.602	44.54	765
3,541	654 (9.37)	119 (1.64)											−82 (.28)	.577	43.78	877
1,434			485 (5.73)	59 (1.32)										.582	60.43	889
2,699	426 (3.49)	43 (.68)	144 (1.12)	56 (1.27)										.610	34.75	870
4,479	484 (4.28)	40 (.50)			−38 (1.04)	−90 (2.65)	−44 (1.45)							.619	28.89	864
3,410	207 (1.07)	−88 (.70)	51 (.34)	93 (1.26)	−40 (.86)	−71 (1.88)	−15 (.37)	−147 (.64)	419 (1.52)	73 (.29)	498 (2.17)	948 (2.71)		.649	13.68	850
2,823			256 (1.84)	85 (1.23)	−33 (.76)	−71 (1.95)	−18 (.51)	−15 (.08)	245 (.88)	−160 (.71)	462 (2.00)			.616	15.58	874
3,579	388 (2.62)	52 (.61)	96 (.72)	41 (.71)	−15 (.37)	−73 (1.98)	−17 (.43)	−15 (.08)						.621	20.74	866
3,046	249 (2.60)			134 (3.61)		−58 (2.02)			514 (2.16)		498 (2.28)	823 (3.23)		.646	27.75	841

[a]Intellectual and manual each at least 1 standard deviation above the mean.
[b]Intellectual and manual each at least .5 standard deviation above the mean.

190

Table A8.2. 1949 Income: Factor Analysis on GATB, GED, and SVP

Intercept	Intellectual	Manual	DATA	PEOPLE	THINGS	LEAD	SALES	HEAVY	INDEP	Int/Man[a]	Int/Data[b]	Int/People[c]	$\bar{R}$	F	$\bar{S}_e$
3,533	661 (11.78)	69 (1.24)								524 (1.82)			.611	70.22	866
3,496	598 (9.12)	7 (.11)											.618	48.39	861
3,401						668 (4.05)	422 (1.51)	-335 (2.21)	304 (1.17)				.424	12.80	994
5,048			-169 (7.86)	-122 (3.29)	-35 (1.60)								.576	38.82	896
4,112	554 (4.50)	73 (.89)	-14 (.37)	-71 (2.05)	-12 (.42)								.622	29.34	862
4,469	384 (2.61)	-65 (.63)	-45 (1.06)	-95 (2.26)	-38 (1.16)					961 (2.07)	-262 (.59)	-304 (.73)	.634	19.30	857
4,343	451 (2.87)	-117 (.90)	-45 (1.00)	-92 (1.90)	-36 (.91)	-178 (.69)	429 (1.51)	199 (.98)	448 (1.95)	1205 (2.43)	-395 (.79)	-350 (.79)	.649	13.72	850

[a]Intellectual and manual each at least 1 standard deviation above the mean.
[b]Intellectual as in (a), and data = 0 (highest level).
[c]Intellectual as in (a), and people = 0 (highest level).

Table A8.3. 1959 Income: Factor Analysis on GATB, GED, and SVP

Intercept	Intellectual	Manual	DATA	PEOPLE	THINGS	LEAD	SALES	HEAVY	INDEP	Int/Man[a]	Int/Data[b]	Int/People[c]	$\bar{R}$	F	$\bar{s}_e$
5,739	1104 (11.53)	246 (2.57)											.610	69.86	1476
5,652	957 (8.61)	101 (.91)								1220 (2.50)			.623	49.71	1460
5,543						1017 (3.55)	727 (1.50)	-531 (2.01)	427 (.95)				.383	10.03	1728
8,623			-269 (7.28)	-220 (3.76)	-96 (2.49)								.565	36.69	1540
6,651	1004 (4.79)	269 (1.93)	11 (.16)	-133 (2.26)	-18 (.35)								.623	29.55	1466
7,299	652 (2.62)	-34 (.19)	-57 (.78)	-166 (2.32)	-72 (1.31)					2036 (2.59)	-658 (.89)	-392 (.56)	.641	20.03	1449
6,990	764 (2.88)	-109 (.49)	-50 (.65)	-149 (1.83)	-75 (1.12)	-204 (.47)	883 (1.84)	306 (.89)	764 (1.96)	2488 (2.97)	-1014 (1.21)	-417 (.55)	.657	14.33	1434

[a]Intellectual and manual each at least 1 standard deviation above the mean.
[b]Intellectual as in (a), and data = 0 (highest level).
[c]Intellectual as in (a), and people = 0 (highest level).

192

Table A8.4. 1949 and 1959 Incomes: Factor Analysis on GATB, E, C, GED, SVP, DATA, PEOPLE, and THINGS

Intercept	Intellectual	Manual	LEAD	SALES	HEAVY	INDEP	Int/Man[a]	Int/Man Lead[b]	$\bar{R}$	F	$\bar{s}_e$
					1949 Income						
3,442	673 (6.14)	65 (.71)	−23 (.11)	385 (1.57)	104 (.57)	410 (1.80)			.628	25.13	858
3,533	668 (11.96)	51 (.92)							.616	72.09	861
3,401			668 (4.05)	422 (1.51)	−335 (2.21)	304 (1.17)			.424	12.80	994
					1959 Income						
5,612	1108 (5.89)	240 (1.53)	−45 (.12)	709 (1.70)	108 (.35)	670 (1.72)			.623	24.53	1470
5,739	1115 (11.67)	202 (2.11)							.611	70.34	1474
5,543			1017 (3.55)	727 (1.50)	−531 (2.01)	427 (.95)			.383	10.03	1728
					1949 Income						
3,484	587 (9.29)	−22 (.36)	−151 (.59)	383 (1.56)	309 (1.58)	467 (2.08)	817 (2.24)	−151 (.35)	.631	38.63	852
3,333	662 (5.57)	−99 (.87)					954 (2.50)	−30 (.06)	.648	20.80	844
					1959 Income						
5,628	931 (8.72)	33 (.32)	−266 (.61)	726 (1.75)	534 (1.62)	788 (2.08)	1923 (3.11)	−470 (.64)	.638	40.09	1441
5,366	1063 (5.30)	−98 (.51)					2156 (3.34)	−262 (.30)	.656	21.69	1425

[a]Intellectual and manual each at least 1 standard deviation above the mean.
[b]Intellectual and manual as in (a), and LEAD = 1.

193

A8.5. 1949 and 1959 *ln* Income: Factor Analysis on GATB, E, C, GED, SVP, DATA, PEOPLE, and THINGS

Intercept	Intellectual	Manual	LEAD	SALES	HEAVY	INDEP	$\bar{R}$	F	$\bar{s}_e$
				1949 ln Income					
8.118	.194 (10.59)	.031 (1.72)					.573	57.64	.283
8.063			.215 (4.03)	.045 (.49)	-.059 (1.19)	.070 (.83)	.365	8.98	.323
8.076	.201 (5.56)	.028 (.95)	.014 (.20)	.037 (.46)	.066 (1.11)	.106 (1.42)	.583	19.89	.283
				1959 ln Income					
8.599	.198 (10.40)	.048 (2.56)					.572	57.44	.295
8.542			.207 (3.67)	.071 (.74)	-.051 (.98)	.068 (.77)	.334	7.32	.340
8.555	.205 (5.45)	.047 (1.50)	.011 (.15)	.068 (.81)	.065 (1.05)	.114 (1.47)	.582	19.84	.295

Table A8.6. 1949 Income and *ln* Income: Factor Analysis on GATB; Time-Equivalent SVP Scale

	Intercept	Intellectual	Manual	GED	SVP	SVP[a]	DATA	PEOPLE	THINGS	LEAD	SALES	HEAVY	INDEP	Int/Man[b]	$\bar{R}$	F	$\bar{s}_e$
1949 income	2,699	426 (3.49)	43 (.68)	144 (1.12)	56 (1.27)										.610	34.75	870
1949 income	3,013	449 (3.71)	39 (.63)	90 (.71)		.24 (2.35)									.619	36.30	862
1949 *ln* income	7.856	.100 (2.50)	.015 (.73)	.059 (1.43)		.00006 (1.63)									.564	27.35	.286[c]
1949 income	3,046	249 (2.60)			134 (3.61)		-58 (2.02)				514 (2.15)		498 (2.28)	823 (3.23)	.646	27.75	841
1949 income	3,447	360 (4.38)				.294 (3.23)	-38 (1.29)				378 (1.62)		491 (2.24)	600 (2.33)	.641	27.03	846
1949 *ln* income	7.984			.054 (1.51)		.00004 (1.19)	-.032 (2.75)						.122 (1.72)	.151 (1.84)	.585	24.21	.282[d]

[a]Time-equivalent SVP scale; see Section 8.2.2.
[b]Intellectual and manual each at least 1 standard deviation above the mean.
[c]The product of $\bar{s}_e$ and geometric mean of the dependent equal 960.
[d]The product of $\bar{s}_e$ and geometric mean of the dependent equal 947.

195

NOTES

1 INTRODUCTION

1. "Maybe it is impossible to say anything new and better, but the dust of time falls on everything that has been written, and so I think it's right if every 10 years someone else draws a line through all those old things and describes the world-of-today in different words" (Boon, 1972).

2. Sattinger (1978b) presents some empirical evidence on the existence of comparative advantage.

3. There is now an abundant empirical literature on the points raised by Lydall regarding the relative influence of genetic and environmental characteristics on ability and the effect of ability, education, and socioeconomic background on earnings. On the nature-nurture discussion, see Taubman (1976) and the critique by Goldberger (1978); for the other points, see Atkinson (1975, Chap. 5) and the further reading references given there. The impact of intelligence on income distribution in the Netherlands was studied empirically by Somermeijer (1965). For an analysis of the impact of education, see Tinbergen (1975).

4. An example of such a questionnaire is the one devised by Berkouwer (see Hartog, 1979a).

2 INDIVIDUAL LABOR SUPPLY

1. This shows the advantage of Keller's formulation over the conventional one, which only covers the Leontief case with input-output coefficients all equal to 1 (in the conventional formulation, the parameters α have exponent 1).

197

2. Note that the solution (2.8) has been assumed to be admissible; the potential effect of the constraint has not been brought in separately.

3. The elasticity is expressed in terms of P_{Lm}; clearly, it is straightforward to express it in terms of w_m, since $\partial P_{Lm}/\partial w_m = P_{Lm}/w_m$.

4. This requires either that the tax rate changes are tailor-made to the individual or that all individuals have identical parameters.

5. In the present specification of the utility function, the elasticity of substitution is equal for all pairs of m and n. Obviously, additional branches would allow the elasticity to vary between pairs. Hence, if empirical evidence necessitates different elasticities, there is no problem in incorporating them.

6. Age-income profiles for the Netherlands are documented in Fase (1969). A decline of income at higher ages, as found there (and elsewhere), may be accounted for by depreciation of capability stocks.

3 LABOR DEMAND

1. Note that the subscripts j and m are running indices, while the subscripts $a, e, k, n,$ and q are fixed.

2. On the basis of interviews with company managers and engineers, Piore (1968) claims that in the sample he studied job design is not very much affected by labor market conditions because the cost would outweigh the benefits.

4 MARKET EQUILIBRIUM

1. Note that this indifference only applies to job combinations *within the standard working period* (e.g., a week). The utility function specified in Chapter 2 thus applies to capability supply over the entire standard working period. The utility loss of an hour's work at effort e^*, compared to the desired level e, is exactly compensated by the utility gain of an hour's work at effort e^{**}, if $e^* - e = e - e^{**}$. This only applies to job combinations within the reference period. In utility terms, then, there is a difference between working half-time in job 1 and half-time in job 2 for two years, and working full-time in job 1 for one year and full-time in job 2 for the second year.

2. Strictly speaking, the conclusions should be stated so that they cover $dw_i/dz = 0$ for at least some i.

3. For an extensive analysis of taxes in a general equilibrium setting, see Keller (1980). For analysis of taxes and behavior of the firm, see Moerland (1978).

4. The vector inequality $x \geqslant 0$ means $x_i \geqslant 0$, all i.

5 THE INCOME DENSITY FUNCTION

1. It should be pointed out, however, that if each worker corresponds exactly to one job, income distribution might equally well be studied as the distribution of jobs by job wage rates; see Section 6.3 on this matter.

2. A time-series analysis of the Dutch income tax since 1914 reveals a distinction in three periods: 1914-1917, 1918-1939, and 1946-1973. Dividing the coefficient of variation of income after taxes by that coefficient before taxes yields, for these three periods, approximate values of .975, .92, and .70, respectively. The implied marginal tax rates would be .025, .08, and .30. The stability of these ratios within the subperiods is remarkable; see Hartog (1979b).

3. Empirically, the gamma density function can give an adequate description of the income distribution; see Salem and Mount (1974) and Bartels and van Metelen (1975). However, Kloek and van Dijk (1978) are less positive about it.

4. The age-income profile can also be used to give a new interpretation to the transition matrix of Markov-chain models. Proportions of individuals moving from one income interval to another can be calculated from assumptions on age-income profile and the age distribution of the labor force. For a specification, see Hartog (1976b); estimates of a transition matrix for the Netherlands are given in Hartog (1973).

5. If $s_0 \neq 1$, the same approach can be applied as the one presented here. However, the results are more complicated and will not be reproduced.

6. An alternative approach is to simulate the income distribution and calculate effects of eliminating some cause of inequality, as Blinder (1974) has done. He estimated that perhaps some 28 percent of inequality is due to differences in (labor-leisure) tastes.

6 A TWO-CAPABILITY ILLUSTRATION

1. Transformation involves defining an additional variable, $u = \beta_2$, transforming the distribution of (β_1, β_2) into a distribution of (P_a, u), and integrating on u, over an area restricted by a nonnegativity condition on P_a (see Hogg and Craig, 1970, p. 125). Note that if $\lambda_1' = \lambda_2' = \lambda$, Equation (6.22) has to be reformulated; in that case, the result is

$$\Phi(P_a) = \lambda^2 \, P_a \, e^{-\lambda P_a}.$$

2. The conclusions can be derived through the method described in detail in Section 5.3.4, now incorporating the assumptions $d\widetilde{w}_i/d\Theta_1 < 0$ and nonzero correlation between capability stocks (see Section M.3, Appendix 3).

7 ON TESTING

1. An interesting historical overview, on which this discussion is based, is given by Bailey and Stadt (1973).

2. The 1955 data were analyzed earlier by Taubman and Wales (1974).

3. An interesting attempt to observe typical career patterns directly is given by Spilerman (1977).

8 MEASUREMENT AND TESTING ON AMERICAN DATA

1. The results are summarized in Hartog (1978a).

2. All quotations in this explanation are from Appendix 5.

3. The first part of the code gives an industrial classification.

4. As mentioned in Appendix 5, there are six components, but the sixth, "working conditions," is not included in the systematic "worker traits arrangement" given in the DOT and is not used here.

5. E and C were omitted there.

6. For some critical remarks on the value of the education and training variables, see Scoville (1966).

7. That occupational mobility is certainly not negligible is clearly illustrated in Sommers and Eck (1977). Analyzing 1970 *Census* data (which also asked for 1965 occupation), they concluded:

> Overall results from the data show that nearly one-third (32.2 per cent) of those working in 1965 had transferred to a different detailed occupation by 1970. Occupational transfers were the most important source of separations, and more than twice as many workers switched occupations as left the labor force entirely.

8. The statistics in the tables with regression results are indicated with the usual symbols. $\bar{R}$ is the multiple correlation coefficient, $\bar{s}_e$ the standard error of estimate (both corrected for degrees of freedom), and F the statistic required for the F-test; t-ratios are always given in parentheses.

9. This conclusion of the F-test applies to all equations presented in the remainder of this chapter and will not be mentioned again.

10. Significance at 1 percent requires a t of 2.38 or more, at 2½ percent of 2.00 or more, and at 5 percent of 1.67 or more.

11. The regressions were estimated with the IBM-SSP routine for stepwise regression.

12. A strict test on the human capital prediction requires that the log of earnings be related to the length of training. This is accomplished in Section 8.3.4, but it is not successful either.

13. Factor analysis is a procedure for finding linear combinations of variables, called factors, so that these factors account for as much variance as possible in the original set of variables (see, e.g., Harman, 1970).

14. The IBM-SSP computer program was used. Factors are estimated from principal components. When rotating, only factors with eigenvalue greater than 1 are retained. Rotation serves to enhance identification of the factors. All variables are standardized to zero mean and unit variance.

15. If z is a vector containing the i-th observation on the original variables, g a similar vector of factor scores, and B the rotated factor matrix, then from $z = Bg$, the scores follow as $g = (B'B)^{-1} B'z$ (see Harman, 1967, Section 16.3).

16. The method used here is rather crude; a more elaborate technique is used in Lucas (1974).

17. Considering the underrepresentation of the occupational group of "laborers," the estimate is likely to be biased downward.

18. Interesting data on the income distribution by ("mathematical") ability level are given in Taubman (1975, Chap. 4). They refer to available ability stocks, not to required levels, however.

19. The variables E and C were also added as input into the factor analysis; a priori, they are not expected to be very relevant for either the labor market structure or for earnings differentials.

20. Lucas (1977) obtained the same result with a different sample from the DOT data. Taubman (1975) documents the opposite case of nonpecuniary rewards in which individually valued job characteristics (such as job security) lead to lower earnings. The evidence is

indirect since he does not measure job characteristics; rather, he measures the individual's motivation for entering the job.

21. A β-coefficient is a regression coefficient obtained when all variables (dependent and independent) have been standardized to unit variance.

22. The same conclusion is obtained by ten Cate (1977), using Dutch data.

23. Note that these remarks apply to the interaction between the factors; all regression equations include the factor requirements separately as well.

24. Note the small negative intercept: this points to a small increase in income inequality (the relative wage structure has widened); similar evidence can be found in Schultz (1972).

9 EVALUATION AND EXPANSION

1. "Oh, richness of the unfinished" (Leopold, 1977).

REFERENCES

Aitchison, J., and J.A.C. Brown. 1957. *The lognormal distribution.* Cambridge: Cambridge University Press.

Arrow, K.J. 1960. Price-quantity adjustment in multiple markets with rising demands. In *Mathematical methods in the social sciences.* K.J. Arrow, S. Karlin, and P. Suppes, eds. Stanford, Calif.: Stanford University Press.

——. 1973. Higher education as a filter. *Journal of Public Economics* 2 (3).

Atkinson, A.B. 1975. *The economics of inequality.* Oxford: Clarendon Press.

Bailey, L.J., and R. Stadt. 1973. *Career education: new approaches to human development.* Bloomington, Ill.: McKnight.

Bartels, C.P.A. 1977. *Economic aspects of regional welfare.* Leiden: Martinus Nijhoff.

Bartels, C.P.A., and H. van Metelen. 1975. Alternative probability density functions of income. Research Memorandum 29, Vrije Universiteit, Amsterdam.

Becker, G.S. 1964. *Human capital.* New York: National Bureau of Economic Research.

Bemis, S.E. 1968. Occupational validity of the General Aptitude Test Battery. *Journal of Applied Psychology* 52 (3):240-44.

Bjerke, K. 1961. Some income and wage distribution theories: summary and comments. *Weltwirtschaftliches Archiv* 86:46-66.

Blaug, M. 1976. The empirical status of human capital theory: a slightly jaundiced survey. *Journal of Economic Literature* 14 (3):827-55.

Blinder, A.S. 1974. *Toward an economy theory of income distribution.* Cambridge, Mass.: M.I.T. Press.

Boehmer, G. 1970. Lerneffekte als Kosteneinflussgrössen und ihre Berücksichtigung in der Kostenplanung unter Kostenrechnung. Ph.D. dissertation, West-fälische Wilhelms – Universität, Münster.

Boissevain, C.H. 1939. Distribution of abilities depending upon two or more in-dependent factors. *Metron* 13 (4):49–58.

Boon, L.P. 1972. *De Kappellekensbaan* [Chapel road]. Translated from Flemish by Adrienne Dixon. Boston: Twayne.

Bowles, S., and V.I. Nelson. 1974. The inheritance of IQ and the intergenera-tional reproduction of economic inequality. *Review of Economics and Statis-tics* 56 (1):39–51.

Bowley, A.L. 1915. *The nature and purpose of the measurement of social phenomena.* London: P.S. King & Son.

Bronfenbrenner, M. 1971. *Income distribution theory.* Chicago: Aldine.

Cain, G. 1976. The challenge of segmented labor market theories to orthodox theory: a survey. *Journal of Economic Literature* 14 (4):1215–57.

Cate, A. ten. 1977. Beroepen: vereisten en beloning. Scriptie, Erasmus Univer-siteit Rotterdam.

Corlett, E.N., and V.J. Morcombe. 1970. Straightening out learning curves. *Per-sonnel Management* 2 (6):14–19.

Cramér, H. 1946. *Mathematical methods of statistics.* Princeton, N.J.: Princeton University Press.

Crossman, E.R.F.W. 1959. A theory of the acquisition of speed-skill. *Ergo-nomics* 2 (2): 153–66.

Dalton, H. 1920. *Some aspects of the inequality of incomes in modern commu-nities.* London: Routledge.

Dhrymes, P.J. 1970. *Econometrics.* New York: Harper & Row.

Direktoraat–Generaal voor de Arbeidsvoorziening. 1973. *Handleiding voor de funktie-analyse.* Den Haag: Staatsuitgeverij.

Droege, R.C. 1967. Effects of aptitude-score adjustment by age curves on pre-diction of job performance. *Journal of Applied Psychology* 51 (2):181–86.

Edwards, R.C. 1976. Individual traits and organizational incentives: what makes a "good" worker? *Journal of Human Resources* 11 (1):51–68.

Fase, M.M.G. 1969. *An econometric model of age-income profiles.* Rotterdam: Rotterdam University Press.

Fozard, J.L., and R.L. Nuttall. 1971. General Aptitude Test Battery scores for men differing in age and socio-economic status. *Journal of Applied Psychol-ogy* 55 (4):372–79.

Freeman, R.B. 1971. *The market for college-trained manpower.* Cambridge, Mass.: Harvard University Press.

Ghiselli, E.E. 1966. *The validity of occupational aptitude tests.* New York: Wiley.

Gintis, H. 1971. Education, technology and the characteristics of worker pro-ductivity. *American Economic Review* 61 (2):266–79.

Goldberger, A.S. 1978. The genetic determination of income: comment. *Ameri-can Economic Review* 68 (5):960–69.

Goodman, L. 1960. On the exact variance of products. *Journal of the American Statistical Association* 55:708-13.

Griliches, Z., and W.M. Mason. 1972. Education, income and ability. *Journal of Political Economy* 80 (3):S74-S103.

Haldane, J.B.S. 1942. Moments of the distributions of powers and products of normal variates. *Biometrika* (1941-42):226-41.

Harman, H.H. 1970. *Modern factor analysis.* Chicago: University of Chicago Press.

Hartog, J. 1973. Een vergelijking van inkomensmobiliteit naar beroepsgroepen. *Preadvies Vereniging voor de Staathuishoudkunde.* Den Haag: Martinus Nijhoff.

——. 1976a. Ability and age-income profiles. *Review of Income and Wealth* 22 (1):61-74.

——. 1976b. Age-income profiles, income distribution and transition proportions. *Journal of Economic Theory* 13 (3):448-57.

——. 1978a. Earnings and capability requirements. Discussion Paper 495-78, Institute for Research on Poverty, University of Wisconsin. Forthcoming in *Review of Economics and Statistics.*

——. 1978b. Wages and allocation under imperfect information. Working paper, Institute for Economic Research, Erasmus University Rotterdam.

——. 1979a. Earnings equations and worker allocation. Working paper, Institute for Economic Research, Erasmus University Rotterdam.

——. 1979b. Income taxes and the distribution of income in the Netherlands, 1914-1973. Working paper, Institute for Economic Research, Erasmus University Rotterdam.

Hogg, R.V., and A.T. Craig. 1970. *Introduction to mathematical statistics.* London: Macmillan.

Keller, W.J. 1976. A nested CES-type utility function and its demand and price-index functions. *European Economic Review* 7:175-86.

——. 1980 (forthcoming). *Tax incidence: a general equilibrium approach.* Amsterdam: North-Holland.

Kloek, T., and H.K. van Dijk. 1978. Efficient estimation of income distribution parameters. *Journal of Econometrics* 8 (1978):61-74.

Leopold, J.H. 1977. *O rijkdom van het onvoltooide.* Amsterdam: Bert Bakker.

Lijftogt, S.G. 1966. De genormaliseerde methode van werkclassificatie. Ph.D. dissertation, Utrecht University.

Lipsey, R.G. 1962. Can there be a valid theory of wages? In *The labour market.* B.J. McCormick and E. Owen Smith, eds. Baltimore: Penguin, 1968.

Lucas, R.E.B. 1974. The distribution of job characteristics. *Review of Economics and Statistics* 56 (4):530-40.

——. 1977. Hedonic wage equations and psychic wages in the returns to schooling. *American Economic Review* 67 (4):549-58.

Lydall, H. 1968. *The structure of earnings.* London: Oxford University Press.

McCormick, E.J., P.R. Jeanneret, and R.C. Mecham. 1972. A study of job characteristics and job dimensions as based on the Position Analysis Question-naire (PAQ). *Journal of Applied Psychology*, Monograph 56 (4):347–68.

McKenzie, L. 1960. Matrices with dominant diagonals and economic theory. In *Mathematical methods in the social sciences*. K.J. Arrow, S. Karlin, and P. Suppes, eds. Stanford, Calif.: Stanford University Press.

Malinvaud, E. 1972. *Lectures on micro economic theory*. Amsterdam: North-Holland.

Mandelbrot, B. 1960. The Pareto-Levy law and the distribution of income. *International Economic Review* 1 (2):79–106.

——. 1962. Paretian distribution and income maximization. *Quarterly Journal of Economics* 76:57–85.

Miller, H.P. 1955. Elements of symmetry in the skewed income curve. *Journal of the American Statistical Association* 50 (269):55–71.

Mincer, J. 1958. Investment in human capital and personal income distribution. *Journal of Political Economy* 66:281–302.

——. 1970. The distribution of labor incomes. *Journal of Economic Literature* 8 (1):1–25.

——. 1974. *Schooling, experience and earnings*. New York: National Bureau of Economic Research.

——. 1976. Progress in human capital analyses of the distribution of earnings. In *The personal distribution of incomes*. A.B. Atkinson, ed. London: Allen & Unwin.

Moerland, P.W. 1978. Firm behavior under taxation. Ph.D. dissertation, Erasmus University Rotterdam.

Olneck, M. 1976. The effects of education on occupational status and earnings. Discussion Paper 358-76, Institute for Research on Poverty, University of Wisconsin.

Pen, J. 1971. *Income distribution*. London: Allen Lane, Penguin Press.

Phelps Brown, H. 1977. *The inequality of pay*. Oxford: Oxford University Press.

Pigou, A.C. 1924. *The economics of welfare*. London: Macmillan.

Piore, M.J. 1968. The impact of the labor market upon the design and selection of productive techniques within the manufacturing plant. *Quarterly Journal of Economics* 82 (4):602–20.

Popper, K.R. 1963. *Conjectures and refutations*. London: Routledge and Kegan Paul.

Praag, B.M.S. van. 1968. *Individual welfare functions and consumer behavior*. Amsterdam: North-Holland.

Raiffa, H., and R. Schlaifer. 1968. *Applied statistical theory*. Cambridge, Mass.: M.I.T. Press.

Rijksarbeidsbureau. 1952. *Classificatie van de beroepen naar hun onderlinge verwantschap*. Den Haag: Staatsuitgeverij.

Roe, A. 1956. *The psychology of occupations*. New York: Wiley.

Rosen, S. 1974. Hedonic prices and implicit markets: product differentiation in pure competition. *Journal of Political Economy* 82 (1):34–55.

Roy, A.D. 1950. The distribution of earnings and of individual output. *Economic Journal* 60:489–505.

——. 1951. Some thoughts on the distribution of earnings. *Oxford Economic Papers* 3:135–46.

Sahota, G.S. 1978. Theories of personal income distribution: a survey. *Journal of Economic Literature* 16 (1):1–55.

Salem, A.B.Z., and T.D. Mount. 1974. A convenient descriptive model of income distribution: the gamma density. *Econometrica* 42 (6):1115–27.

Salvendy, G., and W. Douglas Seymour. 1973. *Prediction and development of industrial work performance.* New York: Wiley.

Sandee, J., and R. Ruiter. 1957. Beroepseisen van de industrie-arbeider. *Economisch Statistische Berichten* 42 (2106):944–46.

Sargan, J.D. 1964. Wages and prices in the United Kingdom: a study in econometric methodology. In *Econometric analysis for national economic planning.* P.E. Hart, G. Mills, and J.K. Whitaker, eds. London: Butterworths.

Sattinger, M. 1975. Comparative advantage and the distribution of earnings and abilities. *Econometrica* 43 (3):455–68.

——.1978a. The assumptions of the human capital model of the distribution of earnings. Working paper, Miami University, Oxford, Ohio.

——. 1978b. Comparative advantage in individuals. *Review of Economics and Statistics* 60 (2):259–67.

——. 1980 (forthcoming). *Capital and the distribution of labor earnings.* Amsterdam: North-Holland.

Schultz, T.P. 1972. Long term change in personal income distribution: theoretical approaches, evidence and explanations. Report P-4767, Rand Corp., Santa Monica, Calif.

Scoville, J.G. 1966. Education and training requirements for occupations. *Review of Economics and Statistics* 48:387–94.

Simmelink, J. Th. 1975. Van functiekenmerken naar functie-eisen. Unpublished report, PTT-.SWO I, 543/1.

Singh, S.K., and G.S. Maddala. 1976. A function for size distribution of incomes. *Econometrica* 44 (5):963–70.

Smith, Adam. 1776. *The wealth of nations.* Andrew Skinner, ed. Baltimore: Pelican, 1974.

Somermeijer, W.H. 1947. Vooroorlogse loonverschillen in de bouwvakken: een poging tot kwantitatieve verklaring. *Weekblad Bouw*, pp. 381–84.

——. 1965. Inkomensongelijkheid: een analyse van spreiding en scheefheid van inkomensverdelingen in Nederland. Ph.D. dissertation, Erasmus University Rotterdam.

Sommers, D., and A. Eck. 1977. Occupational mobility in the American labor force. *Monthly Labor Review* 100 (1):3–19.

Spence, A.M. 1974. *Market signaling.* Cambridge, Mass.: Harvard University Press.

Spilerman, S. 1977. Careers, labor market structure and socio-economic achievement. Discussion Paper 405-77, Institute for Research on Poverty, University of Wisconsin.

Staehle, H. 1943. Ability, wages and income. *Review of Economics and Statistics* 25 (1):77–87.

Super, D.E., and J.O. Crites. 1965. *Appraising vocational fitness.* New York: Harper & Row.

Taubman, P.J. 1975. *Sources of inequality in earnings.* Amsterdam: North-Holland.

——. 1976. The determinants of earnings: genetics, family, and other environments; a study of white male twins. *American Economic Review* 66 (5): 858–70.

Taubman, P.J., and T. Wales. 1974. *Higher education and earnings.* New York: McGraw-Hill.

Taussig, F.W. 1915. *Principles of Economics.* New York: Macmillan.

Thorndike, R.L., and E. Hagen. 1959. *Ten thousand careers.* New York: Wiley.

Thurow, L.C., and R.E.B. Lucas. 1972. *The American distribution of income: a structural problem.* A study for the Joint Economic Committee, U.S. Congress. Washington, D.C.: U.S. Government Printing Office.

Tinbergen, J. 1956. On the theory of income distribution. *Welwirtschaftliches Archiv* 77:156–75.

——. 1975. *Income distribution, analysis and policies.* Amsterdam: North-Holland.

Tolles, N. Arnold. 1964. *Origins of modern wage theories.* Englewood Cliffs, N.J.: Prentice-Hall.

Trattner, M.H., S.A. Fine, and J.F. Kubis. 1955. A comparison of worker requirement ratings made by reading job descriptions and by direct job observations. *Personnel Psychology* 8:183–94.

U.S. Bureau of the Census. 1950. *Census of population,* Vol. 4. *Special reports,* Pt. 1, Chap. B, Occupational characteristics. Washington, D.C.: U.S. Government Printing Office.

——. 1960. *Census of population. Subject reports,* Occupational characteristics, Final Report PC (2)-7A. Washington, D.C.: U.S. Government Printing Office.

——. 1970. *Census of population. Earnings by occupation and education,* PC (2)-8B. Washington, D.C.: U.S. Government Printing Office.

U.S. Department of Labor. 1965. *Dictionary of occupational titles,* Vols. 1 and 2, 3rd ed. Washington, D.C.: U.S. Government Printing Office.

Weber, R.L., and E. Mendoza. 1973. *A random walk in science.* Bristol: Institute of Physics.

Welland, J.D. 1976. An investigation of the role of abilities in the individual earnings function. Ph.D. dissertation, University of Minnesota.

Wiegersma, S. 1958. Gezichtspunten en factoren in de genormaliseerde werkclassificatie. *Mens en Onderneming* 12 (1):200–08.

LIST OF SYMBOLS

Because of the need for many symbols, redefinition was sometimes inevitable. This implies that the symbol has its meaning only in the indicated section; such situations are identified by an asterisk.

Roman Alphabet Symbol	Meaning	*Introduced in* Section
A_i	Number of units labor type i	3.1
$A(\hat{z})$	Asymmetry about $\hat{z}$	Appendix 3
b_i	Semielasticity $(dw_i/d\Theta_1)w_i^{-1}$	6.5
C	Volume of individual consumption	2.1.1
d	Level of demanded capability	4.1
D	Market-equilibrating multiplier	4.3.1
*e	Vector of initial excess demands	4.3.2
e	Effort	4.1
E_i	Number of production units, type i	3.1
E	Matrix of excess demand sensitivities	4.3.2
f_i	Leisure component i	2.1.1
h_i	Time required to perform the i-th operation	2.3

h_{ij}	Individual i's share in standard working hours of job j	4.2
K_i	Volume of capital goods, type i	3.1
ℓ_{ij}	Volume of capability i used in labor type j	3.1
L	Leisure utility	2.1.2
L_i^s	Aggregate supply of capability i[1]	4.3.2
L_i^d	Aggregate demand for capability i[1]	4.3.2
N_i	Volume of intermediate goods, type i	3.1
O	Total cost of production	3.2
p	Price of consumption	2.1.1
p_i	Price of intermediate good i	3.2
P_L	Individual price index, leisure	2.1.2
P_U	Individual price index, overall (leisure and consumption)	2.1.2
P_{Li}	Individual price of leisure component i	2.1.2
P_{ai}	Firm cost index, labor type i	3.2
P_{ei}	Firm cost index, production unit i	3.2
P_Q	Firm cost index, all inputs	3.2
Q	Firm's volume of output	3.1
r	Coefficient of correlation	
$*r$	Reduction fraction, learning curve	2.3
r_i	Unit cost of capital good i	3.2
R	Individual resources: maximum after-tax income	2.1.2
$*s$	Level of supplied capability	4.1
s_0	Elasticity of substitution, leisure consumption	2.1.2
s_1	Elasticity of substitution, leisure components	2.1.2
s_{ai}	Elasticity of substitution, capabilities in labor type i	3.1
s_{ei}	Elasticity of substitution, labor, capital, goods in production unit i	3.1
s_q	Elasticity of substitution, production units	3.1
s_{im}	Individual i's supply of capability m	4.2
S_{it}	Individual supply of capability i, age t	2.2
sk_y	Skewness in the density function of y	5.4
t	Age	2.2

[1] Used without subscript in the one-capability case, Section 4.3.1.

U	Individual utility	2.1.1
ν	Coefficient of variation	Appendix 3
ν_{aj}	Volume of labor type j in production unit j	3.4
ν_{ij}	Volume of capability i per worker, job j	3.1
ν_{kj}	Volume of capital type j in production unit j	3.4
V	Dispersion matrix	Appendix 3
w_i	Wage rate, capability i	2.1.1
$\tilde{w}_i$	Marginal wage rate, capability i, after tax	2.1.2
$*w_s$	Marginal capability price, capability level s	4.1
x_i	Stock of capability i	2.1.1
x_{it}	Stock of capability i, age t	2.3
x_{oi}	Initial level, capability stock i	2.3
x_{di}	Maximum lifetime increase, capability stock i	2.3
y	Individual labor income	2.1.2
$\tilde{y}$	Individual labor income, after tax	2.1.3
z_i	Individual weight of capability profile i	5.3

Greek Alphabet Symbol	*Meaning*	*Introduced in Section*
α_c	Consumption preference weight, utility function	2.1.2
α_L	Leisure preference weight, utility function	2.1.2
α_{Li}	Preference weight, leisure component i	2.1.2
β_{ij}	Weight capability j in labor type i, production function	3.1
β_{ai}	Weight labor type i in production unit i, production function	3.1
β_{ki}	Weight capital type i in production unit i, production function	3.1
β_{ni}	Weight intermediate good, type i in production unit i, production function	3.1
β_i	Weight production unit i in output, production function	3.1
γ_i	Rate of convergence to maximum stock of capability i	2.3
$*\delta$	Distance parameter in asymmetry measure	Appendix 3

*δ	Transformation parameter, indivisible capability	4.1
λ_i	Parameters in bivariate exponential density function, capability demand	6.4
*ν	Exponent learning curve	2.3
μ_i	Arithmetic mean, variable i	
*Π	Proportion of resources R turned into income	2.4
ρ_i	Parameters in utility and production function, associated with elasticity of substitution: $s_i = (1 - \rho_i)^{-1}$	
σ_i	Standard deviation, variable i	
Θ_0	Intercept linear income tax function	2.1.2
Θ_1	Slope linear income tax function (marginal tax rate)	2.1.2

NAME INDEX

215

SUBJECT INDEX

HENRY JAMES'S 'SUBLIME ECONOMY'

Henry James's 'Sublime Economy'

MONEY AS SYMBOLIC CENTER

IN THE FICTION

by DONALD L. MULL

WESLEYAN UNIVERSITY PRESS

Middletown, Connecticut

The poem 'Theory' by Wallace Stevens, which is quoted on page 48, is reprinted from The Collected Poems by permission of Alfred A. Knopf, Inc. Copyright 1923; renewed 1951 by Wallace Stevens.

The publisher gratefully acknowledges the support of the Andrew W. Mellon Foundation toward the publication of this book.

Library of Congress Cataloging in Publication Data

Mull, Donald L   1936–
    Henry James's 'sublime economy'.

        Bibliography: p. [188]– 191,
        1. James, Henry, 1843–1916.   2. Money in literature.
I. Title.
PS2127.M6M8   813'.4   73–6007
ISBN 0–8195–4064–1

Manufactured in the United States of America
First edition

To the R and the Etta

Contents

Acknowledgements

I wish to express thanks to R. W. B. Lewis, who directed the writing of the dissertation from which the present work grew, and to Charles N. Feidelson, Jr., with whom I first studied James intensively; to James H. Wheatley and George R. Creeger, who provided valuable criticism concerning substance and structure, and to Steven Zwicker, who gave sound stylistic advice; to Fran Tallman, my invaluable research assistant; and ultimately to Ruthe and Martin Battestin, Fred Bornhauser, Sam Carmack, Richard Greer, Anne Kiley, Markesan Morrison, the late Bob Orr, Stuart Riggsby, Alan Shavzin, Max Wickert, Viola Winner—even Martha Stephens—and the many other friends whose conversations have illuminated James for me.

The following abbreviations are used in indicating the sources of quotations from James's works. The editions cited are listed in the bibliography.

Am   *The American*
ANS   *The American Novels and Stories of Henry James*
AS   *The American Scene*
Eur   *The Europeans*
EUT   *Eight Uncollected Tales of Henry James*
GB   *The Golden Bowl*
LP   *A Landscape Painter*
ME   *Master Eustace*
MF   *The Madonna of the Future*
NSB   *Notes of a Son and Brother*
NY   *The Novels and Tales of Henry James*
      The New York Edition
PL   *The Portrait of a Lady*
RH   *Roderick Hudson*
SBO   *A Small Boy and Others*
SR   *Sories Revived*
TC   *Travelling Companions*
WW   *Watch and Ward*

HENRY JAMES'S 'SUBLIME ECONOMY'

CHAPTER ONE

Biographical

In *Notes of a Son and Brother* the seventy-year-old Henry James recaptures from his remote past a scene emblematic of his imaginative and artistic nature. The occasion, in comparison to the more celebrated epiphanies in the history of this artist's imagination—the discovery of "Europe" in the juxtaposition of an old peasant woman and a ruined castle, or the confrontation with the "other self" in the dream of the Louvre (*SBO*, 159–161, 195–197)—seems rather pedestrian, merely a young writer's first success in selling his work; but it is, at least in the mature author's rendering of it, as significant as its more patently suggestive fellows in presenting a complex of attitude and meaning central to the whole canon of Henry James.

What simply happened was that Charles Eliot Norton had accepted an unsigned review of Nassau W. Senior's *Essays on Fiction*—the first appearance in print of Henry James, Jr.[1] James, however, recalls the event thus:

> I see before me, in the rich, the many-hued light of my room
> . . . the very greenbacks, to the total value of twelve dollars,
> into which I had changed the checque representing my first
> earned wage. I had earned it, I couldn't but feel, with fabulous
> felicity: a circumstance so strangely mixed with the fact that
> literary composition of a high order had, at that very table
> where the greenbacks were spread out, quite viciously declined,
> and with the air of its being also once for all, to "come" on
> any save its own essential terms, which it seemed to distinguish
> in the most invidious manner conceivable from mine. It was
> to insist through all my course on this distinction, and sordid
> gain thereby never again to seem so easy as in that prime han-
> dling of my fee. (*NSB*, 476)

At the center of the scene are the twelve greenbacks, upon which plays "the rich, the many-hued light," the characteristic Jamesian ambiguity of presentation. The central image of the money becomes a focal point at which converge and from which reflect the conflicting attitudes of the author evinced by the scene—the young writer's elation at having earned his first wage from his craft and the older writer's revulsion at the fact of "sordid gain" (the bluntness of the phrase considerably qualified by that delicate irony which is almost never absent from James's *Autobiography*); the felt felicity of the early composition and the contrasting sense of the disparity between an imposed ideal of "literary composition" and the author's own craft. The method is associational, but everything refers back to and takes its meaning from the image of the money. The conjunction of "literary composition of a high order" and "that very table where the greenbacks were spread out" insists on the relation of the artistic imagination to money, just as it insists on their essential opposition.

If the passage emphasizes James's difficulty in reconciling his art with "sordid gain," the remainder of the paragraph indicates a sense in which the two can be rendered compatible. James proceeds to recall Norton's hospitality following his acceptance of the review:

> I was to grow fond of regarding as a positive consecration to letters that half-hour in the long library at Shady Hill, where the winter sunshine touched serene bookshelves and arrayed pictures, the whole embrowned composition of objects in my view, with I knew not what golden light of promise, what assurance of things to come: there was to be nothing exactly like it later on—the conditions of perfect rightness for a certain fresh felicity, certain decisive pressures of the spring, can occur, it would seem, but once. This was on the other hand the beginning of so many intentions that it mattered little if the particular occasion was not repeated; for what did I do again and again, through all the years, but handle in plenty what I might have called the small change of it? (*NSB*, 477)

The "rich, the many-hued light" of James's room becomes the "golden light of promise" of unknown "things to come," of the possibilities for artistic experience suggested by the conjunction of his first publication and his admission into the literary world. The highly connotative terms associated with money ("rich" and "golden") are taken out of the context of "wage" and "gain" to symbolize, as the light bathing the scene in which the young writer realizes them, the ambiguous potentialities of the imagination. The metaphor becomes overt in the final sentence of the paragraph. The realization of intentions there begun, the fulfilment of the possibilities there glimpsed—these are the "small change" of the "golden light of promise," the fortune of the imagination.

James gradually modulates these terms so that they continually gain nuances of meaning and connote a developing series of attitudes. One can say less that money symbolizes a given particular than that the emotive terms associated with money—ranging from highly favorable ("rich," "golden") to extremely prejorative ("sordid gain")—are brought into significant relation with a complex of varying attitudes (possibly, but not necessarily, attitudes toward the fact of money itself). The image becomes a nexus of meanings, significant in the totality of its relations, rather than a thing determinately meaningful in itself. Abstracting along the lines indicated by the opposed emotive terms we can refer to a commercial and an imaginative sense of money, and indeed, such a distinction proves extremely useful for describing contrasting sets of attitudes in the novels and stories. We must, however, maintain, especially when considering the extremely dense late works, that money is primarily an organic center rather than a thing of fixed aspects.

"If the critics have charged Henry James with being ignorant of the world of business, he largely has himself to blame," remarks Jan W. Dietrichson, who cites the *Autobiography* as the primary source of critical misconception.[2] It is equally true that the *Autobiography* provides the fullest documentation available of James's awareness of the ambiguous fact of money and the sources of that awareness in his father's "ideas." From his own father's world of material acquisition and restricted imagination,[3] Henry James, Sr., had turned to the world of spiritual and imaginative experience, though it was the fruits of his father's acquisitions which permitted him freedom in exploring that world. That complete alienation of the James family from the realm of business which was its base the novelist recorded in A Small Boy and Others:

> The most that could be said of us was that, though about equally wanting, all round, in any faculty of acquisition, we happened to pay for the amiable weakness less in some connections than in others. The point was that we moved so oddly and consistently—as it was our only form of consistency—over our limited pasture, never straying to nibble in the strange or the steep places. What was the matter with us under this spell, and what the moral might have been for our case, are issues of small moment, after all, in face of the fact of our mainly so brief duration. It was given to but few of us to be taught by the event, to be made to wonder with the last intensity what *had* been the matter. This it would be interesting to worry out, might I take the time; for the story wouldn't be told, I conceive, by any mere rueful glance at other avidities, the preference for ease, the play of the passions, the appetite for pleasure. These things have often accompanied the business imagination; just as the love of life and the love of other persons, and of many of the things of the world, just as quickness of soul and sense, have again and again not excluded it. However, it comes back, as I have already hinted, to the manner in which the "things of the world" could but present themselves; there were not enough of these, and they were not fine and fair enough, to engage happily so much unapplied, so much loose and crude attention. We hadn't doubtless at all a complete play of intelligence—if I may not so far discriminate as to say *they* hadn't; or our lack of the instinct of the market needn't have been so much worth speaking of: other curiosities, other sympathies might have redressed the balance. (SBO, 109–110)

At a loss to account fully for his family's total estrangement from the world of business, its complete lack of the "business imagination," the elderly novelist suggests that the "things of the world" were neither plentiful nor "fine and fair enough" to provide significant material for the overactive imagination of his young self. "Convert, convert, convert!" (*SBO*, 123) the elder Henry James had in effect urged his children; and as Robert Le Clair comments, "It was not into gold that they were to convert their experiences. Of that sort of 'success' in life they never heard a word at home, it being a presumption of their parents that they would hear word enough of that idea elsewhere."[4] The things of the world as such were objects of the business imagination, mere "things," unconverted and thoroughly in "the world." Presenting themselves as things (the manner in which, says James, they necessarily presented themselves), they would hardly fail not to satisfy the demands of the creative imagination, the opposite of the business imagination.

James's slight bafflement in explaining away his lack of interest in or understanding of the world of business amounts finally to his failure to recognize, or at least to state, clearly that the mode of thought which he calls the "business imagination" is completely alien to, antithetical to his own mode of thought, the "converting imagination" inculcated in him by his father, which he later analyzed in *A Small Boy and Others*:

> As I reconsider both my own and my brother's early start . . . it is quite for me as if the authors of our being and guardians of our youth had virtually said to us but one thing, directed our course but by one word, though constantly repeated: Convert, convert, convert! With which I have not even the sense of any needed appeal in us for further apprehension of the particular precious metal our chemistry was to have in view. I taste again in that pure air no ghost of a hint, for instance, that the precious metal was the refined gold of "success"— a reward of effort for which I remember to have heard at home no good word, nor any sort of word, ever faintly breathed. . . . We were to convert and convert, success—in the sense that was in the general air—or no success; and simply everything that should happen to us, every contact, every impression and every experience we should know, were to form our soluble stuff; with only ourselves to thank should we remain unaware, by the time our perceptions were decently developed, of the substance finally projected and most desirable. That substance might be just consummately Virtue, as a social grace and value —and as a matter furthermore on which pretexts for ambiguity

of view and of measure were as little as possible called upon
to flourish. This last luxury therefore quite failed us, and we
understood no whit the less what was suggested and expected
because of the highly liberal way in which the pill, if I may
call it so, was gilded: it had been made up—to emphasize my
image—in so bright an air of humanity and gaiety, of charity
and humour. (*SBO*, 122–123)

Experience was not to be converted into gold; "success" in the
world's terms was not what the elder Henry James prescribed
for his children, since that would mean, essentially, being converted by the world. Such an attitude, the business imagination,
maintained an aggrandizing relationship between the self and
the world's things, in which the self was defined by the things
it possessed, its appurtenances. Rather, the James children were
to convert (the paternal dictum itself "gilded" by the father's
humanity) their experience of the world into "Virtue, as a social
grace and value" (James's statement of the unambiguity of
which is sufficiently ambiguous), a quality of the self permit-
ting it the fullest efficacy in social relations, that is, promoting
a rightness of relation with other selves.[5] The elder James's ad-
vocated alchemy was, rather than a conversion of experience
of the world into the hard fact of gold, a conversion of that
fact into another kind of experience, the sort of conversion
which his own father's money had undergone at his hands.

In his attempt to isolate the reason for his lack of business
sense, James lists several possible alternatives to that sense which
—though he finds them possibly concomitant with it and
though he rejects them as the causes of his disinterest—suggest
certain affinities with the converting imagination and the kinds
of relations with persons and things implied by such an imagination. James brackets "the love of life and the love of other persons, and of many of the things of the world, . . . quickness of
soul and sense," as things which "have again and again not excluded" the business imagination, the implication being that
they generally do. The linking of the love of things with the
love of life and the love of persons suggests here not so much

an objectification of persons as a personification of objects—a common relation of the self to life, persons, things, whereby the things of the world are not accepted in the terms wherein they present themselves (their business value, their thingness) but are imaginatively apprehended (the most notable exemplar of such an apprehension being Fleda Vetch in *The Spoils of Poynton*), just as other selves are actually apprehended in a true "love of" them. Conversely, if one is related to things in their thingness—if one possesses, that is, the business imagination— one's relation to other persons will generally parallel one's relations to things; people will become commercial entities, objects possessed by one's self, and, as possessions, the concrete definitions of the self. The business imagination is thus an attitude toward all aspects of life, an attitude which determines the self's loss in its appurtenances and relations. So Henry James, Sr., treats the concept of owning in "Socialism and Civilization": "We degrade by owning and just in the degree of our owning. . . . We degrade and disesteem every person we own absolutely, every person bound to us by any other tenure than his own spontaneous affection."[6] And this belief of the father's became central in the son's great novels.

Another set of possible alternatives to the business imagination James lists as "other avidities, the preference for ease, the play of the passions, the appetite for pleasure." These, leading as they do to immediate satisfaction of the self in the things and persons of the world rather than to a right relation with other selves and externals, may be seen as the obverse of the converting imagination. They are opposed to the business sense in that money is their condition rather than their end; but viewed in regard to the relation of the self and others, they imply the same attitude as the business sense. The avid, the lovers of ease and pleasure, differ from the business-minded only in that they spend money instead of making it. Early in *A Small Boy and Others*, James describes the implications for the world of *not* being in business:

Not to have been immediately launched in business of a rigor-

ous sort was to be exposed—in the absence I mean of some
fairly abnormal predisposition to virtue; since it was a world
so simply constituted that whatever wasn't business, or exactly
an office or a "store," places in which people sat close and
made money, was just simply pleasure, sought, and sought
only, in places in which people got tipsy. There was clearly
no mean, least of all the golden one, for it was just the ready,
even when the moderate, possession of gold that determined,
that hurried on, disaster. (SBO, 30)

To have money instead of making it was, in the eyes of the
world, necessarily to use it wrongly. Leisure and ease led inevita-
bly to pleasure-seeking, and pleasure was not to be sought. One
could always seek more money. James never completely rejects
the possible validity of such an attitude, but its scope, in these
terms, is essentially that of Henrietta Stackpole when she
objects to Ralph Touchett because he doesn't "do" anything.
(Mrs. Touchett, however, who finds her son a failure on the
same grounds, is an example of what Henrietta is, or should be,
driving at, and to an extent is a vindication of Henrietta's point
of view.) It is the failure of the leisured to achieve practical
ends which the business mind objects to. What is potentially
truly objectionable in the leisured attitude, however, is the false
relation to the rest of the world which it can share with the
business attitude.

If money as a means rather than an end is a horror to the
world which is making it—the symbol of unspeakable potentialities and the efficient cause of pernicious effects—it is something
else to those who have it, have it perhaps through the efforts
of their business-minded forbears but are able anyway to see its
potentialities from the inside. For Henry James, Sr., the fortune
which he had, with effort, inherited from his father was the
means whereby his children would be liberated from the need
to make money and hence from the worldly sense of success,
the business imagination; and whereby they would be free to
cultivate that other imagination, the fruit of which was to be
that social virtue which the father valued above all else. Indeed,
the elder James was determined, as Le Clair says, "to spare not